WINE

BOOK

THE *Vintage* WINE BOOK

WILLIAM S. LEEDOM

Vintage Books
A Division of Random House
NEW YORK

VINTAGE BOOKS
are published by ALFRED A. KNOPF, INC.
and RANDOM HOUSE, INC.

 Published in New York by Random House, Inc., and simultaneously in Toronto, Canada, by Random House of Canada, Limited.

Library of Congress Catalog Card Number: 62–12737

MANUFACTURED IN THE UNITED STATES OF AMERICA

Foreword

Hardly a year goes by without the publication, either in this country or in Great Britain, of a major book on wines or wine drinking. In the last few years the tempo has, if anything, increased and there seems to be no sign of a letup in the appearance of new volumes on the subject, whether it be a book on the wines of one particular country or the personal experiences of one particular wine drinker or connoisseur. Many of the books have of course become classics in their own particular field, such as Alexis Lichine's *Wines of France* and Frank Schoonmaker's *The Wines of Germany,* to mention just two that immediately come to mind. Others are intended more for the experienced wine drinker who already knows a great deal about wine and wine drinking, but who nevertheless may be eager to pick up additional bits of information on particular wines or wine-growing regions in which he is especially interested.

Up until now, however, there has been no new book on wines available in an inexpensive, paperback edition that will tell the beginning wine drinker all he needs to know about buying and serving wine, while at the same time avoiding personal anecdotes, reminiscences of great old wines that are no longer obtainable in wine shops, and other such nonessential information. It is hoped that *The Vintage Wine Book* will fill this gap and make the basic information on wines and wine drinking available to a larger public than heretofore. Needless to say, a small volume of this size cannot go into detailed discussions of every wine from every wine-producing country, but it will at least provide the basic information for the intelligent selection of wine in shops and restaurants. Perhaps later the reader will want to delve into other more detailed books as his time and budget may permit, and as his interest in, and knowledge of, wines increases.

Although the author has no ax to grind with anyone or with any country's wines—unless it is with the restaurants that charge such exorbitant prices for the wines they serve—he would, on the other hand, be particularly gratified if *The Vintage Wine Book* could arouse a greater interest among its readers for the fine wines of two much-neglected wine-growing areas: California and Germany. The great wines of France are of course in a class by themselves and certainly need no further praise here, but the reader should bear in mind that other countries produce fine wines too. Most beginning wine drinkers now seem to drink either so-called Beaujolais or else rosé wines, almost to the exclusion of everything else. The present volume should help to broaden the wine-drinker's perspective somewhat, and show him that there are many really fine wines produced not only in Europe, but also right here in the United States, and that they need not always cost four or five dollars a bottle.

The only way to really get to know wine is to buy it and drink it as often as possible. Though *The Vintage Wine Book* will make no one a connoisseur, it *will* keep the novice wine drinker from making the usual beginner's mistakes and at the same time guide him along the way to the selection and enjoyment of really good wines. If it accomplishes this, it will have served its intended purpose.

W. S. L.

Contents

Foreword v

Introduction to Wine Drinking XIII

I. THE WINES OF FRANCE 1

Introduction 1

The Wines of Bordeaux 9

Médoc 20

Graves 27

Saint-Émilion 31

Pomerol 35

Sauternes 36

The Wines of Burgundy 44

Côte de Nuits 52

Côte de Beaune 59

Côte Mâconnais 64

Beaujolais 65

Chablis 66

Champagne 68

Various French Wines 83

Alsace 83

The Loire Valley 84

The Rhône 86

Provence 87

II. THE WINES OF GERMANY 89
Introduction 89
The German Wine Districts 91
The Wines of the Moselle 104
The Wines of the Rheingau 109
The Wines of Rheinhessen and the Famous Liebfraumilch 114
The Wines of the Nahe 118
The Wines of the Palatinate 120
The Wines of Franconia 124
The Wines of the Middle Rhine 126
German Red Wines 127
German Sparkling Wines (Sekt) 128
The Service of German Wines 130

III. THE WINES OF ITALY 135
Introduction 135
Chianti 139
The Northern Provinces 142
Wines from Venetia 148
Central Italy 150
Dessert Wines 153
Vintages 154

IV. PORTUGAL AND ITS PORT AND MADEIRA 157
Port 157
Madeira 168

V. SPAIN AND ITS SHERRY 175

VI. VARIOUS EUROPEAN WINES 185
Introduction 185
Hungary 186

Switzerland 188
Spain 189

VII. THE WINES OF THE UNITED STATES 191
Introduction 191
New York State 195
California 202

VIII. BUYING AND STORING WINE 227

IX. SERVING WINE 239

X. VINTAGES 253

XI. BRANDIES AND LIQUEURS 257

Bibliography 261

Illustrations

1. *The French Wine Regions* 5
2. *The Bordeaux Region* 13
3. *The Burgundy Region* 51
4. *The German Wine Regions* 93
5. *Spain and Its Sherry—Portugal and Its Port* 173
6. *Wineglasses* 236

Introduction to Wine Drinking

Although wine drinking in Europe has been an accepted part of daily living since ancient times, it is only since the repeal of Prohibition that the custom has begun to take hold in the United States to any great extent. To be sure, in colonial days much wine was drunk by the wealthy class in the large cities, but it was pretty much ignored by the average person who had neither the means nor the opportunity to buy wine. Early attempts to make wine from the native American grapes did not meet with much success, nor would the native European vine thrive in our eastern states because of the generally colder winters that we have here, as contrasted with France or Germany. With the election of Andrew Jackson to the presidency in 1828, the colonial era of gracious living, and such wine-drinking tradition as there had been, was replaced by the harder, whiskey-drinking style of living which has more or less dominated the American scene up to the present time.

Since Prohibition ended, and especially in the years following the Second World War, Americans have once again become conscious of wine. This is attributable to several causes: First of all, large numbers of Americans have spent a year or two in Europe as a part of our military forces there, and many more have gone over on their own as tourists. Second, there has been a great deal of advertising and many feature articles in magazines and newspapers not only on wines, liqueurs, and brandies, but also on a more varied style of cooking and eating which takes the serving of wine as a matter of course and not as something special or something "fancy." Finally, our own American wine producers, particularly in California, have made such progress in the last twenty-five years that we can now enjoy, for $1.50 or $2, a bottle of fine domestic wine which is the equal of many European wines selling for a dollar or two more. There is no question, then, that wine drinking in America is becoming more and more popular, and, though it may never reach the proportions that it has in Europe, it will certainly become more a part of our everyday living than it ever has been in the past.

If wine drinking could be made as simple as opening a can of beer or pouring out a shot of whiskey, it would certainly have become even more popular than it already has. Unfortunately, and in spite of many advertisements and newspaper articles to the contrary, it is necessary to know *something* about wine if one is to enjoy it fully and get proper value for the money spent. We often tend to forget that Europeans have a long history of wine drinking behind them, and that their habits and practices in the serving and drinking of various wines are simply common knowledge and established tradition. These same practices and habits when brought to America, however, often seem like affectations and useless falderal, mainly because we don't understand the reasons for them. In this book we hope to guide the wine drinker in a middle course between the exaggerated simplicity of the "any-wine-goes-with-anything" school and the equally exaggerated opposite extreme of worrying about whether the wine was made from grapes grown in the vineyard on the left side of the road or in the vineyard on the right side. A basic knowledge of wine *is* necessary not only to be able to enjoy various types of wine to their fullest, but, even more important, to be able to avoid being cheated or disappointed when purchasing a bottle in a shop or restaurant. One should not be too idealistic and believe that all wine merchants and restaurant waiters are dedicated apostles of the art of good living, interested only in giving you the finest wines at the lowest prices. Just as with buying any other product, it is a case of *caveat emptor*. With wines perhaps a little more so!

Fortunately it is not at all difficult to acquire a sound basic knowledge of wines. It is mainly a question of practice and experience in drinking a number of wines of various types in order to get an overall impression of what they are like, what foods they best accompany, and how they compare with similar wines from other areas or other countries. Some guidance is necessary, especially in the beginning, but the real knowledge and experience can only be gained from the actual drinking of the wines in question. Even the terms "dry" and "sweet" mean different things to different people, and a great French Sauternes, described as "sweet and luscious" by an experienced wine drinker, might not seem sweet at all to someone who had drunk nothing but California muscatel before that. Wine drinking is in any case a very personal kind of experience and one which requires a bit of practice and a bit of concentration. Wine experts are certainly not born with a knowledge of wines, but neither do they acquire their knowledge from books alone. Happily, no great outlay of money is required in the beginning stages of wine drinking, since there is no point in buying expensive wines until one is fully able to appreciate them. Under $1 a bottle it is not possible to get much of anything, even in American wines, and one would do better to figure on an average price of $1.50 a bottle in the beginning, with an occasional excursion into the $2 and $2.50 price classes. The 97-cent specials in the wineshops are never worth bothering with and the wines are rarely, if ever, what the labels claim for them.

We can divide all wines into three main categories, no matter what country they come from or who makes them. These are (1) table wines, (2) sparkling wines, and (3) fortified wines. *Table wines* are produced by the natural fermentation of the juice of freshly squeezed grapes. They may be red, white, or pink (*rosé*) in color and be anywhere from 9 to 14 per cent alcohol, with 11 or 12 per cent about the average. They can be anything from very dry to very sweet and made from any number of different kinds of grapes. The great majority of table wines are dry—the opposite of sweet when talking about wine. One does not say that a wine is "sour" unless it is actually spoiled and is beginning to turn into vinegar. A "white" wine, by the way, is not actually white, but will be anything from a light yellow green to a rich gold in color. *Sparkling wines* are wines that are effervescent, and the best example is of course Champagne. (This is discussed further on page 68.) *Fortified wines* are wines which have had a small amount of grape brandy added to them to stop the fermentation of the wine and thus make them retain a certain amount of the natural grape sugar. Port and Sherry are the best known examples of fortified wines—often called "dessert" wines since many people feel that the term *fortified* might give the impression that the wines had been doctored in some way that was not quite honest. The fortified wines have an alcoholic content of about 20 per cent due to the addition of the brandy. Because of this higher alcoholic content they will also keep longer than any other wines after they have been opened, though they certainly lose some of their freshness if they are left around too long.

Wine can be made from other types of fruit besides grapes, and one often sees such specialties in wineshops as Danish cherry wine or American blackberry wine. There are also the various American "kosher" wines which are made very sweet by adding large quantities of sugar to them. The kosher wines and the fruit and berry wines are outside the scope of this book and in the pages that follow we shall be dealing only with wines made from naturally fermented grape juice.

The great majority of the world's wines are natural table wines and the method of making them has remained virtually unchanged over thousands of years. There are over one hundred fifty references to various wines in the Bible, and we know that even in the time of Christ the knowledge of wine making was sufficiently advanced to permit the making of various kinds of wine: dry and sweet, red and white, and so on. There was of course no such thing as unfermented wine, nor is there today for that matter, since all grape juice will turn into either wine or vinegar as a matter of course if it is not prevented from doing so by pasteurization or freezing—processes which were unknown two thousand years ago. In the last fifty years scientists have learned more about wine and the ways in which it develops than in all the centuries before them. Most of the scientific developments have been directed toward improving the quality of the grape vines, helping the wine to ferment properly, and determining the best vineyard sites for the various species of grapes. The basic process of letting the grape juice ferment into wine remains the same, however, and a vat of grape juice bubbling away, as it slowly turns into wine, looks just the same today to the wine grower in Bordeaux as it did to his Roman predecessor of two thousand years ago when the area was still known as Burdigala.

Wine takes its color from the skins of the grapes

and many white wines are made from blue or black grapes. By letting the grape juice ferment with the skins the wine would of course be red, but, by running it off into another vat and letting it ferment by itself, a white wine is produced. To make a pink (*rosé*) wine, the grape skins are left in contact with the juice just a few hours in order to produce the desired tint, and then the juice is run off and allowed to continue its fermentation away from the skins. When wine is made from white grapes there is no problem of coloration involved, and the juice can be left in contact with the crushed grapes or not, according to what the wine maker decides is best.

Four things go into the making of a great wine: soil, climate, the proper grape variety, and proper cellar care. The soil must be just right for the type of grape which is planted in it, and the climate must offer enough sunshine during the growing season to let the grapes ripen properly. Inferior grape varieties will never produce first-class wines, though they may produce greater quantities of wine than the best varieties, thus tempting the grower to place quantity ahead of quality. Finally, the proper handling of the wines in the cellar is of the greatest importance, not only while they are still in casks, but even after they have been bottled. Without proper storage even the best wines can be ruined. The wine drinker must not think, therefore, that simply because a wine is imported from Europe, it is *ipso facto* a fine, or even good, wine. In all the great wine-producing countries—France, Germany, Italy, Spain, and Portugal—the great bulk of the wine produced is just ordinary common table wine. The really great wines make up but a small fraction of the total annual production, and the average Frenchman or German rarely ever drinks, or even sees, the wines which all our American wine books urge the wine drinker to go out and buy at $5 and $6 a bottle or more.

Since the quantity of great European wines is necessarily limited, the prices will continue to rise as more and more people become interested in them and have the means to purchase them. There is also an increasing demand for the more moderately priced wines, and the point has now been reached where even the cheapest and poorest European wines can be sold here at a good profit simply because they are "imported." American wines, particularly those from California, have not yet achieved the desired degree of respectability to be accepted at their actual face value (which in many cases is considerable), and so the trade in second-rate and downright fraudulent European wines thrives as never before, especially in our eastern cities where a great deal of wine snobbery exists and people are more inclined to "buy labels" than to buy wine. The serious and knowledgeable wine drinker who would like to have a good sound wine as an inexpensive accompaniment to his daily meals should not even look twice at the vast array of 97-cent and $1.19 imported wines in the wineshops, but instead should buy good domestic wines for the same amount of money, or perhaps a few cents more, and be sure in this way of getting real value for what he is spending.

Many people overlook the very practical expedient of buying wines in half-bottles when only one or two people in the household are drinking wine. A full bottle of wine yields about six glasses, and the half-bottle therefore three. Especially in the beginning stages, when you are likely to want to sample a large number of wines, the half-bottles are very practical. Table wines, once they have been opened, are best consumed the same day, though they can be kept in the refrigerator for three or four days without spoiling. By purchasing many of your wines in half-bottles, this will usually not be necessary, however. Remember, though, that really great wines develop better in the larger bottles and it is not wise to buy them in the half-bottle sizes. For any of the wines in the $4 and up category, it is certainly wiser to wait until you have enough people at dinner to warrant opening a regular-sized bottle that can be consumed at one sitting. French wines are very often available in double-sized bottles called *magnums*. These usually cost just twice the price of two single bottles and are very much to be recommended for dinners where five or six people are drinking wine and more than one bottle is required. Wine is even better from a magnum than from a regular-sized bottle, and then, too, such a large bottle adds a certain festive note to the gathering and makes the dinner seem like something very special, even though the wine may not necessarily be the most expensive or greatest of its class.

Though we shall take up the question of vintages and the best years for certain wines in a later chapter, one or two comments on the subject may be of value here. To begin with, far too much importance is laid on the merits of various European vintages in the first place, with just about every importer distributing little cards or booklets telling which wines are "great" and which are merely good. One may usually assume as a general rule of thumb that if a foreign wine is on sale in this country at a fair price—say $2 or over—it is of a reasonably good, if not necessarily great, vintage year. The downright poor wines are always sold off in bulk by the growers and are rarely bottled under their own labels with a vintage date. They are often the 97-cent "bargains" which some stores feature. Second, the *only* thing that determines whether a vintage will be outstanding or not is the weather. There is a popular notion in this country that one should buy only the wines of the odd years, that is, 1951, 1953, 1955, 1957, and 1959, as though there were some actual plan or conspiracy on the part of European winegrowers to produce good wines only in the odd-numbered years and bad wines in the even-numbered ones. This of course is nonsense, since the growers would like to produce fine wines every year if the weather conditions were favorable enough to permit this. It is nothing more than coincidence, therefore, that many of the odd years in the decades of the forty's and fifty's produced fine wines. Nineteen forty-one and nineteen fifty-one, for example, were both below average. In California, most of the best wines also carry vintage dates, but here they are intended only to show the age of the wine and to distinguish one year's wine from the other. Many serious wine drinkers lay these wines away to age in their cellars just as they do with fine French wines, and naturally a vintage date is a necessity in such cases.

The fact that the very greatest French and German wines are described in this book in some detail does not mean that we are contradicting our suggestion that the beginning wine drinker buy only the less expensive wines. There will come a time, however, when you will want to try one of these truly great bottles, and the information will then be of considerable use to you. No book on wines would be complete without mentioning these Great Growths, and the fact that they are very, very expensive does not make them any the less great.

In conclusion we should like to point out that the recommendation of specific wines, vineyards, and producers is one of the main purposes of this book in attempting to guide the wine drinker along the highways and byways of wine drinking and wine buying. The author has no commercial interest in any vineyards, wine-producing firms, or wine-publicity organizations, nor has he received any free cases of wines for favorable mention of specific vineyards or producers. As far as he can ascertain, that recently coined word "payola" has not yet entered into the winegrower's vocabulary. Although some readers may find cause to disagree with certain recommendations or suggestions, the fine wines of the world are pretty generally known and acknowledged as such, and their listing and recommendation here is merely an attempt to make this book as complete and comprehensive as possible.

I

The Wines of France

INTRODUCTION

THE HISTORY OF VITICULTURE in France begins with the first vineyards planted by Phoenician traders and colonists around the year 600 B.C., in the area we now know as the city of Marseilles in southern France. Later, Greek, and then Roman colonizers carried the vines to other parts of France, so that by the year A.D. 92 the Roman emperor Domitian found it necessary to order the uprooting of all vineyards beyond the Alps, so great was the wine production in Gaul. This edict was in force for over a hundred years, until A.D. 210, when it was repealed by the Emperor Probus. (Thus France too has known its period of prohibition, and a much longer one, at that, than we had in this country in the 1920's and 1930's!) Though the vineyards in Bordeaux and Provence were flourishing several centuries before the time of Christ, it was not until the Romans had conquered Gaul that the more northern vineyards, such as those in Burgundy and Champagne, were laid out.

Charlemagne, who ruled over a more or less united Europe, from 771 until 814, did much to encourage winegrowing and made several laws regulating wine production and vineyard cultivation. Most of the wine made at this time was quite ordinary, but some vineyards and vineyard areas did stand out as the source of better-than-average wines. During the Middle Ages, and into the seventeenth and eighteenth centuries, various kings and nobles showed preferences for the wines of one particular area, thus bringing into great prominence wines which had until then been pretty much neglected. Both Champagne and Burgundy were the objects of royal favor at one time or another. Bordeaux had never had any trouble gaining fame for its wines abroad, and, from 1152 until 1453, when the area was for all practical purposes a part of England, huge quantities of Bordeaux wines were shipped to London every year—duty-free, of course, since they were really "English" wines!

Wine production thrived without interruption in France, in spite of wars and invasions, right up until the last century—until the year 1879 to be exact. In that year a very unwelcome little American guest made its appearance in the Bordeaux vineyards—a plant louse known as the Phylloxera vastatrix, which attacked the roots of the vines and killed them. The phylloxera had gotten to England on the cuttings of some native American vines which had been brought to the Botanical Gardens in London. How it ever made its way from London to Bordeaux, and from there to all the other vineyards of Europe, is still an unsolved mystery. At any rate, most of the great Bordeaux vineyards were devastated during the decade of the

1880's, and those of Burgundy and Champagne in the decade that followed. At first no one had any idea what to do about the phylloxera epidemic, and it looked very much like the end of winegrowing in France. Finally, someone hit upon the idea of grafting the French vines onto native American roots, since these, though the cause of all the trouble in the first place, were themselves resistant to the louse as a result of their long exposure to it in this country. Hundreds of thousands of rootstocks were brought to France, and the great vineyards were all gradually replanted after immense outlays of time and money. They have of course long since recovered from the phylloxera blight and are now producing wines just as great as before.

The quantity of wine produced in France each year staggers the imagination: one and a half *billion* United States gallons! There is also a tremendous quantity imported into France from Algeria, equal to about a quarter of the domestic production. This far overshadows the amounts that are exported each year, though in quantity only, it should be pointed out, not in quality. It should always be remembered that fully 90 per cent of this huge quantity of wine is nothing more than *ordinaire*, that is, wine of no particular merit or distinction which is sold in every streetcorner shop and priced according to the degree of alcohol it contains—10 per cent, 11 per cent, or 12 per cent. This is the Frenchman's daily beverage wine, often mixed with a little mineral water, and it is the mainstay of the French wine industry—an industry which employs one out of every seven Frenchmen.

All too often we tend to think that the French drink nothing but great vintage wines from world-famous estates, whereas the opposite is closer to the truth. It is actually easier to find the great French wines in a shop in New York City or even London than it is in Paris.

Most French restaurants feature local wines of their own particular area, whether the area happens to be a famous wine-growing region, such as Burgundy or Bordeaux, or whether it is just a region producing "little" wines of no great distinction. It would be completely unthinkable for a restaurant in Burgundy, for example, to carry anything much but Burgundy wines on its wine card, nor would one expect to find much Burgundy wine in the city of Bordeaux. Foreign wines are just about completely unknown on French wine lists, though an occasional German wine (and even some California wine) is to be found on the wine lists of a few of the top Parisian restaurants. Few Frenchmen would ever dream of ordering such wines, however, and they are listed primarily to give the wine lists an international character that they would not otherwise have. In general, most of the restaurants in Paris feature a cross section of all French wines, though the list often may be heavily weighed in favor of the proprietor's native province if he happens to come from a wine-producing area and is not a native of Paris. Much the same situation applies in New York and other large American cities where there are French restaurants, though in this country there is usually a much smaller selection of wines in most restaurants, and the prices are usually out of all reason. A 300 per cent or 400 per cent markup over the regular retail price of the wine is not at all unusual, and a wine costing $2 in the store would thus cost $6 or more when ordered in a restaurant!

The three great wine-growing areas of France, known to just about every wine drinker throughout the world, are Bordeaux, Burgundy, and Champagne. These are the areas that have made French wines famous and that have given France her reputation as the greatest wine-producing country in the world. Three other wine-growing regions also worthy of special mention

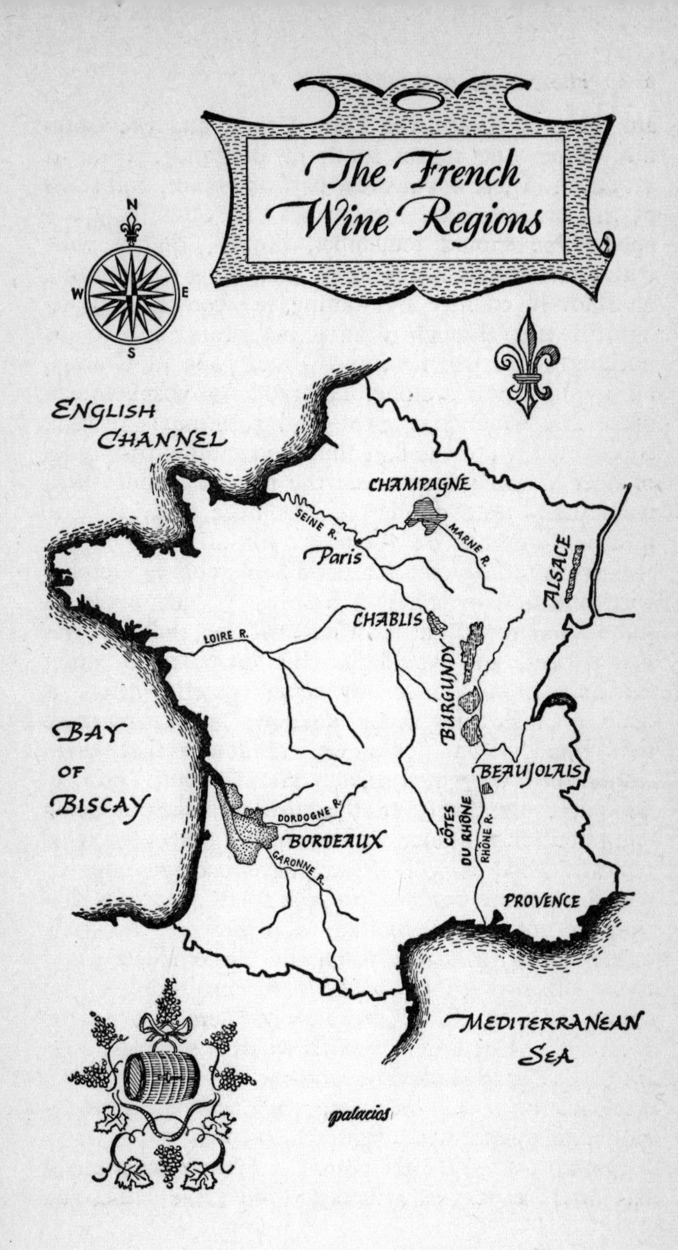
The French Wine Regions
N
W
E
S
ENGLISH CHANNEL
CHAMPAGNE
SEINE R.
MARNE R.
Paris
ALSACE
CHABLIS
LOIRE R.
BURGUNDY
BAY OF BISCAY
BEAUJOLAIS
DORDOGNE R.
BORDEAUX
CÔTES DU RHÔNE
RHÔNE R.
GARONNE R.
PROVENCE
MEDITERRANEAN SEA
palacios

are those of Alsace, the Loire Valley, and the Côtes du Rhône—the region south of Burgundy. Wine is produced in just about every part of France, and some of the obscure little local wines can often be quite good. One should remember, though, that a wine which one thinks is absolutely marvelous when drunk at a lovely country inn during the course of a delightful trip through France may turn out to be nothing at all when sampled again back in Chicago on a cold winter evening. The proper atmosphere can make any wine seem great, and a summer vacation trip is usually not the best time for assessing the values of untried wines, since even the poorest among them will usually taste wonderful. The bane of every wine merchant's existence is the returned tourist who usually appears in the wineshops around September or October with one or two labels or hastily scribbled notes on some "unknown" little wine that he thought was magnificent, and would like the merchant to order for him from France. In actual practice there is really no such thing as an "unknown" wine, any more than there is that "unknown" restaurant that serves wonderful food, which nobody knows about. You may be quite sure that even the smallest wine-producing communities in France are known, and that if the wine is really good it will already have become popular. Many wines are produced in such small quantities that they are not always exported, or, if they are, then only a few dozen cases may reach the United States, and they will perhaps be available in only one or two stores in New York City and nowhere else in the country. The variety of French wines is so great, however, that it is really not worth-while tracking down some relatively unknown wine when there are so many truly magnificent wines from which to choose.

During the past forty years the French government has passed a great many laws to protect the names and reputations of the great French wines, and also to protect the consumer against fraud. Unfortunately, an occasional dishonest shipper or importer can still be found here and there, and some fraudulent wines still manage to get into this country in spite of everything. Usually this is simply a case of an inferior wine being sold as a better-grade wine at a correspondingly higher price. A shipper may go to considerable trouble to evade the French laws if he is dishonest enough and feels that there is enough profit involved to make such trouble and expense worth-while. One way to get around the French law, for example, is to ship the wine in barrels to Amsterdam, where it can then be blended with other wines, bottled, and shipped to the United States, and in this way evade the jurisdiction of the French government completely. Such practices are rather rare, we are happy to say, but many of the very cheapest French wines sold in this country are not really what they claim to be on the label at all. Such wines enjoy an excellent market, however, since a great many people buy wines solely by price and want a "good bottle of imported wine" for not more than $1. They are not really much concerned about where the wine comes from or what it is as long as the label is reasonably attractive. Needless to say, no laws, however strict, will help in cases like this, and, since most wineshops sell hundreds of bottles of such wines each year, and at a very good profit indeed, they can hardly be expected to ban them from their shelves. It is simply up to the buyer to know what to look for on the label and to pay attention to what he is getting for his money. In most cases the salesmen in the wine and liquor shops know next to nothing about the wines they are selling, and in fact have often never even tasted them! The wine drinker must take it upon himself, therefore, to distinguish good from bad, and must not be fooled by pretty labels or bargain prices.

The price range of French wines in the United States runs from about $1 a bottle for the very cheapest wines of no particular quality, up to $17 a bottle for the greatest Burgundy, and up to $8 a bottle for the greatest Bordeaux wines. (Burgundy is always more expensive than Bordeaux since there is much less of it and the supply nowhere equals the demand.) The best vintage Champagne usually sells for around $8.50 a bottle, with nonvintage brands usually about $2 less. There are three or four special brands of Champagne that sell as high as $13.50 a bottle, but these are not encountered everywhere. Until you have acquired a good sound knowledge of French wines, it would be foolish indeed to buy the finest growths, even if price is no object to you. It is simply impossible to appreciate all the finer nuances and subtleties of the greatest French wines without a certain amount of wine-drinking experience and knowledge of what to expect from them. The wine will of course taste good, but then so would a similar wine selling for half the price! Many excellent French wines, both red and white, sell in the $2 to $3 price range, and certainly this is the area where most wine-drinking studies should begin. Buy with care, drink good wines, drink them regularly, and you will soon acquire the foundation and experience for branching out into the great and greatest wines of all, even though you may be able to enjoy them only on very special occasions. Unfortunately, the ever-rising prices of the truly great wines make their frequent enjoyment by the average person just about impossible. A $10 bottle of wine is not usually considered a part of most people's daily wine budget.

THE WINES OF BORDEAUX

Not only does Bordeaux have the largest annual wine production of any region in France—or in the world, for that matter—with an average total of a half billion bottles per year, but it also produces more truly great wines than any other of the world's wine regions. This is one of those rare instances where quality goes hand in hand with quantity. Indeed, it is only the large size of the great Bordeaux wine estates with their production of many thousands of bottles of fine wines that keeps the prices at all within reason. As a typical example, the greatest Burgundy vineyard, that of Romanée-Conti, is four and a half acres in size, whereas one of the greatest Bordeaux vineyards, that of Château Margaux, has about one hundred fifty acres in vineyards with an additional fifty acres resting. Another one of the great Bordeaux vineyards, Château Haut-Brion, has ninety-five acres. The comparison is best seen in the difference between the retail prices of the two types of wine. Whereas the great Romanée-Conti Burgundy will cost about $17 a bottle in the wineshops, one of the very greatest Bordeaux wines will cost around $7 or $8 a bottle. There are sound reasons, therefore, for advising the beginning wine drinker, and in fact any wine drinker on a budget, to buy mainly Bordeaux wines instead of Burgundy.

Needless to say, not all the wines shipped from Bordeaux are great, but there is more good-average wine produced there than anywhere else in the world, and the wine lover can find many delightful Bordeaux wines in the $2 to $3 price category.

Though wine production in Bordeaux has been going on for over two thousand years, it has only been in the past one hundred fifty years that the really magnificent wines, as we know them today, have been produced. In the Middle Ages there was much blending of the Bordeaux wines with inferior wines from the hinterlands, and most of the wine shipped from Bordeaux was of no great merit. However, it was cheap and it was available in large quantities—two factors that were strongly in its favor. The Bordeaux wines became known in England as "claret," from the French word *clairet*, which means a light-colored wine, similar to what we might call a rosé wine today. The wines are no longer this color at the present time, but the name has stuck for several hundred years and seems likely to do so for several hundred more. In this country, many of our very cheapest and poorest American wines are called claret, though they haven't the slightest resemblance to the real thing.

The bulk of the Bordeaux wine trade is handled by many large shippers who maintain cellars right in the city of Bordeaux itself, and who blend the wines of the lesser vineyards to make their own standardized brands of varying degrees of quality. Most of the firms also act as brokers for the great estate-bottled wines, but they have nothing to do with these wines themselves since they have already been bottled by the producers in their own cellars. Such famous firms as Calvet, Cruse, Eschenauer, Delor, Kressmann, and de Luze ship excellent wines for those who want inexpensive claret for their everyday enjoyment. As prices have gone higher and higher in recent years, the shippers' wines are unfortunately not so low in price as they used to be, and often run over $2 a bottle on the American market. They are nevertheless usually a better buy than the wine of some obscure château, which, though selling for less, may still be "château-bottled."

In Bordeaux, almost all the wine-producing estates are called châteaux, even though there may be no actual château on the property. On the large estates, where such buildings really do exist, they are more like what we should call a large mansion or manor house. Certainly there is no Bordeaux château like any of the beautiful châteaux in the Loire Valley of France! The term "château-bottled," as used in Bordeaux, is the same as "estate-bottled" which is used in Burgundy, and on wine labels in other countries as well. It means that the wine is bottled in the cellars of the estate where it is made, thus precluding the possibility that it has been tampered with between the time it is made and the time it finally reaches your table. The term "château-bottled" is *not* an automatic guarantee of quality, however, since any estate can bottle its own wines whether they are good or bad. In general, however, the great estates sell only their best wines under the château label. If the wine of a certain year is really poor, it will in all probability be sold off in bulk to be used in blending by a shipper in Bordeaux. There are occasional off years, such as 1948 or 1954, when some good wines were made, even though the vintage as a whole was not considered very great. Some of the châteaux may sell their wines under their own labels in such years, but at considerably lower prices. Such wines can often be good buys for the knowing wine drinker. If Bordeaux wine is château-bottled, the label will always carry the phrase "*Mis en bouteilles au Château*," or perhaps just "*Mise du Château*." One should not develop a mania for drinking only château-bottled wines, since many good wines would thus be overlooked and one would likewise run the danger of buying second-rate wines of no particular merit merely because the label said they were "Mis en bouteilles au Château."

Bordeaux produces both red and white wines, and, though the red wines are all dry, the white wines range from dry to very sweet. The red wine production is over three times as large as that of white, and it is, of course, the great reds which have brought world-wide fame to the Bordeaux wines. There are many divisions and subdivisions of the wine-growing areas around Bordeaux, but for our purposes here we shall only consider the five most important. One may now and then come across a wine from one of the lesser divisions at a bargain sale in a wineshop, but such wines are usually not worth bothering about. The five most important areas of the Bordeaux region are the *Médoc, Graves, Saint-Émilion, Pomerol,* and *Sauternes.* The Graves area produces a great number of dry white wines along with its large production of red wines. The Médoc is today the outstanding area for the greatest red wines, though the Graves region is by no means second-rate. To complicate matters further, the Médoc region is itself divided into several important townships or "communes"; *Margaux, Saint-Julien, Pauillac,* and *Saint-Estephe.* You will have to be well along in your wine-drinking career before you will be able to distinguish the wines of one of these communes from the other, but it does not require too much experience to be able to distinguish Médoc wine from, say, a Saint-Émilion or a Pomerol. The many names may seem confusing at first, but with a little experience in buying and drinking Bordeaux wines they soon become second nature. The point behind the whole business of dividing the area into such small and still-smaller districts is to locate with absolute accuracy the place from which any given bottle of wine may

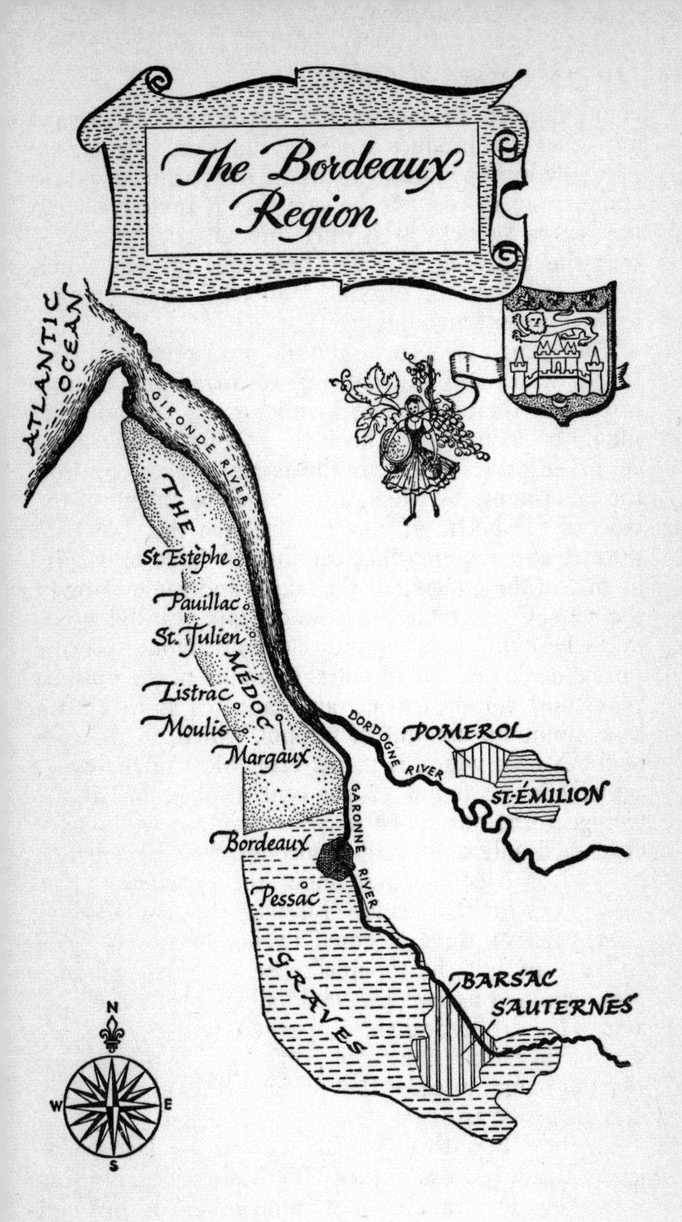
The Bordeaux Region
ATLANTIC OCEAN
GIRONDE RIVER
THE MÉDOC
St. Estèphe
Pauillac
St. Julien
Listrac
Moulis
Margaux
DORDOGNE RIVER
POMEROL
ST.-ÉMILION
GARONNE RIVER
Bordeaux
Pessac
GRAVES
BARSAC
SAUTERNES
N
W
E
S

come. Since every part of the vast Bordeaux vineyard area does not produce wines of the same quality, we naturally want to know just where our particular bottle comes from in order to be sure that it is from one of the better districts. It is only through trial and error over the centuries that the best sites for fine wines have been located, carefully cultivated, and brought to their present high quality.

The French laws governing the production and control of wines and winegrowing are many and complicated, but there is one with which every wine drinker should be acquainted. This is the so-called "*appellation contrôlée*" law, which, as the name implies, controls the exact name by which a wine may be called on the label of the bottle. It goes further than this, however, since it also requires that certain standards of quality be met in the growing of the grapes and the making of the wine. Only certain varieties of grapes can be grown in the best vineyards and only a certain amount of wine can be made per acre of vines. In addition, the finished wine must conform to certain standards as well, such as a minimum amount of alcohol, which, in the case of the Médoc wines, is 10 per cent. Most of the wines actually have around 12 per cent alcohol, but if the vintage turns out to be so poor that the wines have developed only 9 per cent of alcohol, they cannot then be sold as Médoc wines under the *appellation contrôlée* laws for that region. Likewise, the law allows a production of three hundred twenty gallons of wine to the acre, but the top-quality estates rarely produce even as much as two hundred gallons of wine to the acre. The second and third pressings of the grapes are sold off in bulk and are not bottled under the famous château names in order that a high standard of quality may always be assured.

To show how the *appellation contrôlée* law works, let us take a few examples of Bordeaux wines. Starting with the very cheapest wines produced in the area and sold by shippers as everyday table wines, the label would simply say "*Bordeaux rouge*," that is, Bordeaux red wine, and perhaps the vintage date, say 1953. Under this would appear the phrase, "*Appellation Bordeaux contrôlée*." In other words, the wine is guaranteed to be entirely from Bordeaux and not mixed or blended with wine from Algeria or the Midi section of France, but outside of that not much else is said about the wine. One step higher in quality would be a wine from one of the five main wine-growing areas of Bordeaux which we mentioned before: the Médoc, Graves, Saint-Émilion, Pomerol, and Sauternes. If the wine comes from vineyards entirely within the Médoc section of Bordeaux, then the label would say "*Appellation Médoc contrôlée*," which of course pinpoints the source of the wine much more accurately than just the word Bordeaux. The wine will be better in quality and more expensive since it came from one of the finest vineyard areas of Bordeaux, and not from one of the less good areas which produces only second-rate wines. To narrow the whole thing down much closer we can also find wines—and these are the very best—which list the commune or township rather than just the general area in which they are made. Taking one of the five communes of the Médoc for our example, we would then find the label reading "*Appellation Pauillac contrôlée*." The wine must then come entirely from vineyards within the commune of Pauillac, and, since we know that this is one of the really fine wine regions of Bordeaux, we can be reasonably sure that we are getting a good bottle of wine for our money. Unfortunately, not every bottle of an *appellation contrôlée* wine is outstanding, and there are even some good wines which do not carry this phrase, but in general it is best to buy only those wines where this phrase appears on the label. Just about all the really good wines are *appellation contrôlée*, so it is pointless to bother taking a chance on some unknown bottle that the wine merchant may be very anxious to get rid of at a bargain price. The *appellation contrôlée* law applies to wines grown in other parts of France too, with the outstanding exception of Champagne, where the name *Champagne* alone is considered sufficient guarantee of authenticity. It should be pointed out that the *appellation contrôlée* is never narrowed down any further than to the commune. A château in itself is *never* an *appellation contrôlée*, and so we find on the labels of Château Latour, for example, the phrase "*Appellation Pauillac contrôlée*," since the château is located within this commune of the Médoc, but we shall not find such a phrase as "*Appellation Château Latour contrôlée*." This is particularly important to remember in the case of Margaux, where there is a commune by that name as well as a château. Château Margaux is certainly the finest of the Margaux wines, but there are also other excellent wines produced in the commune of Margaux, many of which will carry the name of a château or just the name Margaux alone. All, however, will carry the phrase "*Appellation Margaux contrôlée*" on their labels. There is of course a world of difference between the commune wine labeled simply Margaux, and the wine of Château Margaux itself! The *appellation contrôlée* laws have done a great service in helping to eliminate fraud in the naming of French wines, though now and then some dishonest wines manage to get through. It is obviously impossible to watch what every winegrower does with every bottle of wine that he sells, and often it takes two or three years before a man is caught or enough evidence is collected to make a case against him. The great estates and top-ranking producers would never dare take a chance of endangering their reputations by resorting to fraud, and there is little likelihood that you will ever encounter a dishonest bottle among the wines in this class. The fact that a wine is an *appellation contrôlée* wine, though, does not mean that it will always be great, any more than the fact that the wine was château-bottled can mean this. Even a poor vintage can be bottled at the château or carry the *appellation contrôlée* phrase on the label. It is up to the buyer to determine whether the wine offered for sale is really worth the price being asked for it. In general, the prices usually reflect the quality of the wine, so that a great vintage of one of the leading châteaux will often cost more than twice as much as the same château's wine in an off year.

In 1955, a number of Bordeaux wine shippers devised an additional method of guaranteeing the quality of their wines, over and above the requirements laid down by the French government. This is the so-called ADEB seal, which is about the size of a small postage stamp and is either affixed to the neck of the bottle directly or stamped on the metal capsule which covers the cork. The seal is black and gold and the letters ADEB stand for the name of the sponsoring organization, the *Association pour le Développement de l'Exportation du Vin de Bordeaux*. All the wines which are to qualify for this seal are first sampled by an impartial tasting committee in a blind tasting, that is, the bottles are unmarked so that the committee does not know whose wines are being sampled at any given time. The ADEB standards are quite a bit higher than the minimum legal requirements for the Bordeaux wines, so that none of the inferior growths or blends is ever awarded an ADEB seal. We are told that, in the first year in which the ADEB seals were being used, over 20 per cent of the wines that were sampled were rejected as not being up to the required degree of quality. The ADEB idea smacks a little of chamber-of-commerce type of wine promotion, but as long as the announced standards are maintained it is certainly worth looking for wines which carry the ADEB seal—especially among the lower-priced regional and commune wines. In addition to looking for the name of a reliable shipper, such as one of those we mentioned before, it would be well worth your while to keep an eye out for the ADEB seal as well. It will certainly eliminate much guesswork when buying the lower-priced wines.

There are several different types of grapes grown in the Bordeaux area, four or five varieties for the red wines and about three for the white wines. The most famous of the red wine grapes is the Cabernet Sauvignon, of which there is a subvariety, the Cabernet Franc. Other red wine grape varieties are the Malbec, the Merlot, and the Petit Verdot. All of the red wine vineyards are planted predominantly with the Cabernet Sauvignon, but the exact proportion varies from vineyard to vineyard. Château Mouton-Rothschild is now planted with 85 per cent Cabernet Sauvignon, but the proportion of these grapes may be as little as 45 per cent in some vineyards. Each owner decides which grapes he thinks will do best in his vineyards and also what kind of a wine he would like to make. The Cabernet Sauvignon produces most of the classic, long-lived wines of the great châteaux, whereas those growers who are more interested in making pleasant wines with no claim to greatness and which will be ready to drink in perhaps five years will probably use more of the other grape varieties in their vineyards to attain this end. There is no law which determines the exact proportions of the grapes that may be planted as long as they are among the varieties which are officially approved for the Bordeaux region. The most important grape for the white Bordeaux wines is the Semillon. The other two varieties, the Sauvignon blanc and the Muscadelle, are used in varying proportions with the Semillon.

More has been written in praise of the Bordeaux wines than of any other wines in the world. There are entire books devoted to the subject, with lists of every single wine-producing estate or organization in the area, and attempts to describe them all in almost minute detail. Practically all the cases of wine snobbery which one encounters are based on a highly specialized knowledge of claret, that is to say, the red Bordeaux wines. We very rarely hear of a wine snob who boasts of his knowledge of Champagne, or Burgundy, or German wines, but in the field of Bordeaux wines it is very easy to talk about some unknown château wine which is "every bit as good as the First Growths, but nobody knows about it."

In reading descriptions of some of the great vintages of the past century, we often wonder if the writer is talking about wine at all, and not perhaps about some heavenly nectar which he has been privileged to taste. The various terms which are used to describe wines often sound like complete nonsense to the beginner, and of course, the more effusive they become, the harder it is for the average wine drinker to understand what they are all about. It is very difficult to put taste sensations into plain, everyday language, and even the most modest and conservative attempts to describe wine may sound a trifle silly to the uninitiated wine drinker who is trying to learn exactly what is meant. Thus the terms "light" and "full-bodied," or "dry" and "sweet," which we mentioned before, do not mean anything to someone who has never tasted the wines which are so described. It is only by actually sampling wines, and especially trying one against the other, that one can build up a frame of reference in the matter of taste sensations. In describing the great Bordeaux wines that follow, we have tried, therefore, to be as sparing of elaborate descriptions as possible in order to save the reader from unnecessary confusion. In the beginning, there is enough to remember in just the names and the types of the wines alone. There is certainly no point in trying to memorize taste descriptions of the wines except in the very broadest sense. Everyone should know, for example, that Sauternes is a very sweet wine, but the differences between the wines of the various first-growth châteaux can only be learned by drinking the wines in question and not by reading about them in this or any other book. In general, let us start off by saying that the red wines of Bordeaux are lighter and drier than those of Burgundy, and the white Graves wines are dry, while those of Sauternes are sweet.

MÉDOC

Not only are there carefully delimited wine-growing areas of Bordeaux, such as the Médoc, Graves, Saint-Émilion, Pomerol, and Sauternes (there are of course several others of lesser importance), but, as we have seen, these areas are also divided into various communes. In addition, however, the châteaux in each area have been classified according to the quality of the wine they produce. The most famous of these classifications is that of the Médoc area, which was made in 1855 by a group of Bordeaux wine shippers for the Bordeaux Chamber of Commerce. The list is still in use today, though there is much agitation for a change in the classification and it can hardly be called completely accurate at the present time. The sixty-odd châteaux in the Médoc classification have undergone many changes in the past one hundred years, and a new listing is certainly long overdue. The Médoc wines were divided into five groups known as "growths" or *crus* in French. The division was based on the prices which the wines commanded in the Bordeaux market at that time, and the best wines naturally brought the highest prices. It should not be assumed, however, that because a wine was classified in the Fifth Growth it is only one-fifth as good as a first-growth wine. Too many beginning wine drinkers become slaves to the Médoc classification, just as many become slaves to their little vintage charts, before they know what it is all about and before they are even able to distinguish a Bordeaux from a Burgundy. Remember that this classification lists only the very best of many excellent vineyards and that there are dozens of other outstanding Bordeaux wines which are almost as good as the classified growths, and in some cases actually better! We cannot, for obvious reasons, list those wines which we feel no longer deserve a place in the 1855 classification, but we shall suggest several which deserve higher ratings than they now enjoy, as well as others which many wine experts feel should be included but are not. The only other wine-growing area of Bordeaux to be classified in 1855 was the Sauternes region. The wines from the Graves, Saint-Émilion, and Pomerol areas were not popular enough in the last century to warrant their being classified like the great growths of the Médoc. However, in 1953, the Graves wines were officially classified, and, in 1955, the wines of Saint-Émilion. Neither of these two classifications is like the Médoc classification of five growths, and they are therefore much less complicated and likely to remain valid for a longer time.

First of all, though, let us consider the famous Médoc classification of 1855:

FIRST GROWTHS (*Premiers Crus*)

Château Lafite-Rothschild Château Margaux Château Latour Château Haut-Brion*	These wines still remain today the greatest of all Bordeaux red wines—the standard by which all others are judged.

* Château Haut-Brion is actually a Graves wine and not a Médoc. Because it was so outstanding, however, it was included in the 1855 classification of the Médoc wines. No classification of Graves wines was made at that time.

SECOND GROWTHS (*Seconds Crus*)

Château Mouton-Rothschild	Equal in every way to the First Growths and should be so listed.
Château Rausan-Ségla	
Château Rauzan-Gassies	
Château Léoville-Las-Cases	The Léoville wines are all outstanding, though the Barton is never château-bottled.
Château Léoville-Poyferré	
Château Léoville-Barton	
Château Durfort	
Château Lascombes	Now owned by a group of Americans, headed by Alexis Lichine.
Château Gruaud-Larose	
Château Brane-Cantenac	
Château Pichon-Longueville, Baron de Pichon	
Château Pichon-Longueville, Comtesse de Lalande	
Château Ducru-Beaucaillou	
Château Cos-d'Estournel	
Château Montrose	

THIRD GROWTHS (*Troisièmes Crus*)

Château Kirwan	This wine is never château-bottled.

Château d'Issan	Now owned by the Cruse family and being restored to its former high rank.
Château Lagrange	
Château Langoa-Barton	
Château Giscours	
Château Malescot-Saint-Exupéry	
Château Boyd-Cantenac	
Château Cantenac-Brown	
Château Palmer	Now considered to be equal in quality to a Second Growth.
Château Grand-La-Lagune	
Château Calon-Ségur	Another wine equal in quality to a Second Growth.
Château Ferrière	
Château Marquis-d'Alesme-Becker	

FOURTH GROWTHS (*Quatrièmes Crus*)

Château Saint-Pierre-Sevaistre Château Saint-Pierre-Bontemps	These wines are popular in Belgium, but not often encountered in the U.S.
Château Talbot	An outstanding wine which is often the equal of a Second Growth in quality.

Château Branaire-Ducru	
Château Duhart-Milon	
Château Pouget	
Château LaTour-Carnet	Should not be confused with the first-growth Château Latour
Château Rochet	
Château Beychevelle	Another wine which has outgrown its class. Easily equal to a Third, if not Second, Growth.
Château Marquis-de-Terme	
Château Prieuré-Lichine	Owned by Alexis Lichine since 1952, the wines are much better than ever before.

FIFTH GROWTHS (*Cinquièmes Crus*)

Château Pontet-Canet	The largest estate in all of Bordeaux, with a production of over sixteen thousand cases of wine a year. It is owned by the Cruse family and the wines are never château-bottled, though in quality they are easily equal to a Third Growth, and perhaps sometimes to a Second.

Château Batailley	
Château Haut-Batailley	
Château Grand-Puy-Lacoste	
Château Grand-Puy-Ducasse	
Château Lynch-Bages	Another outstanding wine often the equal of a Second Growth
Château Lynch-Moussas	
Château Dauzac	
Château Mouton-d'Armailhacq, *known since 1956 as* Château Mouton-Baron-Phillipe	An excellent wine. The estate is owned by Baron Philippe de Rothschild, who also owns the great Château Mouton-Rothschild.
Château du Tertre	
Château Haut-Bages-Libéral	
Château Pédesclaux	
Château Belgrave	
Château Camensac	
Château Clos-Labory	
Château Clerc-Milon-Mondon	
Château Croizet-Bages	
Château Cantemerle	Last, but by no means least, the Château Cantemerle wines are fully the equal of a Third, or possibly even Second, Growth.

In addition to the "Great Growths" or *Crus Classés*, there are five additional classifications of the Médoc wines, which in order of descending quality are called:

Crus Exceptionnels
Crus Bourgeois Supérieurs
Crus Bourgeois
Crus Artisans
Crus Paysans

There are several wines in the first two categories, the *Crus Exceptionnels* and the *Crus Bourgeois Supérieurs*, which are often the equal of many of their more illustrious neighbors in the *Crus Classés*. Since it is mainly the quality of the wine which determines its price on the Bordeaux market, these wines will not be cheap. They do, however, lack a certain amount of snob appeal and for that reason will not usually command the same prices that they would if they were officially listed among the *Grands Crus* wines. The following twelve châteaux are worth trying whenever you come across them, though not all of them will be available at any one time or in all vintages. The prices should not be much over $3 a bottle for most of these wines, though some may go as high as $3.50.

Château Chasse-Spleen
Château Gloria
Château Lanessan
Château La Tour-de-Mons
Château Le Boscq
Château Meyney
Château Moulin-Riche
Château Paveil-de-Luze
Château Poujeaux-Theil
Château Rosemont
Château Sénéjac
Château Siran

Not all the great Médoc wines come from the four communes of Margaux, Saint-Julien, Pauillac, and Saint-Estèphe, which we mentioned before. In order to make our listing complete, we should mention here six additional names of communes which produce some of the great growths of the Médoc, though they are much less important than the first four. These are: *Arsac, Labarde, Ludon, Macau, Moulis,* and *Saint-Laurent*. There are about forty more communes in the Médoc area, but since they produce wines of much lower quality than the ten we have mentioned, it is not worth-while listing any of them here. Actually, the first four communes are the really important ones, since the other six have only eight of the Great Growths among them.

GRAVES

The Graves district of Bordeaux begins just north of the city of Bordeaux itself, where the Médoc ends, and runs south as far as the Sauternes region. The word "*graves*" means "gravel" in English, and this is the type of soil which predominates in the region. People who are not familiar with wine-growing methods are often surprised to learn that the vine thrives in the most unlikely types of soil, in soil, that is, where no regular crops could possibly grow. The gravelly soil of the Graves region of Bordeaux is a prime example of this, for excellent wines are made here even though an agricultural expert would probably not consider land of this type suitable for crops of any kind.

Because so much white wine is produced in the Graves region, many people overlook the great red wines and do not associate red wines with this area at all. Nevertheless, there is more red wine produced in the Graves district than white, and the great wine of *Château Haut-Brion* is one of the finest of all Bordeaux wines. It was included in the 1855 classification of the Médoc wines, as we have seen, and fully deserves its reputation and rating as a First Growth. Indeed, there are many wine experts who would claim that Château Haut-Brion is the greatest of all red wines, but this, of course, is a matter of personal opinion. Vintages vary from year to year and in some years one château will be particularly outstanding in the quality of its wine, but the next year it may well be in second or third place. Comparisons are more or less pointless when it comes to the very greatest château wines, since it is often a question of personal taste and nothing is to be gained by trying to select one "best" wine from among so many great ones.

Just as there were four important communes in the Médoc region for the production of fine wines, there are five in the Graves region which are noted for outstanding red wines. These are: *Pessac, Leognan, Martillac, Cadaujac,* and *Talence.* This last one, Talence, is the least important of the five and its wines are often included with those of Pessac. The classification of the various Graves vineyards in 1953 was not completely satisfactory, since many vineyards which produce good wines were not included in the listing. No attempt was made to group the wines into classes, as was done in the Médoc in 1855, but rather the best ones were selected and listed in one group without any attempt to rank them within that group. The following twelve wines, therefore, are listed in alphabetical order, though it goes without saying that Château Haut-Brion is supreme among them and actually in a class by itself.

CLASSIFIED RED WINES OF GRAVES

Château Bouscaut
Château Carbonnieux
Domaine de Chevalier
Château Haut-Bailly
Château Haut-Brion
Château La Mission-Haut-Brion
Château Latour-Haut-Brion
Château Latour-Martillac
Château Malartic-Lagravière
Château Olivier
Château Pape Clément
Château Smith-Haut-Lafitte

Many of these châteaux also produce white wines as well as red, and in some cases, such as *Château Carbonnieux*, the white wine is more easily found than the red in American wineshops. The same might be said of *Château Olivier*, and these two wines are probably the best known of the white Graves. Prices of the Graves wines are about the same as those for the better Médoc wines. Château Haut-Brion, like the first-growth Médoc wines, is in the over $7 class, but the other growths can usually be purchased for around $3 to $5 a bottle.

The white Graves wines are possibly the best known of all French white wines, though they are certainly not the finest. The wines range from fairly dry to fairly sweet, though they are never as sweet as Sauternes, for example, or as dry as a Chablis. Most of the white Graves found on the market today are definitely on the dry side, with few, if any, sweet ones being available in the United States. Under the *appellation contrôlée* law, a regular Graves wine must have between 10 and 12 per cent alcohol. If the alcoholic content is 12 per cent or higher, the wine may then be sold as *Graves Supérieures,* and will be somewhat higher in price. In fine vintage years, therefore, just about all the Graves wines will be entitled to the Graves Supérieures designation, where in poor years, when the wines are thin and lacking in alcohol, even the best estates may have to be content with the designation of Graves alone. Not all the châteaux bother about this difference in nomenclature, feeling that their own names and reputations are sufficient guarantee for the quality of the wines they sell. It is quite possible, therefore, that some of the best Graves wines will never have "Graves Supérieures" printed on the labels, even though they are legally entitled to do so.

Not all the white Graves wines are château-bottled by any means, and there are often great differences in the quality of the wines sold under a shipper's label simply as Graves or Graves Supérieures. When any wine becomes exceptionally popular, the tendency is always to stretch the available supply just as far as possible, usually by blending with other wines. It is of the utmost importance to buy Graves wines only when the shipper has a first-class reputation, or when the wine is château-bottled. There are only a half-dozen châteaux in the official classification of white wines, but there are many others producing very good wines too.

CLASSIFIED WHITE WINES OF GRAVES

Château Bouscaut
Château Carbonnieux
Domaine de Chevalier
Château Laville-Haut-Brion
Château Latour-Martillac
Château Olivier

At the present time the wines of the Domaine de Chevalier command the highest prices for the white Graves—over $3 a bottle. This is partly because of the excellent quality of the wine, but also because very little of it is produced. Also outstanding is the wine from Château Carbonnieux. Château Olivier is often the easiest white Graves to find because its annual production is over eight thousand cases as against only a little over three hundred cases of the Domaine de Chevalier. It is a top-quality wine, and usually commands about the same price as the Château Carbonnieux, around $2.50 a bottle. Other white Graves worthy of your attention are the following châteaux:

Cháteau de la Brède
Château Couhins
Château Ferrande
Château Fieuzal
Château Haut Nouchet
Château Le Tuquet

There is also a superb white wine made at the Château Haut-Brion, and in the Médoc there is the excellent Pavillon Blanc of Château Margaux, the only white wine of this area that can hold its own against the white Graves.

SAINT-ÉMILION

The two remaining red wine districts of Bordeaux, Saint-Émilion and Pomerol, produce wines that are quite similar in character and so we shall consider them together. The Saint-Émilion and Pomerol wines are often called "the Burgundies of Bordeaux," since they are heavier and fuller-bodied than the Médoc and Graves wines. They cannot of course actually be compared with Burgundy wine, but even a beginning wine drinker could distinguish between a Saint-Émilion and a Médoc wine without knowing too much about either one. The Saint-Émilion and Pomerol wines are much less complex than the great Médoc and Graves wines, though the best of them are every bit the equals of the finest Médocs. Because the wines were not too well known a century ago, none of them was ever included in the classifications that were made in 1855. Nevertheless, the best Saint-Émilions and Pomerols now sell at about the same prices as the best Médocs and Graves and certainly rank among the really great wines of Bordeaux. In 1955, the Saint-Émilion wines were finally classified into four groups, but only the first two groups are of interest to us, since the third and fourth, unlike the Médoc classification, are not made up of the top-quality wines. Though there are only twelve châteaux in the first group, there are sixty in the second, but, since many of them are found in the American market, we felt it worth-while to list them all. The first category is known as First Great Growths, and the second simply as Great Growths. One interesting feature of the classifications is that they are subject to revision every ten years. One could only wish that the same condition applied to the Médoc classification! There are many other Saint-Émilion wines on the market, but with such a huge classified list to choose from it is not necessary to take any chances with unknown wines, especially when the better ones are so readily available and at fairly reasonable prices.

SAINT-ÉMILION FIRST GREAT GROWTHS
(*Premier Grand Cru Classe*)

Château Ausone
Château Cheval-Blanc
Château Beauséjour (Duffau-Lagarrosse)
Château Beauséjour (Dr. Fagouet)
Château Belair
Château Canon
Clos Fourtet
Château Figeac
Château La Gaffelière-Naudes
Château Magdelaine
Château Pavie
Château Trottevieille

SAINT-ÉMILION GREAT GROWTHS
(*Grand Cru Classe*)

Château l'Angélus
Château Balestard-la-Tonnelle
Château Bellevue
Château Bergat
Château Cadet-Bon
Château Cadet Piola
Château Canon-la-Gaffelière
Château Cap-de-Mourlin
Château Chapelle Madeleine
Château Chauvin
Château Corbin (Giraud)
Château Corbin-Michotte
Château Coutet
Château Croque-Michotte
Château Curé-Bon-la-Madeleine
Château Fonplégade
Château Fonroque
Château Franc-Mayne
Château Grand-Barrail-Lamarzelle-Figeac

Château Grand-Corbin-Despagne
Château Grand-Corbin-Pecresse
Château Grand-Mayne
Château Grand-Pontet
Château Grandes Murailles
Château Guadet-Saint-Julien
Clos des Jacobins
Château Jean Faure
Château La Carte
Château La Clotte
Château La Clusière
Château La Couspaude
Château La Dominique
Clos La Madeleine
Château La Marzelle
Château Larcis-Ducasse
Domaine de Larmande
Château Laroze
Château La Serre
Château La Tour-du-Pin-Figeac (Bélivier)
Château La Tour-du-Pin-Figeac (Moueix)
Château La Tour-Figeac
Château Le Chatelet
Château Le Couvent
Château Le Prieuré
Château Mauvezin
Château Moulin-du-Cadet
Château Pavie Decesse
Château Pavie-Macquin
Château Pavillon Cadet
Château Petit-Faurie-de-Souchard
Château Petit-Faurie-de-Soutard
Château Ripeau
Château Sansonnet
Château Saint-Georges-Côte-Pavie
Clos Saint-Martin
Château Soutard
Château Tertre-Daugay
Château Trimoulet
Château Trois Moulins
Château Troplong-Mondot
Château Villemaurine
Château Yon Figeac

Of the First Great Growth Saint-Émilion wines, the *Château Cheval-Blanc* is generally considered the finest at the present time. The *Château Ausone* had been able to keep its original French vines intact, in spite of the phylloxera, right up into the present century. Eventually, they too succumbed, and now the vineyard is planted with the grafted vines. These new vines are now old enough to yield fine wines once again, and the quality of Château Ausone's wines should improve from year to year.

Among the many names in the classified lists of Bordeaux wines are several that sound almost alike. It is important not to confuse wines which are completely different in character (and price) just because their names may be very similar. Among the large list of Saint-Émilion wines, for example, *Château Grand-Pontet* should not be mistaken for Château Pontet-Canet in the Médoc. Likewise, the *Château Le Prieuré* has nothing to do with Château Prieuré-Lichine in the Médoc. The Saint-Émilion *Château Moulin-du-Cadet* is likewise no relation to Château Mouton-Cadet, Mouton-Rothschild's "second" wine. If you get the habit of reading labels carefully, such mistakes as these will be easily avoided. The fact that the names are often so much alike does not mean that the growers are dishonest. Often the names have a long tradition behind them and the owners are quite justified in not wanting to change the names of their châteaux simply because there are people who mix up one name with another. Not all of the classified growths of Saint-Émilion are imported into the United States by any means, but most good wineshops carry a representative selection and there should be no difficulty in making a choice using the classification lists as a guide. In the case of the Saint-Émilion wines, we might well say that you should not buy any wine which is not listed in the foregoing classifications if you wish to be absolutely sure of avoiding disappointment. It is possible, of course, that a bad wine from one of the classified châteaux might slip through the various controls which are imposed on it, but the chances of this are much less than with a wine which is not listed as a First Great Growth or Great Growth, and it hardly seems worth-while to take any risk.

POMEROL

Pomerol is the smallest of the major red wine districts of Bordeaux, and for many years was lumped together with Saint-Émilion. It was not until 1923, in fact, that Pomerol actually became independent of Saint-Émilion. The wines are very much alike, though the Pomerol matures more rapidly and can therefore be drunk much sooner than the Saint-Émilion wines. They are usually considered as wines intermediate between the Médoc and the Saint-Émilion in character. Though there is no official classification of Pomerol wines, the local chamber of commerce has made up its own list which is as accurate as any. The best of the Pomerol wines, *Château Pétrus*, ranks among the finest of all Bordeaux growths, and, like Château Cheval-Blanc in Saint-Émilion, it commands a price equal to the top-ranking Médoc wines—usually over $5 a bottle for the great vintage years. Though Château Pétrus is the undisputed leader among the Pomerol wines, it will be seen from the titles of the various classifications that the committee making up the list tried its best to give everyone top billing!

FIRST OF THE GREAT GROWTHS
(*Premier des Grands Crus*)

Château Pétrus

GREAT FIRST GROWTHS
(*Grands Premiers Crus*)

Vieux Château Certan
Château Certan

FIRST GROWTH OF UPPER POMEROL
(*Premier Cru Haut-Pomerol*)

Cru l'Évangile

FIRST GROWTHS (*Premiers Crus*)

Château Beauregard
Château Nénin
Château Petit-Village
Château Trotanoy
Château Guillot
Château Clinet
Château Lafleur
Château La Commanderie
Château Gazin
Château Le Gay
Clos Lacombe
Clos l'Église

There are many other good Pomerol wines as well as those listed above, but here once again it would be foolish for the inexperienced wine drinker to bother with an unknown wine that may be offered at a bargain price when there are over a dozen really good wines from which to choose. Since the Pomerol region is so small, there will not be so many of the wines available as from the Médoc, for example, though several of the châteaux are quite large. *Château Nénin* is often the easiest one to find, since it produces over eight thousand cases of wine a year on the average. *Château Pétrus* is only about a third as large, with an average annual production of under three thousand cases. When high quality is combined with small quantity, the price of the wine is bound to be high, but there are fortunately many other Pomerol wines in the classified list which are in the $2 a bottle price bracket and well worth trying.

SAUTERNES

The last of the great wine-producing regions of Bordeaux is that of *Sauternes.* The wines produced here are all white wines. In discussing Sauternes, we must first of all realize that all the wines produced in this area are sweet and luscious—there is no such thing as a dry Sauternes. In the United States, we have many different types of wines using the name "Sauternes," but none of them really bears any resemblance to the French wine of this type made in the area of Bordeaux. (In this country, the name is often spelled without the final "s" and with a small initial "s" instead of a capital.) Those who have never tasted a genuine Sauternes are usually quite astonished at the unique taste of this wine. It is nothing at all like the sweet, fortified wines made in this country, or for that matter in Spain or Portugal either. As we have already pointed out, Port and Sherry derive their sweetness from the addition of a sweet grape brandy to the wine, which not only stops the fermentation and thus keeps some of the natural grape sugar in the wine, but also raises the alcoholic content from 12 per cent or 13 per cent to about 20 per cent. Sauternes, on the other hand, is a perfectly natural wine with nothing added to it. Its alcoholic content runs around 13 per cent or 14 per cent, and sometimes as high as 16 per cent or 17 per cent. The secret of making a great Sauternes is a mold or fungus which attacks the grapes in the autumn, causing them to shrivel on the vines and thus develop a very concentrated sweet juice. This fungus, known as the Botrytis cinerea, is usually described more picturesquely as the "noble rot"—a rather unpleasant-sounding term—or in French as the *pourriture noble*. It is found only in the Sauternes region of Bordeaux, in Germany, and in the Tokay region of Hungary. Mild, damp weather in the month of September encourages the development of the fungus, and it unfortunately does not occur in our own California wine regions.

Harvesting the grapes in Sauternes is a long drawn-out process, since only the overripe grapes are picked, those, that is, that have been attacked by the *pourriture noble* and have begun to shrivel on the vines. This means that most grapes are individually picked and not gathered in bunches as in other wine-growing regions. The workers must go through the vineyards many, many times and the harvest itself stretches out over a much longer period than is the case in the Médoc, for example, or in the neighboring section of Graves. When weather conditions have been ideal, and the grapes have attained the overripe state without any prolonged period of rain or other mishaps, the fungus can do its work properly and the grapes will develop the sweet, concentrated juice that makes a great Sauternes. If, on the other hand, a period of rain should set in during the harvest time, the whole thing might be ruined and the wines will never have the sweetness which one expects of them. In poor years most of the great châteaux sell their wines to shippers who then market them simply as Sauternes, without any château name or château bottling. Some of the smaller vineyard owners regularly sell their wines to the shippers, even in great years, so it does not necessarily mean that all shippers' Sauternes are made from poor wines. However, if you have never tasted a real Sauternes before, it is best to buy a bottle from one of the famous châteaux, since otherwise you will not get a completely accurate impression of the qualities of these wines. In the United States one often finds labels marked *Haut-Sauternes,* which is supposed to designate a better quality wine than one marked simply *Sauternes.* A shipper might charge $2 a bottle for his regular Sauternes, and perhaps $2.75 for his Haut-Sauternes. This distinction is unknown in France, and the name Haut-Sauternes is legally meaningless. The French government permits it on wines exported to English-speaking countries, however, since it does no real harm.

There is no area called Haut-Sauternes, nor does it mean that the grapes were picked from the top of the vines, as one Frenchman assured an American lady that it did! (The French word *haut,* pronounced *oh,* means "upper" or "top.") The name does get a little out of hand, however, when one shipper in Bordeaux can charge well over $3 a bottle for an Haut-Sauternes, while all the first-growth château wines are selling for $3 a bottle or less. For those occasions when a good Sauternes is called for, it is certainly wisest to buy the château wines and not the bottles marked *Sauternes* or *Haut-Sauternes.* There is not so much difference in price, and in some cases the better wines are actually cheaper. We need hardly add that the wines of Sauternes are not dinner wines, in the sense that one would drink them with the main part of a meal, but rather dessert wines which are best with fresh fruits or other sweet desserts.

The best wine-producing châteaux of Sauternes have been classified as in the other Bordeaux wine regions. The Sauternes classification was made in 1855, at the same time that the Médoc classification was made. There have not been so many changes in the fortunes of the various Sauternes châteaux, however, so that the ratings are still just about as valid as they were over a hundred years ago. Though we shall list the châteaux of the Second Growth here for the sake of completeness, their wines are not too often met with in the United States. This is partly because the output of the first-growth châteaux is so large that the demand for Sauternes can pretty well be met by these wines alone. The custom of having fresh fruit for dessert, together with a glass of Sauternes, is hardly known in this country at all, and the Sauternes wines have never attained the popularity they deserve.

Again in Sauternes there are five communes whose names will be encountered on the labels of the various growths. These are *Sauternes* itself, *Bommes, Fargues, Preignac,* and *Barsac*. There is not a great deal of difference between the wines of the various communes, with the exception perhaps of Barsac, where they tend to be a little less rich and luscious and a little fruitier than the other Sauternes. The beginning wine drinker would be hard put to distinguish any differences in the various growths, and nothing is to be gained by searching for the wines of one particular commune. The *appellation contrôlée* law permits the wines of Barsac to be sold with either the Sauternes or Barsac name, and some shippers feel that the Sauternes name is best used on all their wines, since not too many people would be familiar with the name Barsac. Only wines coming from one of the five above-named communes can legally be called Sauternes under the laws of the *appellation contrôlée.*

When the Sauternes wines were classified in 1855, it was found that one château was so outstanding in its quality that it deserved to be put into a special class all by itself at the top of the list. The quality of the wine has been maintained over the ensuing years and there has never been any reason to question its preeminent place among the great Sauternes.

FIRST GREAT GROWTH
(*Premier Grand Cru*)

Château d'Yquem

FIRST GROWTHS (*Premiers Crus*)

Château La Tour Blanche
Château Lafaurie-Peyraguey
Clos Haut-Peyraguey
Château Rayne-Vigneau
Château Suduiraut
Château Coutet
Château Climens
Château Guiraud
Château Rieussec
Château Rabaud-Promis
Château Rabaud-Sigalas

SECOND GROWTHS (*Deuxièmes Crus*)

Château Myrat	Château Nairac
Château Doisy-Daëne	Château Caillou
Château Doisy-Dubroca	Château Suau
Château Doisy-Védrines	Château de Malle
Château d'Arche-Lafaurie	Château Lamothe-Bergey
Château d'Arche	Château Lamothe-Espagnet
Château Filhot	Château Romer
Château Broustet	

Once again we should emphasize that the classifications of the wines should not be taken too literally. A Second Growth does not mean that the wine is second-rate, nor is there any attempt at classification within the listings—*Château Myrat* is not necessarily the finest of the Second Growths, nor *Château Romer* the poorest. It should also be borne in mind that in great years there are many château wines which are on an equal level of excellence with *Château d'Yquem*, and sometimes one or two are even thought to excel it in certain vintages. Prices run around $7 and $8 for Château d'Yquem, though the off years can be bought for around $3. They are then, of course, not true examples of the fine quality of this wine. First Growths all run around $3 a bottle in the best vintages. *Château Filhot* is the only one of the Second Growths commonly met with in wineshops and usually costs about the same as a First Growth. It is only the huge production of the Sauternes châteaux which keeps the prices within reason for such outstanding wines. Château d'Yquem, for example, is the largest of all, with an annual production of almost nine thousand cases of wine. Were it not for this huge quantity the price would be twice or three times as high. The owner of Château d'Yquem, the Marquis de Lur-Saluces, also owns the two second-growth châteaux, Filhot and de Malle, and no expense is spared in maintaining the high quality of these wines as well. The first-growth Château La Tour Blanche has fallen somewhat from its former high standards since its owner died and the estate was willed to the government of France, which now operates it as a school of viticulture.

The red Bordeaux wines have always been considered the classic accompaniment to lamb or roast beef, though the heavier wines from Pomerol and St. Émilion will certainly go well with steak too. The white wines from Graves are usually best when served with chicken, seafood, or even a baked ham. The sweet Sauternes are at their best when served with fresh fruit, particularly peaches or nectarines, at the end of a meal. Never make the mistake of serving them with fish or chicken simply because they are white wines and are therefore supposed to "go" with white meat! The proper place for a Sauternes is at the end of a meal, as a dessert wine, and not with any of the main courses at dinner. The white Graves are served well chilled, but the Sauternes should be quite cold, since otherwise they will be rather cloying in their sweetness. The red Bordeaux wines are served at room temperature, though this does not mean 80 degrees. If the wine is brought up from a cool cellar it should be allowed to acquire room temperature gradually, away from all radiators or other sources of heat. Never try to warm the wine by plunging it into hot water or putting it on a radiator! It is better to drink the wine a little cool than to treat it in this barbarous fashion.

Always serve the red Bordeaux wines in your largest glasses, so that they need only be filled half full and one can then swirl the wine a little in the glass to fully release the delightful bouquet. The white Bordeaux wines do not require particularly large glasses, but no wineglass should ever be filled more than two-thirds full in any case. Where one may well drink several glasses of a red Bordeaux wine during the course of a particularly fine dinner, most people will not drink more than one, or at most two, glasses of a Sauternes with the dessert because of the richness and sweetness of the wine. A half-bottle of Sauternes will usually be enough for four people if another wine has preceded it with the main course.

Finally, do not feel that you must always serve guests one of the great first-growth wines at dinner. There are many, many other fine Bordeaux wines at half the price of the First Growths which will prove more than satisfactory in every way. If cocktails are served before dinner, it is then a sheer waste of money and fine wine, since no one could possibly appreciate a great Bordeaux wine after having his taste buds numbed by cocktails beforehand. A serious wine drinker, about to serve a fine wine at dinner, will limit the cocktail hour to a glass of Sherry, a glass of *brut* Champagne, or perhaps Vermouth on the rocks, omitting strong drinks altogether. Otherwise, it is best to serve an inexpensive regional wine and no one will know the difference anyway. The mere fact that there is wine with dinner is usually enough in such cases.

THE WINES OF BURGUNDY

Burgundy has become almost a meaningless term in the United States, and is very commonly used to describe wines of no particular quality. The authentic Burgundy wines, however, come only from a very small area of France, what was formerly the Duchy of Burgundy and is today part of several French *départements.* Not only does Burgundy produce some of the greatest red wines of France, but also some of the finest white wines as well. None of these great wines is produced in large quantities, however, and they are always expensive and often difficult to find in wineshops. The area where all the fine red wines, and all but one of the white wines, are produced begins at the city of Dijon, the former capital of the Duchy of Burgundy, about one hundred ninety miles south of Paris. This wine-growing region of Burgundy is usually referred to as the *Côte-d'Or*, or, in English, "slope of gold." The countryside is one of gently rolling hills, and when the vineyards take on their autumnal colors they really do appear golden in the sunshine. The Côte-d'Or itself is subdivided into two other "côtes," the *Côte de Nuits* in the northern half, taking its name from the town of Nuits-St. Georges, and the *Côte de Beaune* in the lower half, taking its name from the town of Beaune. South of the Côte-d'Or region there are two additional wine-growing districts that are still part of Burgundy, though they do not produce any of the really great wines. These districts are known as the *Mâconnais* and *Beaujolais*, the latter being no doubt the best-known French red wine in the United States. To the northeast of Dijon, there is the town of Chablis, where some of the finest of all French dry white wines are produced.

Winegrowing has been known in Burgundy for two thousand years, and the wines have been appreciated for their high quality for the past two or three hundred years at least. The fame of the Burgundy wines is world-wide and there is simply not enough of them to go around. The American wine drinker is at somewhat of a disadvantage, since the Swiss and the Belgians seem to have gotten there first. Switzerland, for example, imports over twelve times as much Burgundy as the United States, and Belgium imports four times as much. Such statistics usually come as somewhat of a shock to American wine drinkers, who have been led to believe that the best of the world's wines all end up on our shores. The days when a French winegrower would do almost anything to get American dollars are long since over, and Belgian or Swiss francs are as readily accepted as dollars. The economic boom in postwar Europe has meant that more people are able to afford the finer things of life, and the demand for fine wines has thus increased tremendously over what it had been in prewar years. Unfortunately for American Burgundy drinkers, the Swiss, and especially the Belgians, have always preferred Burgundy to Bordeaux, and the demand for these wines is therefore at an all-time high.

The greatest single factor that makes the purchase and selection of fine Burgundy wines so difficult, however, is the division of the vineyards into so many small parcels, each owned by a different person. After the

French Revolution most of the large vineyards were divided up among smaller growers, and, in the years since, some of them have been divided and redivided so much that some growers have only a few rows of vines less than an acre in extent. Since most of these small growers had no facilities for bottling their own wines, they were always sold to shippers who performed this operation for them. After Bordeaux wines began to be bottled at the châteaux in the last part of the nineteenth century, the clamor arose for estate-bottled wines from Burgundy too. This method of bottling the wines finally got started at the beginning of the present century, and since the end of the Second World War it has become general practice among those growers with large enough holdings to make it worth-while. The very small growers still of course sell their wines to the *négociants*, or shippers. An estate-bottled Burgundy will always have on the label the phrase, "*Mis au Domaine*" or "*Mis du Domaine.*" Sometimes the phrase, "*Mis en bouteilles par le propriétaire*" is also used, but the first two are more commonly seen. All the greatest Burgundies are now estate-bottled, but they are also the most expensive ones, needless to say. To find a good, medium-priced Burgundy (for there are no low-priced Burgundies any more that are authentic), we must buy the wines of the reputable shippers. If a shipper is completely honest he will market the wines that he has bought from the small growers under his own name without claiming either directly or by implication that they are estate-bottled. If, however, he would like to make his wines look like estate-bottled wines, there are certain phrases that he can use on his labels to give that impression. Some of these are: "*Mise en bouteille sous notre garantie* (Bottled under our guarantee)," "*Mise d'Origine* (Bottled at the place of origin)," "*Mis en bouteilles dans mes caves* (Bottled in my cellars)," or

"*Mis en bouteilles au Château* X (Bottled at the Château X)." There are no châteaux in Burgundy, in the sense that this phrase is used in Bordeaux, and such an expression is obviously an attempt to make people think that the wine is château-bottled in the same way as Bordeaux wines. Another trick of a dishonest shipper is to simply print the English expression, "Estate-bottled," on the labels and leave the French equivalent off altogether. From the English translations of these expressions it can be seen that none of them is actually fraudulent or false in a way to make the shipper liable to prosecution by the government, but rather that they are just misleading enough to trick or deceive the unwary or those unfamiliar with the correct terminology of estate-bottled wines.

There is certainly no other area in France where fraud in wine labeling is so widespread as it is in Burgundy. The large shipping concerns that perpetrate these frauds are constantly being caught, of course, and the fines they pay are a regular part of their operating expenses. It may often be a year or two before a shipper is caught in one of his manipulations, and in the meantime he has managed to make enough profit to make the payment of a fine unimportant. Many shippers operate under several different names and the wine drinker or wine merchant in this country could not possibly locate the source of many of the Burgundy wines that are sold here. Though the *appellation contrôlée* laws are in force in Burgundy, just as they are in Bordeaux and other wine-growing regions of France, the small quantity of really authentic Burgundy wine produced each year makes the temptation to "stretch" it much greater than it would in Bordeaux, for example.

Another factor that complicates the selection of good Burgundy wines is the custom of all the towns along the Côte-d'Or to append the names of their most famous vineyards to the names of the towns themselves. The town of Gevrey has thus become Gevrey-Chambertin, Vosne has become Vosne-Romanée, and Nuits has become Nuits-Saint-Georges. The result of such a practice has been that the wine-drinking public often confuses the secondary wines of Gevrey with the great wine of the Chambertin vineyard itself, or that the wines of Vosne will be considered as identical with those of some of the great vineyards such as Romanée-Conti or Romanée-Saint-Vivant. Under the *appellation contrôlée* laws a "town" wine cannot be sold as the wine of one single vineyard, and there is a great difference between a wine labeled "Saint-Georges Appellation Contrôlée" and one labeled "Nuits-Saint-Georges Appellation Contrôlée." Both wines may be perfectly honest wines, but the one labeled "Saint-Georges" will of course be of finer quality than the one labeled "Nuits-Saint-Georges," since it comes from the finest vineyard in the commune of Nuits.

It can readily be seen that the beginning or inexperienced wine drinker is at a considerable disadvantage when he wants to buy a good bottle of Burgundy. When buying a Bordeaux wine, one need only look for the famous phrase, "*Mis en bouteilles au château*" to be reasonably certain of getting a good bottle of wine. When buying Burgundy, on the other hand, a considerable amount of care and attention to the wording on the label is called for. We cannot always pay from $7 to $15 a bottle for the great estate-bottled Burgundies, but neither should we expect to find good Burgundy for $2 a bottle. The best wines from the top-ranking shippers are usually priced at $3 to $5 a bottle, and you simply cannot expect to find authentic Burgundy wines at prices any lower than these. It is important to know the names of a few of the leading Burgundy shippers in order to have some idea of whose wines are worth looking for. We are listing six of them here, all known for their honesty and integrity, and their wines are certainly to be recommended if you want good value for your money. We cannot of course claim that these are the only honest shippers in Burgundy, but they are certainly six of the best known and their wines can always be relied upon for quality and value. They will usually be somewhat more expensive than wines from other shippers with less reputation, but if you are interested in drinking authentic Burgundy wines you must also be willing to pay the fairly high prices for them that they currently command on the international market. Here, then, are six names to look for when you are not buying the more expensive estate-bottled wines:

Joseph Drouhin
J. Faiveley
Louis Jadot
Louis Latour
J. Morin
J. H. Remy

Some of these shippers also own vineyards of their own, the wines from which they estate-bottle. Do not think that there is anything dishonest, therefore, about a bottle bearing the statement, "*Mis au Domaine*," and one of these shippers' names, since most of them sell both.

In the Côte-d'Or region of Burgundy, the red wines are made from the Pinot Noir grape and the whites from the Pinot Chardonnay. There is also some Pinot Blanc used for the white wines, but the Pinot Chardonnay is the most important. In the Beaujolais region the Gamay grape is grown, a variety that has a much higher yield per acre than the Pinot Noir, but does not produce wines of the same great class as the latter. Not only is the Pinot Noir a very low-yielding grape, but it is also slow to ripen. The Burgundy grower often finds that his grapes could have used another two or three weeks of sunshine when he begins his harvest. The harvest cannot be delayed too long in the fall, since there is always the danger of an early frost. To make up for the lack of sugar in the grapes when there has been a poor growing season, the French laws permit the addition of sugar to the grape juice so that it will ferment into wine with the proper degree of alcohol. This is exactly the same as is done in Germany, except that the German laws permit the addition of water as well as sugar in order to reduce the acidity of the wine, if this should be necessary. In Burgundy, the sugaring of the freshly pressed juice—it is not yet wine, of course—is called *Chaptalisation,* after the Count de Chaptal, who gave the method official government blessing during the time of Napoleon. The French wine laws do not require that the label on the bottle indicate whether the wine was made in this way or not and the purchaser can only assume that, if the wine is of a particularly fine vintage, *Chaptalisation* was not necessary. The wines can still be sold as estate-bottled wines in France, whether sugar has been added or not. (In Germany this is not the case and estate-bottled wines there may not be sugared.)

There are no hard and fast classifications of Burgundy wines such as we have for Bordeaux, but there is a reasonable consensus of opinion on just which Burgundies are the best. They are generally listed as *Tête de Cuvée* (the very finest quality), followed by *Première Cuvée* (First Growth), *Deuxième Cuvée* ("Second Growth"), and *Troisième Cuvée* ("Third Growth"). Very few of the third-growth wines are known in this country, and usually only the top two categories are imported under their own names. The lesser wines are often used by the shippers for blending purposes, and sometimes dishonestly to stretch a better-quality wine of which they have only a limited

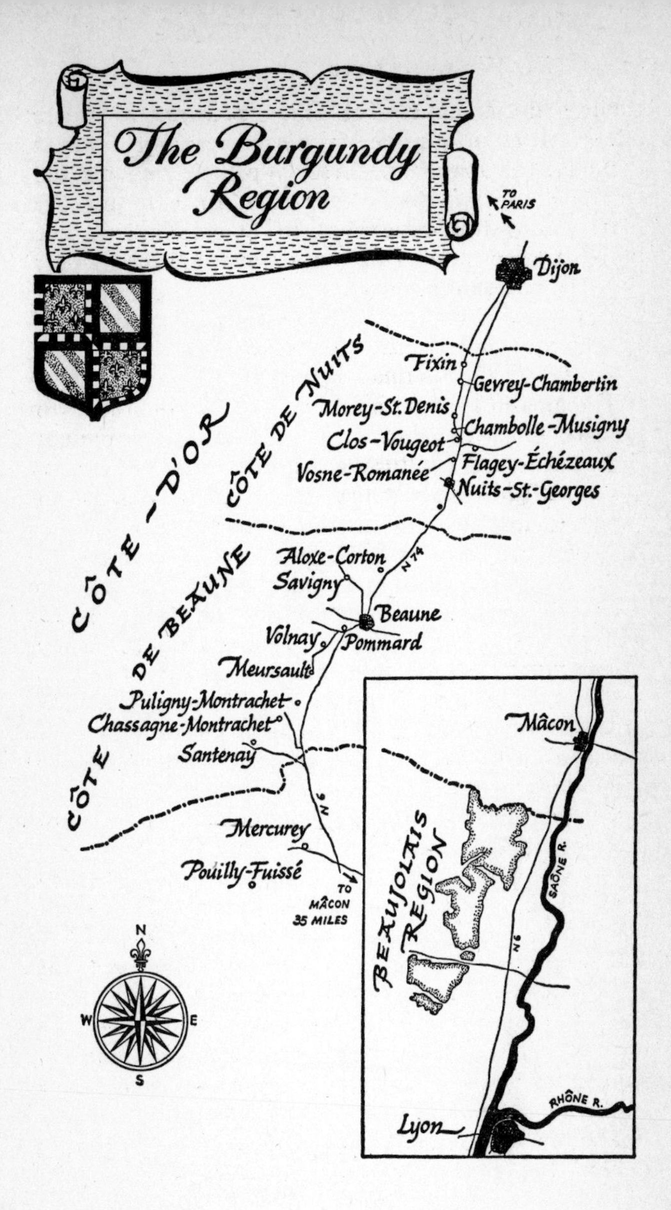
The Burgundy Region
TO PARIS
Dijon
CÔTE-D'OR
CÔTE DE NUITS
Fixin
Gevrey-Chambertin
Morey-St. Denis
Chambolle-Musigny
Clos-Vougeot
Flagey-Échézeaux
Vosne-Romanée
Nuits-St.-Georges
CÔTE DE BEAUNE
Aloxe-Corton
Savigny
N 74
Beaune
Volnay
Pommard
Meursault
Puligny-Montrachet
Chassagne-Montrachet
Santenay
N 6
Mercurey
Pouilly-Fuissé
TO MÂCON 35 MILES
Mâcon
BEAUJOLAIS REGION
SAÔNE R.
N 6
RHÔNE R.
Lyon
N
W
E
S

supply. Just about all the *Tête de Cuvée* wines are estate-bottled now, as well as a good many of the next category, the *Première Cuvée*. We shall list only the wines of the two top classes here, since to list the second- and third-growth wines would only involve listing a large number of wines which are hardly ever seen in this country.

COTE DE NUITS

The area in the immediate vicinity of Dijon used to produce much more wine than it does at the present time, but now the only village worth noting is Marsannay, which for the past few years has been making an excellent rosé wine—something that seems a little strange when we think of Burgundy in this connection.

Proceeding south from Dijon, the first wine-producing town of any consequence is Fixin (pronounced FEE-SAN). Though difficult to pronounce, the name is particularly worth remembering because the two excellent wines that it produces are among the least expensive of fine Burgundies. This is probably because they are not so well known as some of their famous neighbors and also because non-French-speaking people usually shy away from wines whose names they cannot pronounce. This may seem like a strange reason for not buying a wine, but it has proved to be the cause for many a wine's lack of popularity. In any case, the wines from Fixin can often be found for less than $3 a bottle, which we mentioned before as being about as low in price as good Burgundy goes. The *Tête de Cuvée* vineyard of Fixin is the Clos de la Perrière, and the *Première Cuvée* vineyard is the Clos du Chapitre. The wines made by Pierre Gelin are among the best from the last-named vineyard.

The town of Gevrey-Chambertin can boast of having one of the greatest of all Burgundy vineyards, the world-famous Chambertin. The fact that this was Napoleon's favorite wine perhaps helped to spread its fame somewhat, but can have no bearing on the quality of the wine, which was great before he "discovered" it and has remained great since. In addition to the wine sold simply as *Chambertin,* the one from the adjoining vineyard of Clos de Bèze is equally great. It is often sold as *Chambertin-Clos de Bèze* and sometimes as just *Clos de Bèze.* Along with Chambertin itself it is the only other *Tête de Cuvée* wine from this area. Chambertin is a rich, full-bodied wine, dark in color, and with a wonderful bouquet. It is such a wine as this that one thinks of when one thinks of truly great Burgundy. Some of the outstanding owners of these vineyards are Charles Rousseau (son of the late Armand Rousseau, one of Burgundy's greatest winegrowers), Dr. Marion, Louis Latour, Pierre Damoy, J. H. Remy, Léon Camus, and Joseph Drouhin. There are many others, of course, almost twenty-five by actual count, but many of the growers who have very small holdings do not sell their wines under their own names, as we have pointed out before. A bottle of Chambertin or Clos de Bèze from one of these famous producers will usually cost around $7 if the wine is of a fine year. There are seven vineyards in the *Première Cuvée* category of Chambertin, each of which is hyphenated with the name Chambertin as follows:

Latricières-Chambertin
Mazys-Chambertin
Mazoyères-Chambertin
Ruchottes-Chambertin
Chapelle-Chambertin
Charmes-Chambertin
Griotte-Chambertin

Remember not to confuse the town name itself, Gevrey-Chambertin, with any of these first-growth vineyards.

Wines sold as *Gevrey-Chambertin* are definitely *not* on a par with the wines from the vineyards listed here. Also, do not think that the seven first-growth wines are in any way second-rate wines. Many experts feel that they rank as high as the two great *Tête de Cuvée* wines. If you have not had considerable experience in drinking Burgundy, and Chambertin in particular, you will probably notice no difference between the wines from the two classifications. You can also save money by buying the first-growth wines, since they usually sell for around $5 a bottle or less.

The little town of Morey-Saint-Denis can boast three outstanding vineyards that produce *Tête de Cuvée* wines—*Clos de Tart, Clos des Lambrays,* and a small part of the *Bonnes-Mares* vineyard, most of which is in the next town of Chambolle-Musigny. The first two of these are each the property of one single owner, something that is extremely unusual for a Burgundy vineyard. J. Mommessin owns the Clos de Tart, and Madame Cosson owns the Clos des Lambrays. This means of course that no matter where you buy a bottle of *Clos de Tart* or *Clos des Lambrays* it will always be the same wine and of the same quality. These wines are well worth keeping in mind since they are both of outstanding quality and not so expensive as their better-known neighbors from the town of Gevrey-Chambertin. The two vineyards of *Clos de la Roche* and *Clos Saint-Denis* (from which Morey gets the second part of its name) are both classified as first-growth vineyards. The Clos de la Roche is twice as large as the Clos Saint-Denis and its wines are much easier to find than those of the Clos Saint-Denis for that reason.

Chambolle-Musigny, just below Morey-Saint-Denis, would certainly never be known to the world's wine drinkers were it not for the magnificent *Musigny* vineyard which it has added on to its name. The Musigny wines are noted for their outstanding bouquet as well as their light and delicate qualities, often described as feminine. Of all the owners of the vineyard, the Count de Voguë undoubtedly produces the finest wines. Other estate-bottled Musigny will also be found from Adrien & Roblot and from Clair-Daü, to name two of the better producers. The other outstanding wine from Chambolle is *Bonnes-Mares,* still reasonably priced because it is not yet as popular as it deserves to be. The name is certainly not difficult to pronounce, but for some reason or another it just does not seem to have caught on with the wine-buying public, at least not in the United States and Great Britain. There is one first-growth vineyard that we must mention in this commune, that of *Les Amoureuses,* which means "women in love" in English. Only slightly less fine than the Musigny wines themselves, Les Amoureuses is of course considerably cheaper. Whereas a great Musigny costs around $10 a bottle, a Bonnes-Mares or a Les Amoureuses will usually sell for $7 or thereabouts. There is a small amount of *Musigny Blanc* produced in addition to the red wine, but it is difficult to find and also very expensive—around $12 a bottle. All the fine white Burgundies tend to run rather high in price, however, and the white Musigny is not really too expensive when one considers its superb quality.

One of the great landmarks of Burgundy is the Clos Vougeot, formerly a Cistercian monastery dating back to the twelfth century. Taking its name from the Vouge, a small stream which runs near by, the château-like building that still stands was originally the press house of the monastery. The stone wall that the monks built around their one hundred twenty five acres of vineyards is also still intact, except for a few additional entrance ways that have been cut in it since. Those who are familiar with German wines are immediately reminded of the great *Steinberg* vineyard in the

Rheingau, since that too was once a Cistercian property. While the Steinberg has remained intact through all the past centuries right up to the present time, the Clos Vougeot has been broken up into many small plots and is now owned by over fifty different people. This is certainly to be regretted, since not all the owners can make wines of equal quality and many of them must sell their small production to shippers, who in turn are often tempted to blend the wine with other wines of lower quality in order to have that much more *Clos Vougeot* to sell. A genuine Clos Vougeot from one of the best producers ranks as one of the greatest of the Burgundy wines, and so it is particularly important to pay careful attention to the label and look for a "*Mise du Domaine*" wine when buying a Clos Vougeot. The two biggest owners of the vineyard are J. Morin, who has about fourteen acres, and Madame Noëllat, who has about six acres. Champy Père & Fils, G. Grivot, Louis Gros, and P. Missey all own around five acres each, while J. Faiveley, who has only about two acres, also exports his wines to this country. Others may be seen from time to time too, but the wines from most of the smaller growers are usually blended together by the shippers. When the Clos Vougeot was one single domain several hundred years ago, it was divided into a lower, middle, and upper third, with the best wines coming from the upper third. Some of these sections of the vineyard still have names, so that one can often find a *Clos Vougeot Grand Maupertuis,* for example, with the name *Grand Maupertuis* being that of a particular section of the top third of the vineyard. There are many other names used for various parts of the Clos Vougeot, but the name of a reliable shipper or owner is far more important to the consumer.

The commune of Flagey-Échézeaux, next after Clos Vougeot, has one outstanding vineyard, that of *Les*

Grands Échézeaux. The wine is of excellent quality, not as full bodied as the Clos Vougeot, but well balanced and with a lovely bouquet nevertheless. The wines from the other vineyards in this township are usually sold as *Échézeaux* without the word "*Grands.*" They are also excellent wines, by no means second-rate, but Les Grands Échézeaux is the one and only *Tête de Cuvée* and the two names should not be confused. It used to be claimed that the Échézeaux wines were not very popular because the name was too difficult for English-speaking people to pronounce, much like Fixin which we mentioned earlier. In recent years the demand for this wine has been increasing and it now sells for as much as any of the other outstanding Burgundies of equal quality. Apparently there are now enough wine lovers around who *can* pronounce the name and the demand has caused the price to rise. The Grands Échézeaux wines are now in the $7 class for the best vintages. The most famous owner of the vineyard is the Domaine de la Romanée-Conti, but others whose wines are often seen in this country are René Engel and Louis Gros.

The proudest commune in Burgundy must certainly be that of Vosne-Romanée, since it is here that some of the greatest of all Burgundian vineyards are located. Every Burgundy lover knows the name of Romanée-Conti, that small four-and-a-half-acre vineyard which is probably the most valuable piece of agricultural land in all of France. Named for the Prince of Conti, a minister of Louis XV, the vineyard now belongs to an organization or company known as the Domaine de la Romanée-Conti. The name is taken, of course, from the name of its most famous vineyard, but the company also owns other vineyards as well. The famous black and white label of the Domaine can be seen on the wines of La Tâche, which, like the Romanée-Conti, is owned entirely by the Domaine. A part of

Les Grands Échézeaux also belongs to them, as we mentioned before, as well as part of the Richebourg vineyard. There are four great *Tête de Cuvée* vineyards in the commune of Vosne-Romanée:

Romanée-Conti
La Romanée (owned by the firm of S. A. LeRoy)
La Tâche
Richebourg

Because of the very small amount of Romanée-Conti wine produced each year, the price is the highest of any French wine and usually runs around $15 a bottle. Since the vineyard was replanted in 1946, the Romanée-Conti wines have not yet attained their former greatness and the $15-a-bottle price tag does not represent the actual worth of the wine.

Vosne-Romanée has several other Great Growths in addition to the famous vineyards listed above. One of the most outstanding is the *Romanée Saint-Vivant,* part of which is owned by Louis Latour who always makes an excellent wine from his part of the vineyard. Two other outstanding vineyards are *Les Malconsorts* and *Les Suchots,* both of which are fairly easy to find in this country.

The town of Nuits-Saint-Georges, which comes after Vosne-Romanée, is as well known as a shipping center for Burgundy wines as it is for its own vineyards. In spite of all the dishonest blending that goes on in a town like Nuits-Saint-Georges, there are some honest wines made. Most of the outstanding vineyards are fairly large as Burgundian vineyards go, but not all the wines from this commune are seen in the United States. The *Clos de Thorey* is probably the easiest to find, while some of the wines from the *Vaucrains* and *Saint-Georges* vineyards are also seen from time to time. The Nuits-Saint-Georges wines are heavy, full-bodied wines and they develop well with age.

CÔTE DE BEAUNE

The lower half of the Côte d'Or, known as the Côte de Beaune, produces all the fine white wines of Burgundy. Only one really great red wine is produced, that of *Corton,* but the whites rank among the greatest white wines of France. The first town of the Côte de Beaune is that of Aloxe, which has been known as Aloxe-Corton for the past hundred years in honor of its greatest vineyard. In addition to the vineyard of Corton itself, there are several other *Têtes de Cuvées* vineyards whose wines are not quite as expensive. *Corton-Clos du Roi, Corton-Bressandes,* and *Corton-Renardes* are all outstanding. Louis Latour owns most of the Corton vineyard, along with the Prince de Mérode, who also has holdings in the Clos du Roi vineyard as well. Another owner of the Clos du Roi is Baron Thénard. The largest holder of the Corton-Bressandes vineyard is Georges Yard. In discussing the fine red wines of Corton we must also mention the *Château Corton Grancey* which is shipped by Louis Latour. This is one of the very few Burgundy wines that is honestly entitled to the use of the word "château" on the label. It is a blend of wines from several different first-growth vineyards and is always a good buy whenever you can find it.

One of the very great white Burgundy wines also comes from Corton and is known as *Corton-Charlemagne,* since Charlemagne once owned vineyards in this area. The Corton-Charlemagne is not made in large quantities and is always fairly expensive. Since Louis Latour owns about half of the best section of the vineyard, his wines are usually the easiest to find. Another large owner is Louis Jadot.

The wine capital of Burgundy is the city of Beaune. It is here that the great annual wine auction takes place at the charity hospital called the Hospices de

Beaune. In continuous existence since the middle of the fifteenth century, the Hospices de Beaune has been given various vineyard sites over the past five hundred years and the wines are still sold every year to raise money for the hospital. Because of the fact that it is a charitable cause, the prices paid for the wines at the annual auctions are always somewhat higher than the actual value of the wines, though many of them are indeed excellent. Each wine is sold under the name of the original donor of the vineyard, as well as under the commune name itself. For example, one of the greatest and most famous of the Hospices wines is known as *Corton, Cuvée Dr. Peste*. This means that the wine is from several different vineyards in the district of Corton and that these vineyards were originally presented to the hospital by a Dr. Peste. There are almost thirty different *Cuvées* auctioned each year, of which about a half dozen are white wines. Very few of the Hospices de Beaune wines are imported into the United States, and we are listing only twelve of the best known here since the others are rarely seen:

Commune	*Cuvée*
Beaune	Brunet
Beaune	Dames Hospitalières
Beaune	Guigone de Salins
Beaune	Nicolas Rollin
Pommard	Billardet
Pommard	Dames de la Charité
Aloxe-Corton	Charlotte Dumay
Aloxe-Corton	Dr. Peste
Volnay	Blondeau
Meursault-Charmes	de Bahèzre de Lanlay
Meursault-Charmes	Albert Grivault
Meursault-Genevrières	Baudot

As can be seen from the above listing, the Hospices de Beaune owns vineyards in many different towns or communes of the Côte de Beaune, and not just around Beaune itself. This is of course understandable, since not every patient or benefactor of the hospital lived in the immediate vicinity, and over a period of five hundred years a fair general sampling of all the Côte de Beaune communes was bound to be included.

There are many excellent vineyards around Beaune, however, that are still in private hands just as in any other town. Beaune can claim eight *Têtes de Cuvées,* and along with its small neighbor, Savigny-les-Beaune, there are over two dozen *Premiers Crus.* The best Beaune wines come from the vineyards of *Les Grèves de l'Enfant Jésus* (owned by Bouchard Père et Fils), *Les Marconnets, Les Bressandes, Les Fèves,* and *Le Clos-des-Mouches.* Part of this last vineyard is planted with Pinot Chardonnay grapes, and the firm of Joseph Drouhin makes an excellent white wine from them.

Pommard, the next town after Beaune, is probably one of the most famous of all Burgundy wine-producing communes. The wines are a little heavier than those of Beaune, and take longer to develop. Fortunately the Pommard vineyard region is quite large and even the best wines sell for under $5 a bottle. The two finest Pommard wines are the *Têtes de Cuvées* of *Les Épenots,* and *Les Rugiens-Bas.* Les Épenots is sometimes sold as *Grands Épenots,* too, in order to distinguish it from the first-growth vineyard of *Les Petits-Épenots.* Some of the outstanding shippers of Pommard wines are Madame Courcel, the Comte Armand, Parent, and Drouhin. There are other excellent producers of Pommard, in addition to those we have listed, but the most important thing to look for is the statement of estate bottling. The more famous a wine is, the greater is the temptation to blend it and stretch it with other wines of inferior quality!

The town of Volnay is only a short distance south of Pommard, but its wines are lighter and shorter-lived than those of Pommard, though they have a wonderful bouquet. There are five *Têtes de Cuvées* vineyards in Volnay, and the best is the *Caillerets. Santenots* is another that can be found fairly easily in this country, while *Les Champans, Les Fremiets,* and *Les Angles* are not often encountered.

Below Volnay the Côte de Beaune is more famous for its white wines than for its reds. After leaving Volnay, the next town of consequence that we come to is Meursault. The wines from this area are soft and delicate and not quite as austerely dry as some of the other white Burgundies. The best section of vineyard is the *Clos des Perrières,* owned by Madame Grivault. The rest of the vineyard, divided among several owners, is known simply as *Les Perrières.* The first-growth vineyards are excellent here, too, and the wines are often much easier to find than the *Têtes de Cuvées* wines of Les Perrières. Though there are five first-growth vineyards in Meursault, the two wines most often seen in the United States are Les Genevrières and Les Charmes. The names will always appear on the label hyphenated with the name Meursault: *Meursault-Genevrières* and *Meursault-Charmes.* Wines that are simply labeled Meursault are not very reliable and should not be mistaken for wines coming from one of the vineyards that we have named here. There are almost three dozen different owners of the principal Meursault vineyards and not all of them estate-bottle their wines. To be sure of getting the real thing, look for the name of a top vineyard in conjunction with the "*Mise du Domaine*" phrase and the name of the owner.

The two towns of Puligny and Chassagne, south of Meursault, have both added the name of France's greatest white wine vineyard, *Montrachet,* to their own names. We thus have wines sold as *Puligny-Montrachet* and *Chassagne-Montrachet,* as well as wines sold with the vineyard names from each of these towns. The greatest of all, however, is just plain *Montrachet,* without any further designation. The Montrachet vineyard is about nineteen acres in size and is divided among many different growers, as is usual in Burgundy. Some of the owners have only very small holdings and make only about a barrel of wine each. The three largest owners estate-bottle their wines and they are the ones that you will find here in the United States in most cases. They are the Marquis de Laguiche, Baron Thénard, and Bouchard Père & Fils. A genuine Montrachet is always expensive—around $13 a bottle—and you should be absolutely sure that you are getting an authentic, estate-bottled wine when you pay this price. The small amount of Montrachet that is available each year and the great fame that it enjoys help to keep the prices high. The beginning wine drinker may not see just why this particular wine is so magnificent, since many of its qualities can only be appreciated by those who have some experience in wine drinking. Indeed, most wine lovers are better advised to select one of the excellent wines from the surrounding vineyards, since these usually sell for about half the price of Montrachet itself and are still of outstanding quality. The three best wines to look for after Montrachet itself are *Chevalier-Montrachet, Bâtard-Montrachet,* and *Bienvenue-Bâtard-Montrachet.* Two excellent growers whose wines are well worth looking for are Louis Poirier, who makes an excellent Bâtard-Montrachet, and Claude Ramonet, who owns most of the *Les Ruchottes* vineyard, a First Growth of Chassagne-Montrachet.

The red wines of Chassagne-Montrachet are inexpensive but of excellent quality nevertheless. Since most people do not associate red wines with the town of Chassagne-Montrachet, the wines are not much in demand and therefore not high in price. The two top vineyards are *Le Clos Saint-Jean-Morgeot* and *La Boudriotte.* These wines usually sell for under $3 a bottle in this country.

We leave the Côte de Beaune at the town of Santenay, where some very pleasant wines are produced, though they are never of the finest class. A Santenay can often be a good buy at around $2.50 a bottle, but should not cost more than this.

CÔTE MÂCONNAIS

After leaving the Côte d'Or with its two parts, the Côte de Nuits and the Côte de Beaune, we pass through the *Côte Chalonnais* which produces some very nice red wines, the best ones coming from the commune of Mercurey, and then to the *Côte Mâconnais.* Taking its name from the town of Mâcon, the wines from this region are mostly white, though there is some red Mâcon produced too. The most famous of the Mâconnais wines is the *Pouilly-Fuissé,* a dry wine with a wonderful bouquet and flavor that has caused it to lead all white Burgundies in popularity at the present time. Needless to say, there is now far more Pouilly-Fuissé sold than could ever be produced in the region itself. Whenever a wine becomes very popular there is always the temptation to "fill in" with other wines when supplies of the original run out. The authentic Pouilly-Fuissé comes from one of four communes: *Fuissé, Solutré, Chaintré,* and *Vergisson,* though all of the wine is sold as Pouilly-Fuissé, with or without a vineyard name. You are much more certain of getting an authentic wine if you look for one with a vineyard name instead of one merely labeled Pouilly-Fuissé. The authentic wines usually sell for around

$2.50 to $3 a bottle. There is a *Château de Fuissée* in that commune which is quite authentic, and also the vineyards of *Le Clos, Les Vignes-Blanches, Les Chatenays, Les Perrières, Menetrières,* and *Les Brûlets.* The best vineyards in Solutré are *Les Prâs, Les Peloux, Les Chailloux, Les Boutières,* and *Les Rinces,* while Chaintré has a vineyard known as *Les Chevrières,* and Vergisson has one called *Les Crays.* Most of the Pouilly-Fuissé wines that you see in this country, however, will not carry a vineyard or commune name, and you must exercise a certain amount of caution in buying them.

BEAUJOLAIS

If Pouilly-Fuissé is the most popular of the white Burgundy wines at the present time, *Beaujolais* is certainly the most popular of the red wines. The Beaujolais area is just south of the Mâconnais, and, though some white wine is produced, by far the greatest production is of red wine. To Americans the name seems to have become a meaningless name for cheap red wine. The amount of authentic Beaujolais available in the United States is small indeed when compared to the huge quantities of wine sold under this name by every wine and liquor store in the country. There is certainly no genuine wine of this name selling for much under $2 a bottle. Those who buy 97-cent or $1.19 bottles of Beaujolais are certainly not getting the real thing, though no one seems to care much as long as the label says Beaujolais. There are estate-bottled Beaujolais, of course, but you have a better chance of getting the real thing if you buy the wines from one of the towns or communes in the area, rather than a wine just marked Beaujolais. Some of the names to look for are *Moulin-à-Vent, Juliénas, Brouilly, Fleurie, Morgon,*

Chiroubles, and *Saint-Amour*. These are the leading communes of the Beaujolais district, and their wines may also carry vineyard names in addition to the commune name. Some will be estate-bottled, but most are bottled by shippers.

Beaujolais is always drunk young and often slightly chilled. There is no point in buying Beaujolais to lay away, since by the time it reaches this country it is usually quite ready to drink. If kept too long, the wine often loses some of its fresh, fruity quality which makes it so attractive. The Beaujolais wines are made from the Gamay grape instead of the Pinot Noir, and, though the Gamay is not permitted in any of the great vineyards of the Côte d'Or because it is thought to be inferior, it is the only grape used for the wines of the Beaujolais district and the results here are perfectly delightful.

CHABLIS

About ninety miles southeast of Paris is the famous district of Chablis. The wines are considered to be white Burgundy wines, even though the area is not an actual part of the Côte d'Or. Since Chablis is noted for its dry, "flinty" quality, the wine has always been suggested as the perfect accompaniment to seafood, and to oysters in particular. One can drink it with many other light dishes, of course, and it is certainly one of the most delightful of all French white wines. Authentic Chablis is never cheap, for there are only a few hundred acres of vineyards and the wine is much in demand all over the world. All the best wines come from the two top classes of vineyards, the *Grands Crus* and the *Premiers Crus*. Any of these names, together with the owner's name and the statement of estate bottling, is a reasonably good indication that you are getting an honest bottle of Chablis for your money.

Chablis Grands Crus

Blanchots	Vaudésir
Les Clos	Bourgros
Grenouilles	La Moutonne
Valmur	Les Preuses

Chablis Premiers Crus

Beauroy	Montée de Tonnerre
Beugnons	Montmains
Butteaux	Pied d'Aloup
Châpelots	Séchet
Chatains	Roncières
Côte de Fontenay	Troëme
Côte de Léchet	Vaillons
Les Forêts	Vaucoupin
Fourchaume	Vaupinent
Les Lys	Vaulorent
Melinots	Vosgros
Mont-de-Milieu	Vogiras

Many of the *Grands Crus* Chablis run over $4 a bottle, but the *Premiers Crus* can usually be found for around $3. In some years there is very little wine produced because of hail or frost damage in the vineyards during the growing season. For some reason or other, the Chablis vineyards seem to suffer more from these conditions than any other wine-growing region in Europe. The Chablis district is not the farthest north, so there is no geographical explanation for the frosts any more than for the frequent summer hail storms that often destroy large parts of the Chablis vineyards. In any case, when the quantity of wine produced is particularly small and the quality is above average, the prices will often go as high as $5 a bottle.

CHAMPAGNE

Probably no other wine in the history of winegrowing has been made to appear so exotic or glamorous as Champagne has. Ever since the end of the last century, the great Champagne houses of France have spared no expense in making their wines seem to be the epitome of luxurious living and the one indispensable ingredient for successful wedding receptions, ship launchings, diplomatic receptions, and other similar distinguished functions. There is, of course, a more down-to-earth reason for the great reputation of Champagne, and that is its high price as compared with other wines. Not only is Champagne more costly to make than any other wine, but it is also taxed more heavily. Whereas a $17 bottle of Burgundy from the great Romanée-Conti estate is not considered by our customs authorities to be a "luxury," any bottle of Champagne, whether it sells for $5 or $15 a bottle, *is* so classified by our government and is therefore charged an import duty of $1 a bottle, as against the 11-cent duty on the Burgundy, or other table wines that are not sparkling. It is easy to see, then, that good Champagne can never be cheap, and, conversely, cheap Champagne can rarely be good. Many stores sell French Champagne at $4 a bottle, but it is usually raw or acidic and not worthy of the name Champagne.

Wine lovers are divided into two opposing camps as regards Champagne. On the one side, and in the majority, are those who feel that Champagne is a highly overrated wine, unworthy of any serious wine-drinker's attention. The other side maintains that there is nothing finer than a great vintage Champagne and waxes eloquent over fantastic vintages of bygone years in the same way that other wine lovers may discuss a great Burgundy or a great Bordeaux wine. We are inclined to feel that both sides are overdoing it a bit and that the real truth lies somewhere in between.

Because of its price, Champagne will never become a common, everyday wine and we have to think of it as something special whether we want to or not. It *is* a very special type of wine though, and in order to be able to buy it intelligently and with a certain amount of understanding one must know a little about its unique method of manufacture and preparation. Certainly there are times when no other wine will do and Champagne is a must.

To begin with, the wine-producing area of Champagne is very carefully limited and controlled by the French government. Only the wines coming from the area which was formerly known as the province of Champagne—that part of France northeast of Paris, extending from the famous city of Reims to below Épernay—may legally bear the name "Champagne." Through treaties with other European countries, the name "Champagne" is protected by law and cannot be applied to sparkling wines of any other kind or from any other source except those from France. In Germany, for example, the native sparkling wines are known as *Sekt* and do not show the word Champagne anywhere on their labels. This happy condition does not exist in the United States, where any kind of sparkling wine may be called Champagne if its producers so desire, since there is no law to stop them. Today most people refer to genuine Champagne as *French* Champagne or *imported* Champagne in order to distinguish it from the local product from New York State or California. This is not to say that American sparkling wines are no good, but just that it would be better for all concerned if they could be called by some name other than Champagne. However, the word has now taken hold to such an extent that it is synonymous with "sparkling wine" in most people's minds. Many Americans do not even think of Champagne as a type of wine at all, and one has even heard people ask, "Is Champagne a wine?" as though it were a special brew whose origin had nothing in common with other wines.

Wine has been made in the Champagne region for many hundreds of years, but it has only been during the last three hundred years that sparkling Champagne has been known. Before the end of the seventeenth century the wines from Champagne were still wines like those from Bordeaux and Burgundy. Even today some still wine is made in the Champagne area for local consumption, but none of it is exported.

Though Champagne was the first (and is still the finest) of all sparkling wines, there are many imitations of it, not only in France, but throughout the world wherever wine is grown. Some of these other wines are good and some not so good, but none can exactly duplicate the unique qualities of real Champagne. By French law, any wine made like Champagne, but not coming from that delimited area, may carry the phrase *méthode champenoise,* that is, "made by the Champagne method," but the label will never use the word Champagne alone, since this would be a clear-cut case of fraud. The lowest common denominator of sparkling wines, those that are artificially carbonated, should be mentioned briefly in passing. A short-cut method of making a wine sparkling is simply to inject enough carbon dioxide gas into the wine so that it will bubble when the wine is opened. This is the method usually used for making sparkling Burgundy and is nothing like the long and tedious method of making Champagne. Those who like sparkling Burgundy are welcome to it, but they should never imagine that they are drinking a first-class wine by any means.

Champagne as we know it today evolved by a slow and laborious process, and it was not until rather recently—well into the nineteenth century, that is—that the production of Champagne could really be said to be scientifically controlled. In the past it had always been pretty much a hit-or-miss affair with the sound of exploding bottles not at all uncommon. We read of cellars where up to 40 per cent of the bottles exploded while stored away for the necessary development period of three or four years. Bottles still explode now and then even today in the best Champagne cellars, but this is usually because of defective bottles rather than because of any lack of knowledge on the part of the cellar master.

Though popular legend credits the monk Dom Pérignon, cellar master at the Benedictine Abbey of Hautvillers, with the "discovery" of Champagne, it is generally recognized that there was no overnight discovery, but simply that the methods used to make the wines of Champagne "sparkle" were gradually evolved over a period of years, beginning around the end of the seventeenth century. We don't know whether or not Dom Pérignon ever actually said, "I am drinking the stars," as he downed his first glass of sparkling Champagne, but it makes a nice legend in any case. What Dom Pérignon definitely *did* do was to improve the methods of handling the wines and especially the blending of various wines from different vineyards. He was also responsible for the introduction of corks as a means of closing the bottles, rather than the oil-soaked rags or wooden pegs wrapped in cloth which had been used up until then, and which of course precluded the possibility of the wine fermenting in the bottle and building up any amount of gas pressure. In spite of the legends that have grown up around the figure of Dom Pérignon, the truth is that this illustrious monk, who lived from 1639 until 1715, *was* the father of modern Champagne as we know it today.

The initial steps in the making of Champagne are the same as those for any other wine, though it may come as a surprise to many people to learn that Champagne is made mostly from black grapes. Since the skins of the grapes are what give most wines their color, the juice is quickly separated from the grape skins in the making of regular Champagne. For pink Champagne the skins are left with the juice until the proper color has been attained and it is then run off and handled just like any other Champagne. Pink Champagne, once the symbol of a wild and dissolute way of life to many people, no longer enjoys the popularity it once did. It is neither better nor worse than other Champagnes of the same price range, but the shippers never use their finest wines for it, since it is hardly what one would call a connoisseur's wine.

In the spring following the harvest of the grapes, after the wine has fermented and been racked off two or three times in the cellars, the blending of the various wines takes place. In the case of a "vintage" Champagne, such as that made in 1952, 1955, or 1959, where all the wines were of top quality, this blending will be only a blending of wines from different vineyards. All the Champagne firms have holdings in, or buy grapes from, vineyards scattered throughout the area, and so are able to make up a blend for which they have become known over the years. The exact proportion of wines used from the various vineyard areas is kept secret by each firm, since none wants to have its style of Champagne copied by a competitor. If the newly made wine is not of sufficient quality to be sold on its own as a vintage Champagne, the cellar master will blend it with the wines of other years in order to reach a certain level of quality which the public has come to expect from that Champagne. This Champagne will go on the market as a "nonvintage" Champagne, that is, a Champagne which does not carry a date and is therefore a blend of several different years' wines. Nonvintage Champagnes are always about two dollars cheaper than vintage Champagnes from the same firm but are frequently quite as good. They are ideal for large gatherings—wedding receptions, and the like—where one would like to serve a name brand, but because of the nature of the occasion a really great Champagne would go unnoticed and unappreciated. And for ordinary purposes as well, a nonvintage Champagne is usually the best buy. Just be sure it comes from a good house that has a first-class reputation to maintain and you will be on safe ground. Save the great vintage Champagnes for those very special occasions.

The blending of the various vintages or types of Champagne is one of the essential parts of the whole Champagne-making process. The blend that results is known in French as the *cuvée*, and one will often see this word on the labels of Champagne bottles. A phrase such as "English Cuvée," for example, means that the wine was made with the English market in mind, where a very dry Champagne is preferred. Such phrases as "Cuvée spécial" or "Cuvée exceptionnel" may mean little or much, depending on whose Champagne it is, and how reputable the firm is in the first place. Whether the Champagne in the bottle is *really "exceptionnel"* can only be determined by tasting it.

After the *cuvée* has been made, the wine is bottled together with a small amount of pure cane sugar dissolved in older wine, along with a very small amount of brandy. This solution is known in French as the *liqueur d'expédition* and is added in varying amounts according to the type of Champagne desired. This sugar solution does not in any way make the wine sweet, but rather induces a second fermentation of the wine, but this time *in* the bottle. This is the whole secret of Champagne in a nutshell. Since any fermentation will produce carbon dioxide gas, it is simply a matter of keeping this gas imprisoned in the bottle, in a state of suspension in the wine, in order to make the wine sparkling or bubbly. Of course, if too much gas is developed the bottle will explode, but the proper amount will serve to make the wine effervescent to exactly the degree required of a good Champagne. The second fermentation of the wine cannot be hurried if we are to have a first-class wine, and, although the French laws require only a minimum of one year of aging, most of the really fine Champagnes are aged from three to five years before they are considered ready. Those cheap, raw Champagnes which one finds here in the United States for $4.50 a bottle, or in a Paris night spot where Champagne is the required drink at $10 a bottle, are usually in the one-year-minimum class, whereas the great vintage Champagnes from the best houses usually have been aged three or four times as long—all of which of course is reckoned in the price.

As the wines develop during this period of their second fermentation, they throw a sediment which must be removed before the wine can be brought on the market. This is accomplished by gradually sloping the bottles in special racks until they are neck down and the sediment can all accumulate in the neck of the bottle behind the cork. Highly skilled workmen go through the racks of Champagne bottles every day for a period of two or three months, giving the bottles a slight twist and gradually increasing the angle of the racks to work the sediment down into the neck of the bottle. A first-class worker in this particular job can handle up to thirty thousand bottles a day. (It is no wonder that they are the highest paid workers in the entire Champagne-making process!) When the bottles are all in this neck-down position, the very delicate operation of the "*dégorgement*" must be performed. This means that the temporary cork must be removed from the bottle along with the accumulated sediment, whatever sweetening is required must quickly be added, and the permanent cork must be put into the bottle—all without letting the natural gas of the wine escape. Many of the shippers are now resorting to the process of freezing the necks of the bottles in a brine solution so that when the cork is withdrawn the sediment will come with it as a sort of icicle attached to the cork. Whether or not the neck of the bottle is frozen, the whole disgorging process is one which requires very deft manipulation of the bottles on the part of the workmen performing the task. The question of how much sweetening is to be added to the wine is of course decided ahead of time by the requirements of the various markets. A firm which sells large quantities of Champagne to South America will produce mostly very sweet Champagne, since this is the type preferred there. A company dealing mainly with Great Britain, however, would make very dry Champagne with very little sweetening added. The British are noted for their preference for very dry Champagne, and so the terms "British Market," "Reserve for Great Britain," or "English Cuvée" all signify very dry wines.

To be able to select a very dry Champagne or a slightly sweet one from the many bottles displayed on the wineshop's shelf is no easy task. The only sure way of getting what you want is to simply memorize the five basic classifications of Champagne, and, since only the first two or three of them will be encountered in the United States, this is really not a difficult task. Before describing them in more detail let us list them in order, from the driest to the sweetest. They are: (1) *brut*, (2) *extra-sec* or extra-dry, (3) *sec* or dry, (4) *demi-sec*, and (5) *doux*. The word *doux*, which means "sweet" in English, will never be encountered on a Champagne label in the United States, since the *doux* Champagnes are sent mainly to South America. The *demi-sec* wines are likewise rarely seen in this country, so we need not concern ourselves with them here.

A *brut* Champagne is the driest type made and is always the most expensive for the simple reason that any possible defects in the wine cannot be covered up or masked by the addition of sweetening. This means that the producers must use their best wines for their *brut* Champagne, and all the great vintages are sold as *brut*. One sees, for example, "1955 *Brut*" or "1953 *Brut*," but never "1955 Extra-Dry." For a *brut* Champagne, up to 1 per cent sweetening by volume may be added, but it is often only one-half of 1 per cent if a very dry finish to the wine is desired. Each firm has its own formula and the individual vintages differ as to the amount of sweetening they require. There is no such thing as "*extra-brut*," though sometimes the phrase "*brut extra*" is seen. This supposedly means an extra-*quality* wine and not an extra-*dry* one.

It is when we come to the phrase "extra-dry," our second classification, that the confusion is apt to be at its worst. First of all, the phrase "extra-dry" on a Champagne label definitely does not mean what it says! The wine is *not* drier than *brut*, but rather a little sweeter. For an extra-dry (also encountered in French as *extra-sec*) Champagne, up to 3 per cent sweetening may be added, and such Champagnes are usually considered to be dessert Champagnes because of this little bit of extra sweetness. At one time, before the present terminology was well established, an extra-dry Champagne was just what the name implied, but this is no longer the case. To add a little more to the confusion in the use of these terms, we must point out here that the very fine Champagne firm of Krug ships its vintage *brut* Champagne as extra-dry. Krug is generally considered by most people to be among the very finest Champagne houses and one should bear in mind that their best vintage *brut* wines will be labeled extra-dry. They have been using this term for so many years that they just do not see any reason to change it now. Their less expensive, nonvintage wines *are* marked *brut,* which may or may not make the whole thing more complicated.

We see few *sec,* or dry, Champagnes in this country, and with their sweetening of up to 5 per cent this is understandable. Only those who have a real sweet tooth will enjoy these wines, or those in the two categories above them, *demi-sec* with up to 7 or 8 per cent sweetening, and *doux* with up to 10 per cent and sometimes over. During the middle of the nineteenth century, Champagnes with 15 per cent sweetening were all the rage! They were of course considered only as dessert wines. By the 1870's, however, the drier Champagnes were becoming more popular, and extra-dry wines soon became the fashion. When even these Champagnes were found to be too sweet, the *brut* designation was then introduced for the very driest wines of all.

When ordering Champagne in Europe, or on board one of the trans-Atlantic liners, one should be careful of two other phrases which pop up occasionally and may cause confusion among the uninitiated. They are "*Gout Américain*" and "*Drapeau Américain.*" The *Américain* referred to here is the American from South America, and not from the United States. Champagnes with either of these two designations are usually quite sweet—at least *sec*, and perhaps even *demi-sec*—so do not be misled by the description into thinking that they are very dry wines for our North American tastes.

There are no official classifications of various Champagnes in order of quality, such as exist for the wines of Bordeaux, and no one could say with absolute certainty that brand X was *the* finest Champagne made. There are several top-notch producers, but the final choice of which Champagne is the best for your taste must be your own. Each shipper has his own style of Champagne, and the individual must decide for himself which of these best suits him. There are supposed to be one hundred seventy-eight Champagne producers in France today. Some of these are of course small shippers who supply cheap wines for the inexpensive blends, while others of them rank among the finest in their field. Still others may be quite good but are only known in certain markets, such as Scandinavia or South America. If we had to select the top three or four firms among all of those who ship their Champagnes to the United States, we should say Krug, Bollinger, Roederer, and Pommery & Greno. The Pommery Champagnes are much better known in Europe than they are here, but of course that has nothing to do with their quality. We have long felt that *Pommery Extra-Dry* was the finest of the extra-dry Champagnes at present available in this country. All these firms market a vintage *brut* Champagne as well as a non-vintage *brut*, which is of course cheaper. The Roederer firm puts out a special Champagne in a clear bottle which was first designed for the late Czar Nicholas II of Russia. It is always a vintage *brut* and is known as *Roederer Cristal*. Krug is the most expensive of all the regular Champagnes—around $10 a bottle for the vintage *brut*, or "*Extra-Sec*" as they call it.

Quite in a class by itself is the fabulous *Dom*

Pérignon Cuvée of Moët & Chandon. This Champagne, costing around $13.50 a bottle, is one of the finest Champagnes that one can find on the market today. Not only is it made from carefully selected wines to begin with, but it is also aged longer in the cellars than most other Champagnes. That is, the "disgorgement" is not made for six or seven years instead of after only four or five years, as is customary for most other fine Champagnes. Once the Champagne has been disgorged and has been recorked it no longer develops to any great extent and can just as well be drunk as laid away for some future celebration. The Moët & Chandon *Dom Pérignon* is bottled in a distinctive old-fashioned-style bottle instead of in the regular bottles currently in use.

Besides the firms we have already mentioned, there are several other outstanding houses which also deserve to be listed here. Mumm and Piper-Heidsieck are probably the two most famous and the two best-known shippers to the average American. Then there are Veuve Clicquot, Lanson, Perrier-Jouët, Irroy, Pol Roger, Charles Heidsieck, Taittinger, and Heidsieck Dry Monopole. Note that the firm name is Heidsieck Dry Monopole, but their Champagnes may be *brut*, extra dry, and so on, just as with any other shipper. The "dry" in their name does not refer to the Champagne in the bottle. In the same way, the firm of Moët & Chandon markets a Champagne known as *Dry Imperial*, both as a vintage and nonvintage *brut*. There, too, the "dry" is only part of the name and has nothing to do with the type of Champagne inside.

In buying Champagne, just as in buying any other wine, it pays to buy the biggest bottle you can use, rather than several small bottles. This is because the wine is better in the bigger bottles, since there is less air coming in contact with it in proportion to the amount of wine which a magnum (double bottle), or

Jeroboam (four bottles), contains. Certainly as far as Champagne is concerned, one should avoid at all costs the "split" (the small 6¼-ounce quarter bottle). No wine can develop or keep in a tiny bottle of this size, and splits are in most cases just a waste of money. They often turn out to be flat and, since they only contain two scant glasses of Champagne anyway, they are hardly worth the trouble.

With the great variety of Champagne-bottle sizes, one should have no difficulty in selecting the proper size for any given occasion. Just bear in mind that the Champagne should be drunk within about a half-hour after the bottle has been opened, so buy accordingly. One bottle contains about eight glasses, and the other sizes are all multiples of this. The list that follows is the complete range of Champagne-bottle sizes, but the last four, magnificent though they may be, are not very practical to handle and are no longer imported into the United States, except on special order. If you want a Nebuchadnezzar for your wedding reception, therefore, be sure to notify your wine merchant in plenty of time so that it can be imported from France for you. Here, then, are the bottle sizes with their picturesque names:

Split (a quarter bottle—
forget about this one!)
Half-bottle—four glasses
Bottle—eight glasses
Magnum—double bottle
Jeroboam—four bottles
Rehoboam—six bottles
Methuselah—eight bottles
Salmanasar—twelve bottles
Balthazar—sixteen bottles
Nebuchadnezzar—twenty bottles

Fine Champagne never needs to be served ice-cold. It should of course be well chilled, but not so cold that there is no taste left to the wine. It also helps if the glasses can be chilled as well, since this keeps the wine cool that much longer. Let the glasses be dry, though, since the Champagne keeps its sparkle better than when served in a wet glass. Nobody wants to be handed a glass which has just been dunked in ice water anyway! Although a nice loud pop of the cork is part of the fun to many people when they drink Champagne, it is much better to open the bottle slowly and carefully with only the minimum of pop. This keeps the gas from all rushing out of the bottle and the Champagne will sparkle that much longer. At a very festive moment, such as the stroke of midnight on New Year's Eve, we doubt whether even the fussiest Champagne connoisseur would object to a big, loud pop, but in general it is best to let the Champagne retain its natural sparkle for as long as possible by opening the bottle carefully.

Though it may seem hard to believe, there are actually people who claim that they like Champagne, but yet can't stand the effervescence in it. They have therefore equipped themselves with ridiculous little whisk-type gadgets known as swizzle sticks, with which they calmly stir their Champagne until it has become flat! In other words, they are taking out of the wine what nature and the Champagne maker spent three or four years putting in. This hardly makes much sense, of course, but then if one has a solid gold or platinum swizzle stick one must no doubt put it to some sort of use.

It is claimed for Champagne that it is the one wine that can be served right through the meal without any regard for the various foods being eaten. This is essentially true, although it is a lazy way out as far as selecting wines is concerned. It would seem rather boring to be served a delicious meal of several courses and to be offered nothing but Champagne all the way through. Any real wine lover could not help but think of the various other wines that he *could* be drinking with the different foods. Since many-course dinners are now largely a thing of the past, this is hardly a serious problem for most of us, though.

The ideal time to enjoy a glass of fine vintage *brut* Champagne is before dinner instead of cocktails. The Champagne can then be appreciated to its fullest extent, and it stimulates the digestion for what is to follow, without in any way being heavy on the stomach or spoiling the palate for other wines that are to come afterwards. The slightly sweeter extra-dry Champagnes are, as far as we are concerned, strictly dessert wines. Since they are two or three dollars cheaper than the best *brut* Champagnes, they can also be enjoyed that much more often.

It is encouraging to the cause of good Champagne drinking to see the graceful tulip-shaped glass becoming more and more popular. One sees these glasses in the advertisements of many of the leading Champagne shippers, and they have been written up and described in many articles and books on wine. Not everybody can afford the beautiful Baccarat glasses, of course, but there are now at least two American-made glasses of this type on sale in many stores, and they are quite reasonable in price. The saucer-type glass has the great disadvantage of offering a wider surface of Champagne to the air, and thus letting it get flat that much sooner. The hollow-stem glasses are not only difficult to clean, but also let the hand warm the Champagne, since very few people hold the base of the glass with just their thumb and forefinger. Not only is the tulip-shaped glass the most beautiful, therefore, but it is also the most practical.

VARIOUS FRENCH WINES

ALSACE

The easternmost province of France, Alsace, was under German rule from 1870 to 1918, and again during the Second World War. While it was a part of Germany, the Alsatian wines were used mainly for blending purposes to make *Liebfraumilch* and such other ordinary wines as were required, whether for the home market or for export abroad. No attempt was made to really develop Alsatian winegrowing in any way, since it was obviously not desirable to have the region producing wines in direct competition with the German Rhine wines. After suffering considerable damage toward the end of the last war, Alsace is now almost completely rebuilt and the growers have been giving more and more attention to the production of quality wines. The best grape varieties, such as Riesling, Sylvaner, Traminer, and Gewürztraminer are now being planted wherever the soil is suitable for them. The Alsatian wines are sold by the name of the grape variety from which they are made and the name of the producer or shipper. Here one does not have to look for town or vineyard names, but merely for the type of wine wanted. The Riesling is the finest of all, just as in Germany, though it rarely attains the same quality that it does in the German vineyards. Also quite popular is the Gewürztraminer, or spicy Traminer. This wine has a very pronounced flavor and bouquet, though not everyone likes such a strong, spicy quality as this. The Sylvaner is a milder wine and is the least expensive of the three. The best Alsatian wines run around $3 a bottle from one of the leading shippers such as Hugel or Dopff. When a wine is a blend of several different grape varieties, it is usually given a name of its own, such as the *Fleur d'Alsace,* which Hugel puts out. Such wines always cost a little less than those made only from the Riesling or only from the Traminer.

THE LOIRE VALLEY

Southwest of Paris, in one of the most beautiful provinces of France, many charming wines are produced along the Loire River as it flows from Nevers north to Orléans, and then west to the Atlantic Ocean at Saint Nazaire. Tourists who travel through this region and sample the many different wines along the way usually manage to find an "unknown" wine that was better than any other they tasted in France. Wine merchants in this country are quite used to these stories by now, and, as we have already mentioned, there is no such thing as an unknown wine in France today. There are many wines from the Loire, as from other parts of France, which are not exported to the United States for one reason or another, but you can be sure that they are known to everyone in the wine trade. If a wine is reasonably good and produced in sufficient quantity, it will usually be imported into this country sooner or later.

Just north of Nevers, before the Loire turns to flow west, are the three famous vineyard areas of Pouilly-Sur-Loire, Sancerre, and Quincy. A fourth region, that of Reuilly, is right across from Quincy, but the wines are not seen in this country very often. The best wines from Pouilly-Sur-Loire are sold as *Pouilly-Fumé* or sometimes as *Blanc-Fumé de Pouilly*. These are both made from the classic Sauvignon Blanc grape of Bordeaux, while those simply called *Pouilly-Sur-Loire* are made from an inferior grape variety called the Chasselas. The best of the Pouilly-Fumé wines is that of the *Château du Nozet*, owned by Baron de Ladoucette. The *Sancerre* wines are much like those of Pouilly, while the *Quincy* is extremely dry and light in alcohol.

The best known of all the Loire wines is certainly *Vouvray*, found as both a still wine and a sparkling wine. The Vouvray vineyards are located a short distance upstream from Tours. The wines here are soft and fresh, but not always completely dry. In especially great years the wines tend to have a slight trace of sweetness to them. The sparkling Vouvray, often made by the Champagne method, is generally on the sweet side and is best for people who do not like dry Champagne of the *brut* type. The Vouvray wines are best drunk young and they often lose some of their freshness and charm if kept too long.

On the other side of Tours, the two areas of Chinon and Bourgueil both produce very pleasant red wines, but the best ones are not often exported. What we find in this country under a Chinon or Bourgueil label is rarely worth bothering about.

Saumur, the next town down the river, is noted for its sparkling wines, most of which are on the sweet side. The wines are heavier-bodied than those of Vouvray, and they are also made by the Champagne process in most cases. The sparkling Saumur and Vouvray wines must pay the same duty as Champagne when they are imported into the United States, and this often puts the best brands into the $4 to $5 class. The sparkling *Saumur*, as well as most sparkling Vouvray, should be drunk as a dessert wine because of its sweetness. Some of the drier types can of course be served with a meal just as Champagne would be, but the sweet varieties should be saved until the end of the meal.

The area around Saumur, and down along the river to Angers and beyond, is the old province of Anjou. There are many different wine-producing districts in Anjou, but today the region is most famous for its rosé wines. Rosé wine at its best is never a great wine, and the Anjou rosés are certainly not the best that France has to offer. Many of these wines do not have a high enough alcoholic content to be shipped properly, while others are not true rosés at all, having been made pink by the addition of cochineal dye. Sometimes they appear more orange than pink in color.

The region near Nantes, almost at the Atlantic coast, produces the undistinguished white wine known as *Muscadet.* It is very dry and goes quite well with the seafood from the coast when one is visiting in that area. Some Muscadet is imported into the United States, but it should not cost over $1.50 a bottle if it is to be worth buying. Otherwise it is better passed by in favor of a good white Burgundy, or one of the other wines from the Loire, if a wine from this region is wanted.

THE RHÔNE

South of the Burgundy region and beginning below the city of Lyon is the Rhône Valley. This region is noted for three outstanding red wines, as well as the most famous French rosé, *Tavel.* The first of the red wine areas that we come to is the *Côte Rôtie,* or "roasted slope" in English. The wines really do soak up the sun here and they are all big and full-bodied. One characteristic of Rhône wines in general is that they take a long time to develop properly and then keep well for many, many years. The *Hermitage* is the second of the Rhône reds and many people have failed to appreciate it properly because they drank it when it was too young. Most of these wines are aged five years in the barrel before being bottled, but even then another five years in bottle will be required before they can really be said to have come into their own. There is some white Hermitage made too and it has the same characteristics as the red—big, full-bodied, and long-lived. The most famous of the white Hermitage wines is *Chante-Alouette.* The best known of all the Rhône wines is certainly *Châteauneuf-du-Pape,* which takes its name from the former residence of the popes near Avignon. The castle is now in ruins, but the vines still thrive and produce wines of outstanding quality. The Châteauneuf-du-Pape is ready to drink much sooner than the Côte Rôtie or Hermitage wines and is also a little cheaper. The average price for the wine of a good shipper like Chapoutier is around $3.50 a bottle, whereas the other Rhône wines will be nearer to $4. Those who like rich, full-bodied wines could not do better than to try some of the excellent Rhône wines. They are certainly far better buys than some of the low-priced Burgundies of questionable origin.

PROVENCE

Most travelers in France include the Riviera in their itinerary and are charmed by the wines they find there. Very few of the wines from this region are exported, since local demand more than takes care of the limited supply. Around the little fishing village of Cassis there are many vineyards and it is here that the finest of the Provence rosé wines is produced. There is also an excellent white wine made, but most people seem to prefer the charming rosé to the white wine. Another excellent rosé is produced in the coastal town of

Bandol, while the vineyards in Bellet, not far from Nice, supply more quantities of rosé wines to all the Riviera resorts. Farther back from the coast are the vineyards of the Palette region, where red and white wines are made as well as rosé. Though the wines will be found in the hotels and restaurants along the Riviera, they are of no particular quality and are not exported. When you travel in France, however, it is always interesting to try such local wines and not always insist on great Bordeaux or Burgundy growths wherever you go. The wines of Provence certainly make no pretense of being in any way great, and if one does not expect too much from them they can be quite enjoyable.

II

The Wines of Germany

INTRODUCTION

GERMAN WHITE WINES have long been known and appreciated for their superb quality, and, indeed, the best German wines are considered by many wine experts to be the finest white wines grown anywhere in the world. The many varieties and types of these wines, however, can often confuse the beginning wine drinker, especially if he has too little knowledge of the German language to understand what the words on the label tell him about the wine. To get to know German wines well, and—even more important—to be able to select a good bottle of German wine in a shop, requires some little effort on the part of the wine drinker. There are no established classifications of German wines, such as exist for many wine-growing areas in

France, nor are there any large estates producing only a single wine of uniform quality such as one finds in the case of Bordeaux with its famous châteaux.

Good German wine will certainly repay the effort it may take to learn about it, however, and with a little practice even the inexperienced wine drinker should be able to distinguish the good wines from the merely drinkable. It is very unfortunate that so much poor German wine is imported into the United States, and the prospective purchaser is warned right from the start that very few wineshops handle the best German wines at all. Thousands of bottles of *Liebfraumilch,* the lowest common denominator of German wines—contrary to what some advertisements may tell you about it—are sold in this country for every bottle of really fine Rhine or Moselle wine that is sold. There are a number of reasons for this unfortunate state of affairs, but the main one is probably the fact that good German wines are in general more expensive than French or Italian wines. For example, a bottle selling at $1.50 or $2 cannot possibly be anything more than Liebfraumilch or Moselblümchen, both of which are simply blends of various wines from second-rate vineyards.

It is hoped that the following pages will help to clear up the many misconceptions about German wines, and, by explaining some of the more common German wine terms, enable the reader to select a good bottle of German wine without any doubts or uncertainties about what he is getting.

THE GERMAN WINE DISTRICTS

There are many different wine-growing districts in Germany, and just the Rhine wines alone come from four separate areas. Before considering the German wines in any detail, therefore, it will be worth-while for us to have an idea of the German vineyard districts so that we do not think simply in terms of Rhine wine and Moselle wine.

The northernmost white wine vineyards in the world are those growing along the steep slopes of the Moselle River (*Mosel* in German) and the two smaller rivers that flow into it, the Saar and the Ruwer. The wines from all three river valleys have the same general characteristics, so that the bottle labels always carry the three words "*Mosel—Saar—Ruwer,*" regardless of which one the wine comes from.

Let us consider next the Rhine and its major wine areas. We come first to the *Rheingau,* a small area about ten miles long on the right bank of the Rhine, which extends from Rüdesheim to a point just about south of Wiesbaden. The wines from the town of Hochheim, a short way up on the Main River, are also classified as Rheingau wines.

On the other side of the river is Rhine-Hessia (in German, *Rheinhessen*), which begins at Bingen, runs across to Mainz, and extends as far south as Worms. The Rhine-Palatinate (in German, *Rheinpfalz*) continues down the same side of the Rhine south of Worms, and extends as far south as the town of Schweigen, almost at the French frontier. It would be well to remember these three important Rhine wine districts by their German names: Rheingau, Rheinhessen, and Rheinpfalz, since this is the way the names will always appear on bottle labels.

The fourth Rhine wine area, the vineyards of the middle Rhine, from Assmannshausen up to Koblenz, are located on the most picturesque stretch of the entire Rhine River, but they do not produce wines in either quantity or quality to match those from the three major Rhine wine districts farther to the South.

Some distance east of the Rhine, on the Main River, are grown the wines of Franconia (in German, *Franken*). The Franken wine district is centered about the city of Würzburg, and the wines are bottled in distinctive flagon-shaped bottles which are always quite easy to identify.

The Nahe River, flowing into the Rhine at Bingen, is located between the Mosel and Rheinhessen areas and produces wines combining the characteristics of the two. The wine trade here is centered around the pretty little town of Bad Kreuznach. Though still not very well known abroad, the Nahe wines rank among the finest in Germany.

In southern Germany, there are large vineyard areas in Baden and Württemberg, extending all the way to Lake Constance on the Swiss border. Most of the wines produced in the area are consumed locally, and they vary widely in their character and quality. They are very seldom found in American wineshops.

READING AND UNDERSTANDING THE LABEL

To those who do not know German, selecting a good bottle of German wine may often seem like a hope-

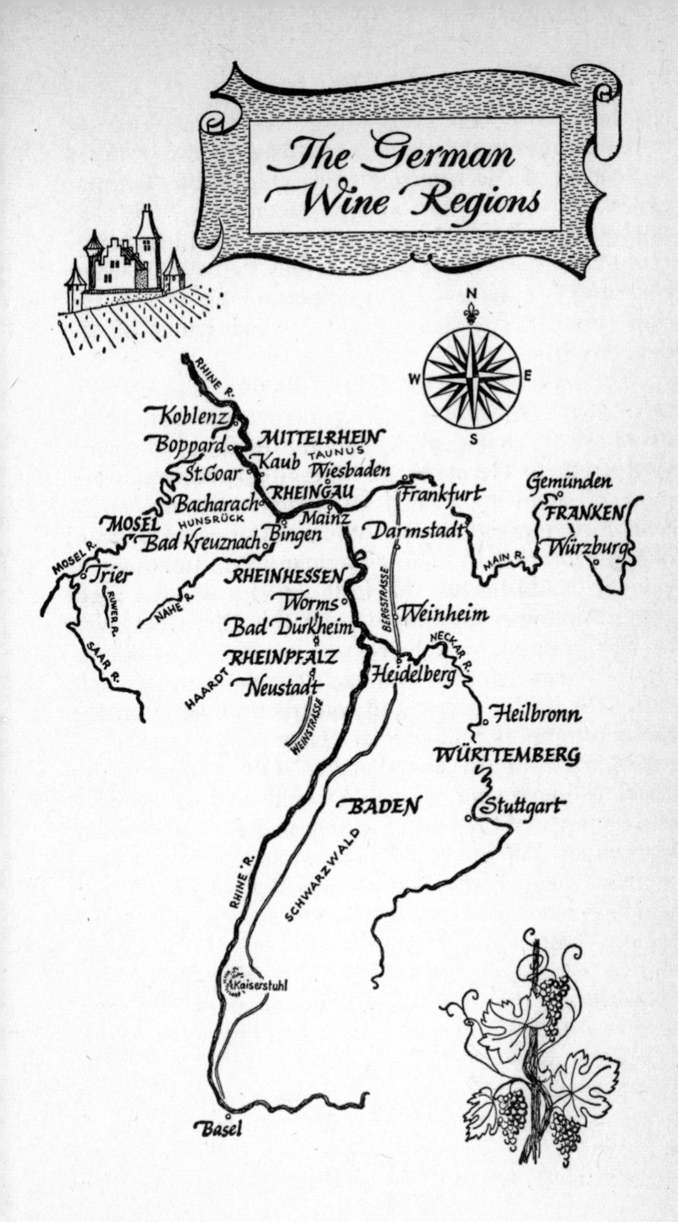
The German Wine Regions
N
W
E
S
RHINE R.
Koblenz
Boppard
MITTELRHEIN
Kaub
TAUNUS
Wiesbaden
St. Goar
RHEINGAU
Frankfurt
Gemünden
FRANKEN
Bacharach
MOSEL
HUNSRÜCK
Mainz
Bingen
Darmstadt
Bad Kreuznach
Würzburg
MAIN R.
MOSEL R.
Trier
RHEINHESSEN
RUWER R.
NAHE R.
Worms
BERGSTRASSE
Weinheim
Bad Dürkheim
SAAR R.
RHEINPFALZ
NECKAR R.
HAARDT
Heidelberg
Neustadt
WEINSTRASSE
Heilbronn
WÜRTTEMBERG
BADEN
Stuttgart
SCHWARZWALD
RHINE R.
Kaiserstuhl
Basel

less task. Although every word on the label of the bottle is important, one does not need to have a fluent knowledge of the language to be able to buy German wines with intelligence and understanding.

The label should be thought of as the birth certificate of the wine. First of all, it tells the year in which the wine was made—a very important bit of information, since every year does not yield wines of the same quality.

The second thing the label tells us is the place of birth, that is, the wine-growing district, the community or village in that district, and the name of the vineyard itself. In Germany, all vineyards have names and most of them are owned by several different people. This fact, more than any other, is the cause of most of the confusion in buying German wine. Just imagine what it would be like, for instance, if a popular make of an American automobile, say the Chevrolet, were to be produced by a half-dozen other companies besides General Motors, and each company made slight variations in the design and construction, yet all called their automobiles Chevrolet. How would one know which make of car was the best? Other things being equal, the only sure guarantee would be the reputation and integrity of the manufacturer, and so it is with German wines. When ten different winegrowers own parts of one vineyard, the best wine will naturally be that which is made by the most skillful and the most reputable grower.

The parentage of the wine then is the final thing we look for on the label, and it is the most important factor in determining the quality and character of what has been produced. One does not customarily think much about who bottled the wine, since it is usually taken for granted that the same man who made the wine has also bottled it. When we are discussing top-quality wines, we can be sure that this is the case, but many of the middle-grade wines, and just about all the very cheapest wines, are sold to large wholesale companies who then bottle them in their own cellars.

In the case of German wines, however, the very strict wine laws make it unnecessary to be in any doubt as to who actually did bottle the wine you are planning to buy. If the label carries the word "*Originalabfüllung*" (in English, "original bottling"), you may be sure that the wine was bottled in the cellar of the grower and that it is a natural wine, that is, a wine that has not been made with the addition of sugar. It is necessary to remember, though, that the word *Originalabfüllung* in itself is not a guarantee of the quality of a wine. In poor years, when the grapes have not been able to produce sufficient sugar of their own, enough extra sugar must be added to the freshly pressed grape juice to make it ferment into wine with the proper alcoholic strength. Such wines are nearly always better than natural wines of the same vintage and they do not taste at all sweet, as many people think. The added sugar ferments into alcohol right along with what natural grape sugar there is, and the wine is thus able to develop as it would in a normal year. (Sugar is never added to the wine itself, but only to the grape juice before it starts to ferment.) There is thus no point in insisting on an *Originalabfüllung* wine from a poor year when the corrected wines are better in every respect, and also much cheaper.

In addition to the word "*Originalabfüllung*," there are other words that are sometimes used, but which mean the same as *Originalabfüllung*. Some of the bigger estates that have castles or large manor houses on their properties—mainly in the Rheingau—may use either the word "*Schlossabfüllung*," or the word "*Schlossabzug*," both of which mean "bottled at the castle." Two other variations that are often encountered are the terms "*Original-Kellerabfüllung*," or

"*Original-Kellerabzug.*" It is very important in these last two versions that the word *Original* appear as the first part of the compound, since the words "*Kellerabfüllung*" and "*Kellerabzug*" by themselves mean nothing more than that the wine was bottled in a cellar. Since even the poorest wines are bottled in a cellar, the important thing to know, of course, is in *whose* cellar. Several of the less honest German shippers make quite a point of printing the word "*Kellerabfüllung*" in an obvious place on their labels in order to make the unwary wine drinker think he is getting an *Originalabfüllung* wine when such is not the case at all. The word "*Originalabfüllung*" and all combinations with the word "*Original*" are protected by German law for natural wines bottled by the grower in his own cellars, so that one may purchase these wines with complete confidence that they are just what the label says they are. Since the word "*Original*" is the same in English as it is in German, it should not cause any problem in trying to remember what it means, or in recognizing it on the label of the bottle.

The words, "*Wachstum,*" "*Gewächs,*" and "*Kreszenz*" (all of which mean "growth" in English), are often seen on labels too. When one of these words appears before the name of a grower, it simply means that the wine is a natural, unsugared wine from his estate or vineyard, but not necessarily bottled by the man whose *Wachstum* or *Gewächs* the wine is. Likewise, the words "*naturrein*" and "*Naturwein*" (meaning "naturally pure" and "natural wine") both signify that no sugar was added to the wine. These words are often used by companies or restaurants who buy a wine from a small grower and then bottle it themselves. Such wines, by the way, are often to be preferred to an *Originalabfüllung* from a small grower who may not have the modern equipment and sanitary facilities to bottle the wine properly himself. The beginning wine drinker would do well, however, to buy his better wines only from the large estates and growers who have a reputation for quality which they must maintain at all costs.

Finally, we come to the terms "*Cabinet-Wein*" or "*Cabinet-Füllung*," which signify, or at least *should* signify, wines of topmost quality. Needless to say, such wines will always be *Originalabfüllung* wines as well! The term "*Cabinet-Wein*" originated in the Rheingau, and is still used almost exclusively in that area. In the days when the dukes of Nassau ruled the territory now known as the Rheingau, the best wines from each community and vineyard were selected for the ducal court at Wiesbaden. These wines were designated as being for the duke's private *Cabinet*—actually a special section of the wine cellar—and thus the term "*Cabinet-Wein*" came into existence. Over the years, as the *Cabinet* became full, some of the wines were sold to the general public and the term gradually became a synonym for wines of better than average quality. The practice of selling *Cabinet-Wein* has now been adopted by other growers in the Rheingau, especially by the State Domains, and the designation is restricted by general agreement to the best-grade wines. Since a *Cabinet-Wein* always brings a higher price than a regular wine from the same vintage and vineyard, many producers tend to stretch this designation a little thin and often call an ordinary wine a *Cabinet-Wein* when they really have no right to do so. The buyer should beware, therefore, of seeming bargains in wines advertised as *Cabinet-Wein* for "only" $2 a bottle or thereabouts. An authentic *Cabinet-Wein* will hardly ever be available for under $3 a bottle in the United States.

The State Domains, by the way, use still another variation of the term "*Originalabfüllung*" on their labels. They prefer the phrase "*Eigener Kellerabzug und Korkbrand,*" which means "Our own cellar bottling and branded cork." Nowadays all wine producers brand or stamp their corks with their names and the vintage date of the wine, but the government apparently feels that it should emphasize this point as far as its own wines are concerned. A branded cork simply serves as an additional proof of authenticity of a wine, since it would be exceedingly difficult to replace a cork in a bottle once it had been pulled. Where people are careless or unconcerned about having a bottle of wine opened at the table in front of them, the purpose of a branded cork is completely lost, since it would then be possible for a dishonest restaurant owner to pour out the wine and replace it with an inferior one before bringing the bottle to the table. Such things *do* happen, especially in some of the crowded tourist areas of Europe, where the bustle and excitement make it easy to deceive unknowing foreigners.

The variety of grape used in the making of a wine is one of the principal factors that gives to every wine its own distinctive character. (Climate, type of soil, and cellar care are important too, of course.) In Germany, as in all wine-growing countries, there is a large number of grape varieties grown for wine-making purposes. Some types of grapes yield large quantities of wine of no particular distinction; other types will only grow in certain kinds of soil, while others are particularly resistant to cold and frost. The wine drinker need only remember about three of the most important varieties to be able to select a good bottle of German wine.

First and foremost is the Riesling (pronounced REES-LING). This is the grape from which all the greatest German wines are made, and it is noted for its wonderful bouquet and aroma. The grapes are small and late to ripen, but they are more resistant to frost than many other varieties. All the best vineyards are planted with Riesling grapes, and more and more are being planted every year as growers switch over from quantity production to quality production of wines.

The Traminer and Gewürztraminer ("spicy" Traminer) grapes are found mainly in Baden, the Rhine Palatinate, and Franconia. They can be grown only on good sites, and the wines have a very powerful bouquet which many people admire. The taste of these wines, however, does not appeal to everyone.

The Sylvaner is the mass-production grape and is usually found in the lesser vineyards which yield many of the wines for Liebfraumilch. It gives a mild and pleasant type wine which often can be quite good.

Whenever a German wine is made from the great Riesling grape it will always say so on the label, except in the case of the Moselle wines where it is taken for granted, since no other grape variety is planted in the quality-wine area of the Moselle. If no grape name is given on the label of a bottle of Rhine wine, it can generally be assumed that the wine is a blend of two or more varieties or perhaps just made from the Sylvaner grape alone.

The unique method of harvesting the grapes in the German vineyards makes it possible to find German wines ranging from very dry to honey sweet. They are divided by law into five categories, according to their degree of sweetness. For a thorough understanding of the matter, let us consider first how the German winemaking methods differ from those of other countries.

We know that when the grapes are gathered in the autumn it is quite impossible to pick them all in a single day or even in a single week. Realizing this, it follows that the grapes picked at the beginning of the harvest will not make as sweet a wine as those picked at the end of the harvest, since the longer the grapes stay on the vines, the riper and sweeter they become—assuming, of course, that the weather remains warm and sunny during this time. If the wine made from the various gatherings of the grapes during the harvest period were all to be mixed together, we should have one standard quality wine as a result, and every bottle of a given wine would taste like any other. This is the method used in France, and in most other wine-growing countries. On the other hand, when the wine made from the various pressings is *not* blended together, but rather is kept in separate barrels and bottled separately, as is the case in Germany, we are, naturally enough, going to have wines of quite different quality from barrel to barrel, even though they may all have been made by the very same grower from grapes grown in one single vineyard. This practice often causes confusion and even disappointment among inexperienced wine drinkers, but when the system is once understood there need be no cause for any misunderstanding, since every German wine label provides exact information about what kind of wine the bottle contains.

The German method of separately harvesting and pressing the grapes has its justification in a perfectly natural development which occurs toward the end of the growing season. Anyone who has ever seen a grapevine in the late summer and early autumn knows that the grapes begin to shrivel and dry out if left too long on the vines. Oddly enough, this is just what the German winegrower would like to have happen to his grapes. One type of fungus, known in German as *Edelfäule* (in French, the afore-mentioned *pourriture noble*), attacks the grapes when they are fully ripe and causes them to shrivel and dry out as they hang on the vines. By this perfectly natural process the grapes lose some of their water content, and the remaining juice becomes sweeter and more concentrated as a result. It need hardly be added that such a development will only take place when weather conditions are extremely favorable. Without plenty of late autumn sunshine the grapes will never reach the degree of ripeness which is necessary for the *Edelfäule* to do its work.

How can you tell whether the wine you are ordering was made from grapes picked early in the harvest, or from the overripe grapes picked at the end of the harvest? Fortunately for the wine drinker, the very strict German wine laws make a most careful distinction among the five categories into which the wines are divided. Once you know the key words or descriptive terms, you can easily tell from the label what type of wine you are getting. Let us consider the five categories individually, starting with the lowest and working up to those rare bottles that few of us will ever have the opportunity to drink.

For lack of an official designation for the lowest category, we shall call this wine simply the "regular" or "ordinary" wine, since the label bears no additional quality designation. Since it is made from the first gatherings of the grapes, it is the driest type of wine that we can get. There is certainly nothing inferior about such wines as these, and they are the kind we usually prefer to drink with our meals. The wines should, of course, come from a reliable producer and should be of a good vintage year if one is to derive the fullest amount of pleasure from them, but then that is true of all wines no matter where they come from.

The second category of German wines is *Spätlese*. This word means "late picking" or "late gathering" in English, and implies that the wine was made from grapes picked after the regular harvest. Since the grapes have had more time to ripen on the vines, the wine made from them will naturally be somewhat sweeter than the ordinary wine. In recent years there has been much abuse of the *Spätlese* term on labels, since the German wine laws say only that the wine must be made from fully ripe grapes picked after the regular harvest, and no one can say exactly when this fully ripe state is reached. One grower may wait two days after the regular harvest and another may wait two weeks, and yet each one can call his wine *Spätlese*. Fortunately, the growers themselves have got together in the last year or two and have to a considerable extent curbed the abuse of the *Spätlese* designation. At any rate, a *Spätlese* wine should always be a little bit sweeter than the regular wines of the same vintage.

The third category is *Auslese*. The word means a "selection" in English, and the wine is made from carefully selected bunches of overripe grapes, from which all unripe, damaged, or sick grapes have been removed. Although *Auslese* is usually sweeter and richer than *Spätlese*, it may nevertheless have been made during the regular harvest, that is, before the *Spätlese* was made. It is important to remember here that it is the very careful selection of only the best and ripest grapes which makes the difference between *Auslese* and *Spätlese*.

As we come to the two top categories of German wines, it should be pointed out that we are dealing here with what the Germans refer to as *Spitzenweine*, that is, wines of the very highest quality. These wines rank among the greatest wines in the world and are rare, sweet, and expensive.

In the fourth category, then, we have *Beerenauslese*. We already know that *Auslese* means a selection, and, if we add the word *Beeren* (English, "berries") to it, we get "berry selection," which is just what this wine is. Each individual grape is separately picked! Before this, we have been dealing with grapes gathered in bunches, but to make *Beerenauslese* the picker selects only those individual grapes that have been attacked by the *Edelfäule* and have begun to shrivel into raisins. We have already mentioned that the juice from these grapes is sweeter and more concentrated than the juice from the ordinary grapes, but we should also remember that the *quantity* of juice is a good bit less than is obtained from the regular pressings. This is one reason why the wine is so expensive, but what is lacking in quantity is more than made up for in quality.

At the topmost rung of the ladder we have *Trockenbeerenauslese*. Don't be confused by the length of this word if you don't know German. The word *trocken* means "dry" in English, and when we put it in front of *Beerenauslese*, we can easily see that the entire word then means "a selection of dry berries." In other words, this wine is *Beerenauslese* carried to the ultimate degree. To make a *Trockenbeerenauslese* the grapes are left to dry out on the vines until they have become almost raisins. It is perhaps difficult to realize how many of these raisinlike grapes are required to make a single bottle of this magnificent wine, and, just as a matter of interest, we should perhaps mention here that a person picking grapes in a vineyard for an entire day can gather only enough of these dried-out grapes to make *one* bottle of *Trockenbeerenauslese*. These wines are of course the rarest and most expensive of all German wines, and indeed, of all wines anywhere. The few bottles that can be found in wineshops here in the United States cost anywhere from $25 to $40 each! A fine *Trockenbeerenauslese* is golden in color, rich, very sweet, and really more of a natural liqueur than what we ordinarily think of as wine.

It cannot be too strongly emphasized that the sweetness of the great German wines is a natural sweetness —no sugar is ever added to them. They should never be compared with Port wine or Cream Sherry, for example, both of which are sweetened by the addition of a special brandy, which also raises their alcoholic content to 20 per cent, as against 12 per cent for the German wines.

THE WINES OF THE MOSELLE

The Moselle River flows through one of the most beautiful river valleys in Germany, yet few travelers visit the area because it lies somewhat away from the usual tourist routes. The vineyards along the Moselle and its two small tributaries, the Saar and the Ruwer, are the northernmost white wine vineyards in all of Europe, and the wines which are produced there rank among the greatest in the world.

Although the wine-growing area of the Moselle River extends all the way from Koblenz, where the Moselle empties into the Rhine, to beyond Trier, the lower and upper Moselle do not produce the top-quality wines which are produced in the middle Moselle section. We shall therefore confine our survey to the area extending roughly from Enkirch up to Klüsserath, and to the vineyards of the Saar and Ruwer.

Grown in light, slaty soil, the Moselle wines are noted for their wonderful bouquet, delicacy, and fragrance. We think of them as being light and elegant, and they are often very slightly effervescent or "prickly" on the tongue—a quality known in German as *spritzig.* There is no other white wine which can match them in these qualities, and they are always much sought after in wineshops and restaurants throughout Germany. Because of this great demand for the wines in Germany, and to a lesser extent in

England and the United States, fine Moselle wines can never be cheap. The shippers and importers can justly claim, therefore, that they are filling a real need by bringing in second-rate, blended wines and selling them as *Moselblümchen* or *Bernkasteler Riesling* for $1.50 or $2 a bottle, even though these brands are certainly not the ones that gave the Moselle its great reputation for magnificent wines, any more than *Liebfraumilch* enhances the reputation of Rhine wines. As long as the consumer realizes that he is not getting the best, no great harm can result in buying and drinking the shippers' wines, but one should never pay over $2 a bottle for any of them. Above that price it should be possible to find estate-bottled wines, that is, wines marked *Originalabfüllung* on the label and stating the name of the grower. The best vintages to look for among the fine wines would be 1964, 1962, and 1966, in that order. Wines older than 1959 will no longer be of much interest to the average drinker, unless they are one of the great 1959 wines of *Auslese* class or above. It is quite ridiculous, by the way, to think of Moselle wine as being in any way sour. Those who have drunk sour Moselle wine have obviously not drunk a good wine. All Moselle wines have a certain natural tartness, but they should never have so high an acid content as to taste sour. If they do, they are certainly not worth drinking even if purchased at a so-called bargain price.

Although the words "*Mosel—Saar—Ruwer*" always appear together on bottle labels, there are some small differences in the wines from the three different river valleys. The outstanding characteristic of the Saar wines is a certain "steely" quality which is easy to recognize and is much enjoyed by wine connoisseurs. They have a great amount of fine flavor but are not so "soft" as the wines from the Moselle. The Ruwer wines are also every bit as fine as the wines from the Moselle itself, but they are often a little lighter and drier than the Moselle wines, yet with perhaps even more bouquet.

Which are the outstanding Moselle wines to look for? There are many small growers who produce excellent wines every bit as good as those of the big estates, but they are not so easily found as the wines from the big estates. The wines from the Reichsgraf von Kesselstatt are among the finest of the Moselle wines, as are those from the various Prüm estates in Wehlen, or the Bergweiler estate also located there. In Bernkastel we have the famous Doktor vineyard, whose two most famous producers are the Thannisch and Deinhard estates. Because the *Bernkasteler Doktor* wine is world famous and the quantity produced is relatively small, the prices are always very high and do not reflect the actual worth of the wine. A price of $7 a bottle is not unusual, even though the wine may be worth only $4 a bottle, but you must be willing to pay a little extra for the prestige value of the wine if you are interested in such things. Other well-known and reliable estates are those of von Schorlemer, the Friedrich-Wilhelm Gymnasium, the St. Nikolaus Hospital, the Bischöfliches Priesterseminar (a Catholic seminary in Trier), and any of the various Berres and Ehses-Berres clan. Most of these producers have holdings in several vineyard areas, such as the towns of Graach, Wehlen, Zeltingen, Erden, or Uerzig, to name some of the most important.

In the list that follows, we have named most of the best vineyards in the leading wine-producing communities of the Moselle, Saar, and Ruwer. The fact that any particular wine may not be found on this list does not mean that it is not good, nor should you take for granted that its inclusion here is an automatic guarantee of quality. Each wine must be judged on its own merits with due consideration of price, vintage, grower, and whether it is an *Originalabfüllung* or not. The listing, like all such listings in this book should be taken as a guide and not as an endorsement of any particular wines or wine producers.

THE WINE-PRODUCING COMMUNITIES OF THE MIDDLE MOSELLE AND THEIR BEST VINEYARDS

Wehlen: Sonnenuhr, Nonnenberg, Rosenberg, Klosterlay, and Lay

Bernkastel: Doktor (and Graben), Lay, Badstube, Rosenberg, Schwanen, and Schlossberg

Graach: Himmelreich, Domprobst, Abtsberg, Stablay, Münzlay, and Goldwingert

Piesport: Goldtröpfchen, Lay, Falkenberg, Taubengarten, and Güntherslay

Erden: Treppchen, Herrenberg, and Busslei

Brauneberg: Juffer, Falkenberg, and Hasenläufer

Ürzig: Würzgarten

Zeltingen: Himmelreich, Schlossberg, Sonnenuhr, Kirchenpfad, and Rotlay

Trittenheim: Apotheke, Laurentiusberg, Falkenberg, and Altärchen

Traben-Trarbach: Königsberg, Schlossberg, Hühnerberg, and Ungsberg

Dhron: Hofberg (or Dhronhofberger)

Josephshof: This is not the name of a town, but rather the name of an excellent wine estate owned by the Count of Kesselstatt (Reichsgraf von Kesselstatt). The wines are sold as *Josephshöfer*, and the vineyards are located between the towns of Graach and Wehlen.

THE COMMUNITIES AND THEIR BEST VINEYARDS OF THE SAAR

Wiltingen: Scharzhofberg (mainly owned by the Egon Müller estate, and probably the finest of all the Saar wines), Braunfels, Klosterberg, and Kupp

Ockfen: Bockstein, Geisberg, and Herrenberg

Ayl: Herrenberg, Kupp, and Neuberg

Niedermennig: Euchariusberg, Herrenberg, and Sonnenberg

Oberemmel: Altenberg, Scharzberg, Rosenberg, and Hütte

Kanzem: Altenberg, Kelterberg, Wolfsberg, Sonnenberg, and Berg

Wawern: Herrenberg and Goldberg

Serrig: Antoniusberg, Hindenburglei, Kupp, Wingertsheck, and Schloss Saarfelser Vogelsang

THE COMMUNITIES AND THEIR BEST VINEYARDS
OF THE RUWER

Mertesdorf: Maximin Grünhaus (owned entirely by the excellent von Schubert estate), Lorenzberg, and Treppchen

Eitelsbach: Karthäuser Berg, Marienholz, and Sonnenberg. (The best wine from the Karthäuser Berg vineyard is sold as *Eitelsbacher Karthäuser Hofberg* and the vineyard is the property of the Rautenstrauch family.)

Avelsbach: Altenberg, Dom-Avelsbach, Dom-Herrenberg, Herrenberg, and Hammerstein (owned entirely by the State Domains)

Kasel: Kehrnagel, Niesgen, Hitzlay, and Taubenberg

THE WINES OF THE RHEINGAU

Probably no other German vineyard area produces so many famous wines as does the Rheingau. On a ten-mile stretch of land, extending from a point just about opposite Mainz up to the town of Rüdesheim, are grown most of the wines that people think of first when they talk about Rhine wine. There is certainly no doubt that the Rheingau wines deserve their great fame and the reputation for quality which they enjoy. The Rhine flows from east to west as it passes through the Rheingau, and not due north as it does elsewhere along its course. This is a very important factor in the making of wine, for it means that all the vineyards in this area have a southern exposure. In addition to this considerable advantage, the vineyards are also sheltered by the hills of the Taunus Mountains, which protect them against cold winds from the north. The Rhine River itself does its bit by providing a broad, heat-reflecting, and moisture-giving surface along this part of its course. Thus the Rheingau enjoys a unique combination of natural advantages that make it an almost ideal wine-growing region.

The town of Hochheim, located on the Main River a short distance away from the Rheingau proper, is also included among the communities of the Rheingau as far as its wines are concerned. They have all the characteristics of the Rheingau wines, and the excellent estate of Domdechant Werner, as well as the vineyards of the State Domains, both produce wines of topmost quality. It is from the town of Hochheim, incidentally, that the British name for Rhine wines, *Hock*, is derived. Wine lists in Great Britain always list "Hocks and Moselles," rather than "Rhine Wines and Moselle Wines," as in the United States. Queen Victoria once visited Hochheim and had a vineyard named for her—unfortunately not a very good one—and one can even today buy a bottle of *Hochheimer Königen-Viktoria-Berg,* though one should not expect it to live up to its royal name.

A great many of the German nobility still have wine estates in the Rheingau, and their wines are always among the best that are produced there. In Eltville, there is Graf zu Eltz and Freiherr Langwerth von Simmern; in Hattenheim, Graf von Schönborn; in Erbach, Prinz Friedrich Heinrich of Prussia; at Schloss Johannisberg, the Fürst von Metternich; and at Schloss Vollrads, Graf Matuschka-Greiffenclau, who is also president of the German Winegrowers' Association and a very active figure in German viticulture in general.

In addition to these famous growers, there are also a great many smaller growers who enjoy a reputation for wines of the highest quality. Finally, we should not fail to mention the State Domains—those vineyards which are owned by the state governments of Hessen (Hessia), and Rheinland-Pfalz (the Rhine Palatinate). Formerly the property of the Prussian crown, it need hardly be said that the State Domains own parts of all the finest vineyards in the principal Rheingau communities.

All the best sites in the Rheingau are planted with the Riesling grape. The wines here are full, harmonious, rich, well rounded, and they all have the wonderful Riesling bouquet. In fine years, the great *Auslese,*

Beerenauslese, and *Trockenbeerenauslese* wines are among the finest in all Germany, and are much in demand by wine lovers in all parts of the world.

THE WINE PRODUCING COMMUNITIES OF THE RHEINGAU AND THEIR BEST VINEYARDS

Hochheim: Domdechaney, Kirchenstück, Rauchloch, Stein, and Hölle

Eltville: Sonnenberg, Sandgrube, Taubenberg, Kalbspflicht, and Langenstück

Rauenthal: Baiken, Gehrn, Langenstück, Siebenmorgen, Rothenberg, and Kesselring

Kiedrich: Sandgrube, Turmberg, Gräfenberg, Klosterberg, and Scharfenstein

Erbach: Marcobrunn, Herrenberg, Steinmorgen, Hohenrain, Siegelsberg, and Honigberg. (NOTE: Some of the owners of the Marcobrunn vineyard sell their wine as *Erbacher Marcobrunner,* and others market it simply as *Marcobrunner.* Either way, the wine is one of the greatest of the Rheingau.)

Hattenheim: Nussbrunnen, Engelmannsberg, Wisselbrunnen, Mannberg, Hinterhaus, and Rotenberg

Halfway between Hattenheim and Erbach, some distance back from the Rhine, is Kloster Eberbach, a former Cistercian monastery, and the near-by vineyard known as the Steinberg. This is without a doubt the most famous single vineyard in the Rheingau, and it is owned entirely by the State Domains. Some of the finest of all German wines are produced from its sixty-six acres (which are still surrounded by the original six-foot-high stone wall built by the monks several hundred years ago), and the best of them are always expensive.

Hallgarten: Schönhell, Würzgarten, Hendelberg, Jungfer, Mehrhölzchen, and Deutelsberg

Oestrich: Lenchen, Doosberg, Pfaffenberg, and Rosengarten

Mittelheim: Edelmann, Gottesthal, and Honigberg

Winkel: Hasensprung, Dachsberg, Steinchen, and Ansbach

A short distance above Winkel is located Schloss Vollrads, the excellent wine estate belonging to Graf Matuschka-Greiffenclau. Ranking among the best of the Rheingau wines, the *Schloss Vollrads* is not difficult to find since the production is quite large.

Near by is another famous estate, Schloss Johannisberg, the property of the Fürst von Metternich. The manor house itself was badly damaged during the war, and has now been almost completely restored. From the terrace overlooking the vineyards there is a beautiful view of the Rhine with the surrounding vineyard country, and the estate is well worth visiting when touring through the Rheingau area. Even though there is a very large annual production at Schloss Johannisberg, the wines tend to be somewhat overpriced because of their immense popularity abroad, especially in Great Britain. Not all the wines are of the same quality by any means, and it takes a little bit of study on the part of the buyer to know with certainty just what he is getting. Eight different types of *Schloss Johannisberg* wines are currently being marketed! The wines most often met with are sold as regular *Originalabfüllung* wines and are three in number. All have the coat of arms of the Metternich family on the label, which helps make them easy to recognize. The ordinary wine is called *Rotlack,* and the label is white. This wine is seldom very distinguished and should not be too high-priced if it is to be worth buying. The next best quality is called *Grünlack,* and has a green label. In very good years the *Grünlack* will correspond to the *Spätlese* wines of other producers. After the *Grünlack* comes the *Rosalack*, which carries a peach-colored label. This is the *Auslese* wine of fine vintages.

In addition to the above three types of wine, there are five additional types sold as *Cabinet-Wein*. They all carry a label showing a mid-nineteenth-century view of the castle as seen from the Rhine, and the words *Cabinet-Wein* above. The label is the same for all, but the lead foil around the top of the bottle varies in color. The ordinary wines have orange-colored foil, the *Spätlese* wines have white foil, the *Auslese* wines have blue foil, and the *Beerenauslese* and *Trockenbeerenauslese* wines have gold-colored foil. These last three categories also have an extra label around the neck of the bottle to show which type of wine it is—*Auslese, Beerenauslese,* or *Trockenbeerenauslese*. It probably never would occur to Prince Metternich or his cellar master that such a multitude of labels and colors might confuse the wine-drinking public! There is unfortunately no short cut to the "system" and one must either learn the classifications or just skip the whole thing and buy some other wine.

Johannisberg (village): Erntebringer, Klaus, and Hölle

Geisenheim: Rotenberg, Mäuerchen, Rosengarten, Katzenloch, and Kirchgrube

Rüdesheim: (The best Rüdesheimer wines come from the section known as the Rüdesheimer Berg.) Bronnen, Hinterhaus, Paares, Schlossberg, Hellpfad, Burgweg, Bischofsberg, Lay, Roseneck, Zollhaus, Rottland, and Bienengarten.

THE WINES OF RHEINHESSEN AND THE FAMOUS LIEBFRAUMILCH

Rheinhessen, or Hessia, in English, is one of the largest of the Rhine wine areas, but the top-quality wines are limited to the vineyards along what is usually called the "Rhine Front." Of the three main types of Rhine wines, those from Rheinhessen are the mildest, and therefore they enjoy a reputation of being ideal luncheon wines. In Germany, the Rheinhessen wines are often referred to as *Damenwein*, that is, wines which especially appeal to women because of their mild and pleasant qualities. This is not to say that men don't, or shouldn't, drink the Rheinhessen wines, but the term helps describe the wines more accurately.

The greatest of all the Rheinhessen wines are those which come from Nierstein. But please don't think of *Niersteiner Domthal* as typical of fine-quality Nierstein wines! *Domthal* is merely a general, catch-all name for second-rate wines which may or may not have been grown in the Nierstein area. To enjoy the really good Nierstein wines, one should select a bottle bearing one of the famous vineyard names listed a little further on, and one which has been estate-bottled by such an outstanding producer as Franz Karl Schmitt, Freiherr Heyl zu Herrnsheim, or the State Domains. There are several other Schmitt families in Nierstein, by the way, so remember the Franz Karl part of the name to be sure of the best wines. Some of the Nierstein producers own vineyards in the neighboring community of Oppenheim, which also produces some of the best of the Rheinhessen wines. Less often met with, but nevertheless very good, are the wines from the village of Nackenheim, just north of Nierstein on the way to Mainz.

Of all the Rheinhessen wines, *Liebfraumilch* is certainly the most famous. As a result of some fancy publicity in American magazines and much promotional work on the part of importers and wine dealers, most Americans now believe that this wine is one of Germany's finest, whereas Liebfraumilch is actually just a blend of various Rheinhessen wines (and often of other wines as well!), which are *supposed* to be of a fairly good and pleasant quality. They are often just that, but then the price asked for them is almost as high as for an estate-bottled (*Originalabfüllung*) wine. There is actually one brand of Liebfraumilch on the market today selling for $3.75 a bottle! Even though this is the price of a good estate-bottled wine from one of the top growers, people will pass over the much superior wines of these estates and choose the Liebfraumilch instead, mainly because they don't know which the really good wines are. Certainly a sad state of affairs in the world of German wines! In Germany, Liebfraumilch is the *vin ordinaire* which every housewife buys at the corner grocery for 35 cents, or perhaps 50 cents, a bottle. Serious wine drinkers never touch it.

Liebfraumilch had its origin in Worms, where the wines from the vineyards of the Liebfrauenkirche (Church of the Blessed Virgin) attained such great popularity in the last century that the supply nowhere equaled the demand. Wines from other vineyards were soon being sold as Liebfraumilch too, and the original wines were thus overshadowed by the huge quantities of cheaper wines using the original name. When the German wine laws were put into effect in the year 1909, the name Liebfraumilch had become too well known to restrict it to the original wines from the church vineyards, and a compromise was reached to the satisfaction of all concerned. It was forbidden to use labels for ordinary Liebfraumilch which carried a picture of the church in Worms or its vineyards. Furthermore, the wine actually produced in the church vineyards at Worms was to be designated as *Liebfrauenstift* wine by the three companies owning the vineyards: W. Mahler, Langenbach & Co., and P. J. Valckenberg—the oldest and largest of the three. The real Liebfrauenstift wine always has the name of one of these three firms on the label, together with the words *Liebfrauenstift-Wein* and perhaps one of the vineyard names. Although Valckenberg uses the picture of the church and vineyards on their labels, Langenbach does not, and their labels resemble very closely their labels for ordinary Liebfraumilch. Many people mistakenly believe that when the word "*Liebfraumilch*" is spelled "*Liebfrauenmilch*" it means that the wine is from the original vineyards in Worms. This is not so, as the above discussion has attempted to make clear, but it is one of those erroneous statements that is often printed in articles on German wine and wine buying (just as *Auslese* is listed before *Spätlese* in the ascending order of quality, though this last mistake is met with more often in England than in the United States for some strange reason). It would be nice if we could say in conclusion that the real Liebfrauenstift wines from Worms were wonderful wines worth seeking out, but unfortunately this is not the case. None of the vineyards in Worms can begin to compare with the great wines of Nierstein, and the search for a genuine Liebfrauenstift wine is hardly worth the trouble, though most of the larger wineshops carry one or more of them. The wines have a rather unpleasant "earthy" taste which many people do not like. In short, the entire question of Liebfraumilch versus Liebfrauenstift wine is of purely academic interest, and the informed wine drinker will pass over the whole lot of them and choose a good Niersteiner instead.

THE WINE-PRODUCING COMMUNITIES OF RHEINHESSEN AND THEIR BEST VINEYARDS

Nierstein: Auflangen, Fuchsloch, Glöck, Orbel, Kehr, Ölberg, Heiligenbaum, Rehbach, Kranzberg, Brudersberg, Pettental, and Hipping. (*Not* Domthal!)

Oppenheim: Sackträger, Goldberg, Krötenbrunnen, Kreuz, and Schlossberg

Nackenheim: Engelberg, Rosenberg, Fenchelberg, and Weyershorn

Laubenheim: Hitz, Dammsberg, Edelmann, and Steig

Bingen: Rheinberg, Rochusberg, Anberg (and especially the wines from the Villa Sachsen estate)

The vineyards of the Liebfrauenkirche in Worms: Liebfrauenstift, Liebfrauenstift Kirchenstück, Liebfrauenstift Klostergarten, Liebfrauenstift Kreuzgang, and Liebfrauenstift Kapitelhaus. (These last three are owned entirely by the P. J. Valckenberg Co. in Worms, who also own the two other Worms vineyards, Katterloch and Luginsland.

THE WINES OF THE NAHE

The wines from the Nahe Valley are not so well known as those from the Rhine or Moselle, yet they rank in quality among the best of the German wines. The Nahe River flows into the Rhine at Bingen, and from there to its source back at Birkenfeld, and along its two small tributaries, the Alsenz and the Glan, are grown wines which are described as fruity, elegant, full-bodied, and fragrant. In great years the wines have a pleasant sweetness in many cases, and wonderful *Beerenauslesen* and *Trockenbeerenauslesen* are produced. The Nahe Valley is not one of the largest wine-producing areas in Germany—its production is about equal to that of the Rheingau—but fortunately for the wine drinker, quantity has nothing to do with quality in this case.

Some of the Nahe wines remind one of Moselle wines, others are more like the Rheingau wines, and still others resemble the wines of Rheinhessen. This is easy to understand when one realizes that the Nahe lies just between the Moselle and Rheinhessen areas, and that the Rheingau is just across from it on the other side of the Rhine. There is hardly any other German wine region where such a wide variety of wines can be found in such a small area, and one could make an interesting study of various types of German wines just by working one's way through the Nahe Valley. The great variety comes from the many different types of soil which are found in the Nahe vineyards from one community to the next. We know that the type of soil in which the grapes are grown is one of the main factors in determining the character of a wine, and so it is easy to understand that the wines will not all taste the same when they are grown in slaty soil in one place and in rich loam in another.

In Germany, the Nahe wines are often said to be wines for connoisseurs. This is not just because there are so many fine points in the wines which connoisseurs appreciate, but also because the average wine drinker has not been much aware of the Nahe wines. The result has been that many of the wine lovers and wine connoisseurs in Germany have been able to buy the Nahe wines somewhat more cheaply than wines of the same quality from the Rhine or Moselle. As these wines become better known, however, and their quality is discovered by more wine lovers in other countries as well as in Germany, they will almost certainly increase in price. At the present time they are among the best buys of all German wines, although not always easy to find in wineshops.

Among the top-ranking producers of Nahe wines we should mention the estates of Graf von Plettenberg, Paul Anheuser, Ludwig Herf, and August Anheuser, all in Bad Kreuznach, and the State Domains at Neiderhausen. The *Schloss Böckelheimer Kupfergrube* from the State Domains is probably the most famous Nahe wine, although a 1953 *Bretzenheimer Kronenberg Trockenbeerenauslese* from the estate of Graf von Plettenberg won a prize in 1956 as the best wine from the Rheinland-Nassau area.

THE WINE-PRODUING COMMUNITIES OF THE NAHE AND THEIR BEST VINEYARDS

Schloss Böckelheim: Kupfergrube, Königsfels, Felsenberg, and Mühlberg

Bad Kreuznach: Narrenkappe, Kahlenberg, Brückes, and Hinkelstein

Niederhausen: Hermannshöhe and Rosenhecke

Ebernburg: Erzgrube and Schlossberg

Bretzenheim: Steinweg and Kronenberg

Norheim: Hinterfels, Hafels, Kirschheck, and Götzenfels

Rüdesheim (don't confuse this with the Rüdesheim in the Rheingau): Rosengarten

Roxheim: Höllenpfad and Birkenberg

Langenlonsheim: Rotenberg and Löhr

Odernheim: Disibodenberg and Kappellenberg

Wallhausen: Johannisberg and Pastorenberg

Monzingen: Frühlingsplätzchen

THE WINES OF THE PALATINATE

We now come to the southernmost of the three Rhine wine areas—the Rhine Palatinate, or, as it is known in German, the *Rheinpfalz*. We shall use the German name in discussing this area, since it will be the word "*Rheinpfalz*" which one will find on bottle labels, and not the English equivalent.

The Rheinpfalz has the largest vineyard area in Germany, and enjoys a most favorable location as far as weather and climate are concerned. The vineyards are situated in an ideal position between the Rhine

River and the Haardt Mountains. These mountains —really more hills than mountains—shelter the vineyards from cold winds from the western part of Europe, just as the Taunus Mountains keep the north winds from the vineyards of the Rheingau. Another important advantage which the Rheinpfalz enjoys is that, since the vineyards here are farther south than the other Rhine vineyards, they get more hours of sunshine during the growing season. In the Rheinpfalz the spring comes sooner and the warm autumn days last longer than in any other German wine-producing area.

We could probably best describe the Rheinpfalz wines as being full, ripe, luscious, and having a fine bouquet and body. They are also distinguished by a certain spiciness and can often resemble the wines of the Rheingau very closely. Even in such great years as 1953 or 1959, they will still keep traces of this distinctive spiciness.

Just as we think of the Moselle area as being divided into three parts, so too do we consider the Rheinpfalz as being divided into three general vineyard areas. And just as on the Moselle, it is also the middle section here which produces the best wines. Taking their names from the Haardt Mountains which shelter them on their western side, the three areas are known simply as the Upper Haardt, Middle Haardt, and Lower Haardt. The area farthest south, the Upper Haardt, runs from the French frontier up to the town of Hambach. From Neustadt to Herxheim am Berg, we have the Middle Haardt, and from there on up to Zell, the Lower Haardt. The wines from the Upper and Lower Haardt regions are seldom exported, and are usually consumed locally as table wines. We shall concern ourselves here only with the wines from the Middle Haardt section.

Three towns in the Middle Haardt should be kept in mind as being the source of most of the finest

Rheinpfalz wines: *Deidesheim*, *Forst*, and *Ruppertsberg*. As far as the production of top-quality wines is concerned, three outstanding producers deserve to be mentioned here. They are known in the German wine trade as the "three B's" because their names all begin with that letter. In Deidesheim are the estates of Geheimer Rat Dr. von Bassermann-Jordan and Reichsrat von Buhl. In Wachenheim is the estate of Dr. Bürklin-Wolf. These three estates have a well-earned reputation for producing wines of finest quality, and the inexperienced wine drinker need not hesitate in buying a bottle bearing one of these famous names. In connection with this, it might be of interest to mention here that at a special auction of top-quality German wines held in Wiesbaden, in May of 1955, a 1952 *Deidesheimer Hohenmorgen Riesling Trockenbeerenauslese* from the Bassermann-Jordan estate attained the highest price among all offered wines of the past thirty years—62 marks or $15.50 a bottle. This wine was generally acknowledged to be the greatest 1952 wine from the Rheinpfalz area. It is only when one has drunk such a wine, or perhaps the other great gem from the Bassermann-Jordan collection, a *Forster Jesuitengarten Trockenbeerenauslese*, that one fully realizes just what heights these magnificent German wines can attain. Even such an eminent wine authority as the Marquis de Lur Saluces, owner of the world famous Château d'Yquem in Sauternes, was frank to admit the superiority of these wines over his own Great Growths, and also relieved to know that the production of such fabulous *Trockenbeerenauslesen* was so small that it would not afford any serious competition to the French Sauternes.

Only the finest vineyards in the Rheinpfalz, as in the other wine-growing districts, are planted with the Riesling grape. A few good vineyards are planted with the Traminer or Gewürztraminer, but they are rare.

Altogether, not more than 15 per cent of the entire Rheinpfalz area is planted with the Riesling, and if the wine is made from this variety of grape the label will always say so. If no grape variety is mentioned on the label at all, the wine was probably made from Sylvaner grapes, a variety which has a higher yield than the Riesling but never attains such great class.

Keep in mind that the poorer vintages, the so-called off years, are usually somewhat better in the Rheinpfalz than in the other German wine districts. Even such a generally poor year as 1954, for example, yielded several good wines there, and in 1955, one of the estates even made an excellent *Beerenauslese*.

THE WINE-PRODUCING COMMUNITIES IN THE RHEINPFALZ AND THEIR BEST VINEYARDS

Deidesheim: Hohenmorgen, Grainhübel, Kieselberg, Kränzler, Kalkofen, Leinhöhle, Geheu, Langenmorgen, and Hofstück

Forst: Jesuitengarten (owned entirely by the Bassermann-Jordan estate in Deidesheim), Kirchenstück, Ungeheuer, Ziegler, Kranich, and Langenmorgen

Ruppertsberg: Reiterpfad, Hoheburg, Spiess, Kreuz, Hofstück, Mandelacker, and Gaisböhl

Wachenheim: Goldbächel, Gerümpel, Böhlig, and Wolfsdarm

Dürkheim: Michelsberg, Spielberg, and Frohnhof

Ungstein: Spielberg, Michelsberg, and Herrenberg

Kallstadt: Kobnert, Annaberg, and Saumagen

Königsbach: Idig

Gimmeldingen: Meerspinne

THE WINES OF FRANCONIA

When we think of Franconian wines, we usually think of Würzburg and its excellent vineyards—particularly the *Stein*—and never stop to realize that the wine-growing area takes in a great deal more territory than just Würzburg alone. The vineyard region of Franconia (*Franken* in German) begins all the way down at Hörstein, just above Aschaffenburg, and continues along the Main River almost as far as Schweinfurt. The principal wine area, however, is the so-called "Main Triangle," with Gemünden, Ochsenfurt, and Schweinfurt as the three corners.

The Franconian wines are the strongest of all the German white wines, and most of them are described as being "hard." They are quite often compared to French Chablis, though such a comparison should not be taken to mean that the two types of wine are in any way alike. They are never so sweet as some of the Rhine wines can be, and those who prefer dry wines which are firm and strong, yet with an excellent bouquet, could not do better than to sample the Franconian wines. The Sylvaner grape is highly cultivated here, although in the finest vineyards the Riesling is grown.

One should always order a Franconian wine by name, just as one would do in ordering any other wine. Never order just a *Bocksbeutel,* since this is merely the

German name for the flagon-shaped bottles in which the Franconian wines are sold, and has nothing to do with the quality of the wine inside. Likewise, the term "Stein wine" is not in itself a guarantee for the best quality Franconian wines. The Stein may well be the best of all the Franconian vineyards, but unless the wine is an *Originalabfüllung* from a leading producer with holdings in this vineyard, such as the State Domains for example, the wine will seldom be from the real Stein vineyard. The practice of using the term Stein wine as a general name for any Franconian wine is forbidden in Germany, but there are still some of these wines sold on the American market when the importers have been able to get away with this designation. In any case, you would certainly not want to limit yourself to just this one wine when there are so many other excellent wines grown throughout the entire Franconian region. The three best wine-producing estates in Franconia, all located in Würzburg, are the State Domains, the Bürgerspital, and the Juliusspital. Any one of these three names on a Bocksbeutel of Franconian wine is an automatic guarantee of authenticity, and one can be sure of getting a first-class bottle of wine for the money.

THE WINE-PRODUCING COMMUNITIES OF FRANCONIA AND THEIR BEST VINEYARDS

Würzburg: Stein, Innere Leiste, Harfe, and Schalksberg

Randersacker: Pfülben, Lämmerberg, Teufelskeller, Spielberg, Neuberg, and Hohbug

Escherndorf: Kirchberg, Lump, Fürstenberg, and Hengstberg

Iphofen: Kronsberg and Julius-Echter-Berg

Castell: Schlossberg

Hörstein: Reuschberg, Abtsberg, and Langenberg
Sommerach: Engelsberg, Katzenkopf, and Rothenbühl

THE WINES OF THE MIDDLE RHINE

From where the Rhine turns north after leaving Rüdesheim and Assmannshausen in the Rheingau until it reaches Koblenz, we pass through what is unquestionably the most beautiful section along the entire course of the river. If one makes the trip by steamer, one sees castles and vineyards on both sides, and the many small towns along the way seem to be ideal spots for a Sunday afternoon excursion or a short break in the summer trip through Germany. The wines of the Middle Rhine, however, do not have much to offer the wine-drinking tourist, and many of them are used to make German *Sekt* because of their light, thin and "steely" character. Probably the best wines from the Middle Rhine come from the vineyards around the town of Bacharach, and the two adjoining communities of Steeg and Oberdiebach. In the Middle Ages, the town of Bacharach was a very important wine center, since many wines from the Rheingau, Rheinhessen, and the Rheinpfalz used to be shipped out from Bacharach to England, Holland, and Scandinavia. Nobody paid any attention to the place where the wine was grown in those days, and since it was shipped from

Bacharach it was all called *Bacharacher*, thus giving the town a reputation for having much better wine than it really produced. The wines from the Middle Rhine are rarely exported today and one will seldom see them in the United States.

GERMAN RED WINES

Most of the best German red wines are made from the same variety of grape which is used in France for Burgundy wines, the Pinot Noir, or, as it is known in Germany, the *Spätburgunder*. The different soil and climate of the German wine regions, however, causes the grapes to produce a wine altogether different from that which is grown in France.

Two of the best German red wine districts are those of Assmannshausen, just above Rüdesheim, and the Ahr Valley, above Koblenz. Red wine is also produced in the Rheinpfalz area, and the best one is the *Dürkheimer Feuerberg*. In just about every German wine region some red wine is made, but none of it can compare to the great red wines of France. The finest German red wines, such as the *Walporzheimer* from the Ahr or the *Assmannshäuser Höllenberg*, can easily be recognized as Burgundy-type wines, but the vineyards are just too far north for the grapes to soak up the sun as they do in France, and the wine never develops into the full-bodied wine we know as Burgundy.

The German wine laws permit the addition of up to 25 per cent of foreign red wine to all German red wines. This is done to give the German wines the necessary dark red color, since otherwise they would look too pale and weak to interest the prospective consumer. The great majority of German red wines are consumed locally and few are exported. When given a choice, the wine drinker would do best to select a good French Bordeaux or Burgundy wine rather than pay a high price for a German red wine which never will be really first-class as red wines go. When such wines are sold at over $3 a bottle in this country, they certainly cannot be considered good value for the money.

GERMAN SPARKLING WINES (SEKT)

In the United States we can call any wine that bubbles champagne, and we don't often realize that the real thing comes only from the delimited area in France which used to be known as the province of Champagne. The wines made in New York State, California, or Germany are similar, but they are not Champagne. International agreements exist in Europe which prevent the abuse of various wine and vineyard names, and it is for this reason that German sparkling wines are known as *Sekt*—an invented name first used in

Berlin around the turn of the century—and may not be called German Champagne.

Most German *Sekt* is not as good as Champagne because the wine that is used to make it is generally of a poorer quality than that which is used in France for Champagne. There is no area in Germany where grapes are grown just for the production of *Sekt*, as is the case in France for Champagne. In poor vintage years most of the great German estates sell their entire production of wine to the *Sekt* firms, since the wines are not of high enough quality to bottle and sell as *Originalabfüllungen*, that is to say, they require the addition of sugar to bring them up to the proper degree of alcohol. In great vintage years, such as 1953 or 1959, none of these wines is sold for *Sekt* production and the *Sekt* producers are thus forced to buy up the poorer, thinner wines from the second-rate vineyards. The wines used for *Sekt* have usually been sugared, therefore, to a considerable extent, and the resulting sparkling wine is never so light nor so delicate as true Champagne. Some of the German producers have resorted to importing French wines from the Champagne area to use in their best grades of *Sekt*, and to be perfectly fair we must say that some of the best German *Sekt can* hold its own with the lesser brands of Champagne. In the United States, however, the import duty on *Sekt* makes it almost as expensive as Champagne, since all sparkling wines are taxed at the same rate of about $1 a bottle, regardless of the country of origin. If one wants an inexpensive sparkling wine, our own California or New York State champagne-type wines will do perfectly well at around $4 a bottle. In all other cases the great Champagnes of France still remain the unchallenged leaders as far as quality is concerned.

THE SERVICE OF GERMAN WINES

One of the reasons that German wines are not more popular in this country (aside from their often hard-to-pronounce names) is the fact that there are so few foods that really go with them. All the best German wines are more suited to drinking by themselves than they are as accompaniments to food. This applies particularly to the great *Auslese*, *Beerenauslese*, and *Trockenbeerenauslese* wines, and to many of the *Spätlesen* as well. Only the dry German wines really go well with food—the Rhine wines with chicken or veal dishes, and the Moselle wines with fish, particularly with filet of sole. Because the German wines are light and delicate they are easily overpowered by highly seasoned dishes or rich sauces. Most Americans just would not feel comfortable about serving their guests a bottle or two of Rhine wine instead of the usual drinks during the course of an evening's visit, and it would require a lot more wine to produce the same effects that can be obtained from two or three drinks of hard liquor. Those seeking the effects of the alcohol more than anything else will certainly never switch to wine, especially German wines where the alcoholic content is often the lowest of any of the world's great wines. Some Moselle wines, for example, have only 9 per cent alcohol, with an average of around 10 per cent. For a group of wine-loving friends, however, nothing could be more delightful than to serve them a fine bottle of an *Auslese* wine from the Rhine or Moselle and omit the stronger drinks altogether.

German wines should be served well chilled, but never ice-cold. If these delicate wines are overchilled they lose all their wonderful bouquet and flavor, and of course if they are served too warm they will be insipid—especially the sweeter wines, which can always stand a little more cooling than the drier ones. If the bottles are placed in the bottom part of the refrigerator for two or three hours they will usually be properly chilled by the time they are to be served. Never put them in the freezer. Those who have the opportunity to dine out of doors in the summer will find that a bucket of ice water—or a regular wine cooler, if you have one—will serve to keep the wines chilled throughout the meal. Certainly nothing is more annoying to the wine lover than to find his well-chilled bottle of white wine getting warmer and warmer as the meal progresses and no bucket at hand in which to keep it chilled!

Remember that the great *Beerenauslese* and *Trockenbeerenauslese* wines, like the great Sauternes of France, are dessert wines only. They are at their best when served with fresh nectarines or peaches, or simply drunk alone as one would drink a liqueur.

It is extraordinarily difficult to find the really fine German wines in restaurants in the United States. Most of the top restaurants in the large cities are French and one does not often encounter much besides French wines on their lists.

There is always a Liebfraumilch or Moselblümchen available in first-class restaurants, but the German part of the wine list usually begins and ends right there. Those who have the good fortune to travel in Germany should not pass up the opportunity to drink some of the great German wines while they are there. Prices are much less than here in the United States, and the selections in some of the most famous restaurants run into the hundreds. It is not the purpose of this book to serve as a restaurant guide to Europe, but since most travelers know nothing at all about eating in Germany, even though they may have memorized every two- and three-star restaurant in the *Guide Michelin* for their tour of France, we feel that a listing of a half-dozen of the most famous German restaurants would not be out of place here. All of these establishments have wine lists covering the entire range of German wines from the very cheapest at 50 cents a bottle, up to the fabulous *Trockenbeerenauslesen* for $25 a bottle or more. Here are a few places to keep in mind on your next trip to Germany:

In Bremen: The *Ratskeller*—one of the greatest and most famous wine restaurants in all of Germany.

In Frankfurt: The *Kaiserkeller*—an excellent restaurant with a huge wine list. Rather expensive.

In Assmannshausen: *Hotel zur Krone*—an outstanding restaurant with an open-air terrace for warm-weather dining. Excellent food and a wonderful wine list.

In Kronberg (Taunus): *Schloss Hotel*—A beautiful parklike setting for what used to be the castle of Kaiser Wilhelm's mother. First-class food and wines. Favored by the diplomatic set from Bonn.

In Munich: *Hotel Vier Jahreszeiten*—famous for fine food with an excellent French chef in charge of the kitchen. Small, but outstanding wine list. Expensive.

Schwarzwälder Restaurant—One of Germany's finest wine restaurants located here in the beer capital of the world. Excellent food and a huge wine list.

There are many excellent restaurants located in the various wine regions themselves, and, unlike France, where the best wines are never available in their native villages, one can find all the finest growths in these local inns and wine houses. Whether it is the *Ratskeller* in Bernkastel, the *Rhein Hotel* in Nierstein, or some of the delightful Rheingau establishments, such as the *Weinpump* in Eltville, the *Schwan Hotel* in Oestrich, or the *Pfortenhaus Restaurant* out at Kloster Eberbach, one can be sure of finding many delightful and outstanding bottles.

Here at home we should not fail to mention the famous German restaurant in New York City, *Lüchow's*, located at 110 East Fourteenth Street. This is the next best thing to a trip to Germany, and those who have the opportunity to eat here should certainly do so. This restaurant probably has one of the finest cellars of German wines in the United States.

We can only urge once again that in your selection of German wines you skip Liebfraumilch, Moselblümchen, Bernkasteler Riesling, Niersteiner Domthal, and one or two others of like character, and that you look for the estate-bottled (*Originalabfüllung*) wines instead. They are certainly worth the extra amount that they cost and are actually better buys than the cheaper wines of no particular merit.

III

The Wines of Italy

INTRODUCTION

EVERYONE WHO HAS TRAVELED in Italy has come home with glowing reports of the wines that he has found there. Even among those who have never been to Italy, there are many enthusiastic Chianti lovers who find a great deal of charm in those straw-covered bottles, known in Italian as *fiaschi*. Whether this is because of the attractive flasklike bottles themselves, or because the wine in them is so good, we cannot say. In most cases, however, it would seem to be the former, since the same, or better, wine when bottled in regular-shaped bottles never sells as well as the wine in the *fiaschi*. No matter where you may have drunk Italian wine, or however much you may enjoy it, it is important to remember that Italian wines are never great wines, that is to say, they never achieve the greatness of a fine Bordeaux or Burgundy from France, or a fine Rhine or Moselle from Germany. They are nevertheless perfectly delightful on many occasions and we should simply accept them for what they are and not demand too much from them. A good Chianti, Bardolino, or Valpolicella seems to be just the perfect wine to go with Italian food, for who would want Burgundy or Bordeaux with spaghetti?

We often hear reports of Italian wines which were perfectly delightful in their native province but unfortunately don't travel well. This has become a catch-all expression in recent years, and is often used by wine snobs to give the impression that there are many wonderful wines in Europe which for some mysterious reason cannot stand the strain of shipment to this country, and of course these wines are always supposed to be better than the ones that are available here. In actual fact, a wine that won't "travel" well is simply a wine that is deficient in alcohol and will not keep very long, whether in the United States, Italy, or anywhere else. Such wines are made all over Italy by every farmer who has a patch of grapevines on his little plot of land. These wines are not much more intoxicating than beer and can often be very pleasant to drink on a warm day. They are usually mixed with mineral water and this makes them so much the more refreshing. These are obviously not fine wines, and how ever much they may capture your fancy on a summer vacation trip in Italy, there is no point in expecting importers to bring them into this country when there are so many other Italian wines, well made and with sufficient alcoholic content to keep them from going bad during their life in the bottle. There are some wines that don't travel simply because they are produced in such small quantities that there would be no point in an importer trying to establish a market for them in the United

States. It may also be that the wines are simply not good enough to bring onto the American market, and the explanation that they don't travel is nothing more than an alibi on the part of the grower. All reports about such "wonderful" wines can usually be written off, therefore, as uninformed opinion on the part of the person making the statement and should not be taken as an incentive to search out the particular wines in question on your next trip to Europe.

There are a number of reasons that keep the Italian wines from attaining the classic heights of the great French and German wines. One of these is the fairly lax system of control by the Italian government, in spite of the very modern wine laws that were put into effect back around 1930. It is easy to have model laws, of course, but if they are not strictly enforced they are not of much use to anyone. There is probably no other major wine-producing country where so much manipulation of wines and wine names is practiced as in Italy. The most notorious example in this respect is that of Chianti, far more of which is sold than could ever possibly be produced in the Tuscan vineyards of the Chianti region. This means that the buyer must exercise a certain amount of care—not to say common sense—in buying Italian wines, if he is to get true value for his money.

The main reason that keeps the Italian wines from becoming "great" wines, however, is to be found in the attitude of the people toward their wines and toward wine drinking in general. In Italy, wine is regarded simply as an everyday household beverage, and, though this is true in France as well, there is no stress laid on the prestige of great estate-bottled wines, great vintages, or even the wines of any particular region. Whereas a Frenchman will have a very great château-bottled Bordeaux or estate-bottled Burgundy for that "special occasion," the Italian will simply drink an older bottle of the same wine he always drinks, and this will be considered "special" enough for the wedding feast, communion dinner, or whatever it may be that requires a good bottle that is a little above the average. The emphasis on great cooking is also missing in Italy, and without great cooking there is naturally no reason to have great wines. The Italian takes his wines when and where he finds them and has a very much more relaxed attitude toward the subject than his neighbors across the Alps in France, or even in Switzerland for that matter. There are no public outcries against wine fraud in Italy, such as we read about from time to time in France or Germany. If people find that a certain grower is watering his wine, they simply stop buying from him and go to another grower up the road who may be somewhat more honest. It is very doubtful, however, if the offender would be hauled into court and fined, or forced to stop making wine for a period of several years as punishment. In Italy, it seems that just about everybody makes wine of some kind, if not for sale, then at least for his own family consumption. Some of these wines can be quite good, and some are barely drinkable. Everything depends on the skill of the grower, the kind of soil he has in his vineyard, and the variety of grapes he uses for his wine.

Italy has given less attention to the cultivation of the finest grape varieties than other countries have, and as a result the growers usually tend to concentrate on high-yielding grapes rather than on the varieties of the very highest quality, such as the Germans do with their Riesling on the Rhine and Moselle, or the French with their Pinot Noir in Burgundy. Even the best grapes, however, do not grow equally well in every type of soil or in every climate, and the planting of the so-called "noble" grape varieties would not in itself solve the problem of raising the quality of Italian wines. Most of us, though, are pretty much satisfied with Italian wines the way they are, and we certainly wouldn't want all the growers there to start imitating French and German wines and trying to equal them in any way. Our whole attitude toward Italian wines should be more lighthearted and carefree than it is with the wines of other countries. We should not take the Italian wines too seriously, that is, and no one should feel aghast if his companion at dinner decides that the wine would be improved by the addition of a little *Pelligrino* mineral water. If we don't expect too much from Italian wines we shall certainly not be disappointed, and there can be many pleasant surprises in store for those who have never ventured much beyond the 97-cent Chianti in their local wineshop. It is unfortunate that the best Italian wines cost between $2 and $3 in this country, when they are so inexpensive in Italy, but transportation, duty, and taxes must all be added to the American prices, and if the wines were really good to begin with they were obviously not purchased in Italy for 25 cents a bottle, tourist tales notwithstanding!

CHIANTI

The most famous Italian wine is undoubtedly *Chianti,* of which it can be said, like Beaujolais in France, that far more is sold than is ever made in the region of that name. The actual wine-growing area for the so-called *Chianti classico,* or classic Chianti, is located between the cities of Florence and Siena, in the province of Tuscany, and comprises about one hundred fifty thousand acres. It is certainly the largest of the Italian vineyard regions devoted to one wine, and because of its large annual production Chianti is known in almost every country of the world where wines are drunk. *Chianti classico* is easy to identify since every bottle carries a seal showing a black rooster on a gold background with the statement of authenticity printed on a red border around this. Once you begin to look for this seal you will be surprised at how few of the Chianti wines have it. There are imitations of the seal, of course, and it should not be confused with the Italian government's seal of origin, which is merely a red seal with black printing, but no rooster. This seal has the word "*Italia*" printed in large letters and the words *Marchio Nazionale* ("National Trademark" in English). It guarantees that the wine really comes from Italy, and supposedly from the region that the label on the bottle claims for it. Any Italian wine can have this trademark label and it has nothing to do with Chianti in particular.

All the finest Chianti wines are bottled in regular Bordeaux-type wine bottles so that they can be properly stored away just like any other wine. The lesser brands, and all the inferior wines without exception, are bottled in the *fiaschi*. This is not to say that the Chianti wines in *fiaschi* are never any good, for some of the top producers bottle their wines in these bottles as well as in the regular bottles, and both carry the rooster seal of authenticity. Usually, however, the wines in the regular bottles are those of the very finest vintages that will repay laying away and aging for a few years. The three top estate-bottled Chiantis that are generally available in this country all cost around $3.25 a bottle, about the highest price of any Italian wines sold here. The most famous of the three is the wonderful wine from the vineyards of Baron Ricasoli: *Brolio*. The label carries the seldom-seen statement (for Italian wines) of estate-bottling. In this case it reads "*Imbottigliato al Castello di Brolio in Chianti*," or in English, "Bottled at Brolio Castle in Chianti." Other producers may simply use the phrase, "*Imbottigliato alla tenuta*" (estate-bottled), which of course amounts to the same thing. Baron Ricasoli also markets another Chianti, not very often seen in this country, called *Meleto*. The Ruffino people call their estate-bottled wine *Riserva Ducale*, or "Ducal Reserve" in English. The wine from the Antinori family is sold as *Villa Antinori*, named for the ancestral family estate. It would be impossible to say which of these three great Chiantis—Brolio, Ruffino, or Antinori—is the best, but one should bear in mind that each of these estates produces other Chiantis in the straw-covered *fiaschi*, as well as the superior wines just described. In former years the wines from Chianti were noted for their hardness, but this has now given way to the production of a softer, better-balanced wine because of changes made in the types of grapes used and different methods of making the wine. Chianti, by the way, is not made from a single classic grape variety, but rather from a blend of three or four different kinds of grapes. Many of the wines now on the market are also a little "prickly" on the tongue due to a slight secondary fermentation induced in the wine. This *frizzante* quality, as it is known in Italian, serves to give the wines a certain freshness in their taste that they would not otherwise have. It is most obvious in very young wines and disappears after the wines have attained a certain amount of bottle age.

Since the classic Chianti is not produced in sufficient quantity to satisfy world-wide demand, it was soon decided that other vineyards outside the main Chianti region yielded wines enough like the classic Chianti to be allowed to use the name Chianti too. Since they were not, however, from the *Chianti classico* region, they were not allowed to use the rooster seal, but were instead given one showing a little white cherub on a blue background. These wines are also in a sense authentic Chiantis, but will be a little lower in price than the *Chianti classico*. If the bottle of Chianti that you are about to purchase has neither the rooster seal nor the cherub seal, you may be fairly sure that it is not authentic Chianti. Most of the 97-cent *fiaschi* are simply coarse, hard red wines not worth bothering about at all.

There is some white Chianti produced by several of the leading growers, but the wines are not outstanding and we feel that they are too high in price for what they are—ordinary wines of no particular distinction.

THE NORTHERN PROVINCES

Before proceeding any farther south into the Italian vineyard country, we shall explore the northern districts where all the finest Italian wines are produced, with the exception of Chianti of course. Crossing into Italy from Austria, we come first to the much-disputed province of Alto Adige, better known to English-speaking people as the Italian Tirol. Even though we hear much German being spoken in this area, we cannot help feeling that we are really in Italy once we have crossed the Alps, and we can have little sympathy for those who feel that this region should be given back to Austria once again. Political considerations aside, however, there are some very pleasant wines produced in this lovely region, the best of which are white and often like some of the German or Alsatian wines. The most outstanding example is the *Terlano*, made not far from Bolzano, the capital city of Alto Adige. The Terlano is not merely an Italian version of Rhine wine, and in fact is made mostly from the Pinot Blanc grape of Burgundy rather than from any of the German varieties. A soft, dry wine with an attractive bouquet, the Terlano runs to around 12 or 13 per cent alcohol like many of the white Burgundy wines. In the same area there is also a pleasant red wine produced called *Santa Maddalena*. The other red wine of the area, *Lago di Caldaro*, is also of good quality, somewhat lighter in color than the Santa Maddalena, but none the less delightful. It is also known in German as *Kalterer*, and is seen on all wine lists in Germany as *Kalterer See Auslese*. The term "*Auslese*" has no meaning here, and steps have recently been taken to stop the use of this word on the wines sent to Germany, since it obviously gives an impression of superior quality that the wine does not deserve. The methods used for making an *Auslese* wine in Germany are certainly not employed by the Italians for their Kalterer wines and the term has no meaning when used in this way. The famous German and Alsatian Gewürztraminer grape is grown here too, and the wine it yields is very much like the same wine made in Alsace. It has the strong, spicy bouquet that is its chief characteristic and is rather full-bodied.

Finally, the Alto Adige region can also boast a very pleasant rosé wine called *Lagarino Rosato*. Many other rosé wines are made in the province too, but this one is the best of all. When young, it is fresh, has a delightful bouquet, and can often be distinguished by its *frizzante* quality, which makes it so much the more refreshing to drink on a warm summer day. The wines from this section of Italy are not easy to find in the United States, and most American wine drinkers will not have a chance to try them until they are able to drink them on their native ground.

When we come to the other northern province of Italy, Piedmont, the situation becomes quite different, and almost all the fine wines of this region are readily available in the United States. The province of Piedmont borders France and Switzerland, and lies to the west of the province of Alto Adige. The industrial city of Turin is its capital, and it is here that all the famous Vermouth firms have their plants. The oldest of these (and the first to begin the manufacture of Vermouth) is Carpano. Connoisseurs of Vermouth, if one may use this word in connection with a "manufactured" drink, consider the Carpano Vermouth to be in a class by itself as far as sweet Vermouths are concerned. The two other popular brands, Martini & Rossi and Cinzano, are better known in the United States, however, probably because they lack the slight "bitter" quality that distinguishes the Carpano Vermouth. This company also produces a variation of their regular Vermouth called *Punt e Mes*. The name means "point and a half" in English and dates back to 1786, when the Carpano "bar" was located near the Turin Stock Exchange. The term was used by the stockbrokers, and, when the Carpano people decided to make a Vermouth with a little more of the bitter quality to it than was usual at the time, they took this expression of the brokers as the name for their new product. Most Americans do not like to drink Punt e Mes straight and they usually mix it with either a regular sweet Vermouth or with a dry Vermouth of the French type. All Vermouth is basically a wine that has been infused with various spices and herbs and slightly fortified so that the alcoholic content is raised to about 18 per cent —just a little less than the 20 per cent of Sherry and Port. The wide variation in degree of sweetness and in quality among the different brands of Vermouth results mainly from the amount and types of the various herbs and spices that are added to the wine base by the different makers. Each firm keeps its blend a secret, of course, and in the case of dry Vermouth each one tries to make a "drier" one than the other, at least for the American market, with its obsession for "dry" martinis—actually nothing more than straight gin. Since the French preference is supposed to be for dry Vermouth and the Italian for sweet, many people call all sweet Vermouth "Italian" and all dry Vermouth "French." Actually, the major Vermouth concerns, whether in France or Italy, make both dry and sweet Vermouths, and one can just as easily buy a sweet Noilly Prat Vermouth from France as a dry Martini & Rossi Vermouth from Italy. Regardless of the brand chosen, a Vermouth "on the rocks"—served over ice, that is, with a twist of lemon peel—makes an ideal *apéritif* before a meal at which fine wines are to be served. It does not dull the taste buds as stronger drinks do and so leaves one fully able to enjoy the wines that follow—something that would not be possible after a few cocktails of the usual type. Many people prefer a mixture of half-sweet and half-dry Vermouth when they use it as an *apéritif*, since one type alone would be either too dry or too sweet to drink by itself.

In addition to its Vermouth production, the province of Piedmont also produces what is generally regarded as the greatest red wine of Italy, equaled only by the estate-bottled Chiantis of Tuscany. This is the famous *Barolo*, a rich, full-bodied wine that reminds one a little of the Rhône wines of France. Barolo is unfortunately made in rather limited quantities and is not too easy to find in the United States. The very finest of the Barolo wines are made from the vineyards around the village of that name, but the vineyards of several other villages in the immediate area produce wines that can also be sold as Barolo. Though fairly high in alcohol, often as much as 15 per cent, the Barolo wines are wonderfully soft and smooth. They require at least five years of aging before they are ready to drink, and the best growers do not market them until five or six years after the vintage in order to be sure that they will not be consumed too young. They can age much longer, of course, and the best ones should certainly be drunk when they are ten years old or more, rather than at the minimum age of five. (Do not confuse the name *Barolo* with the name of Baron Ricasoli's Chianti, *Brolio!* Both are excellent wines in their own right and do not deserve to be mistaken for one another.) The Barolo wine is made from the Nebbiolo grape, as are two other outstanding red wines from this province. Northeast of Turin, near the beautiful Laggo Maggiore, the excellent *Gattinara* is made. Not so dark in color as the Barolo, it is nevertheless a full-bodied wine and one that is also slow to mature like the Barolo. We have never seen it in the United States, though it is well worth watching for when shopping for Italian wines. An importer may sometimes get just a few barrels, of which your store may be lucky enough to receive two or three cases. Much easier to find is the *Barbaresco*, a wine grown in the region south of Turin, not far from where Barolo is made. Though not as velvety smooth as Barolo, it matures faster than the latter wine, and is also a little lower in alcohol, usually around 12 to 13 per cent. It is nevertheless an outstanding wine and well worth trying. Besides the three outstanding wines made from the Nebbiolo grape—the Barolo, Gattinara, and Barbaresco—there is also much ordinary table wine made from this grape throughout the entire Piedmont area. It is sold simply as *Nebbiolo* and is also found as a sparkling wine—a sort of slightly sweet Italian version of "sparkling Burgundy" called *Nebbiolo Spumante.* (The word *spumante* is Italian for "sparkling," and all their Champagne-type wines are so labeled.) Ordinary Nebbiolo is a pleasant enough everyday table wine, but should not cost much over $1.50 in this country if it is to be a good value for the money. The *spumante* version is best forgotten.

The most popular wine of Piedmont is surely the *Barbera,* thousands of gallons of which are produced every year. It is a pleasant wine, dark in color, high in alcohol, but somewhat coarse. (It should not be confused with the much better *Barbaresco* that we mentioned before.) The Barbera grape, from which the wine takes its name, is one of those high-yielding varieties that will grow just about anywhere, and is therefore dear to the hearts of the smaller growers. The wine is perhaps better than a run-of-the-mill Nebbiolo, but should not be any higher in price. Better than either of these two wines, however, is the *Freisa,* a charming wine made from the grape of that name. It has much fruit, is not heavy in body, and has a delightful bouquet. There is a semisweet, *frizzante* version of this wine too, but most people will prefer it as a dry wine.

Around the town of Asti, southwest of Turin, the vineyards are mainly planted with the *Moscato* grape, better known to us in English as Muscatel. This is the source of the famous Italian sparkling wine, *Asti Spumante.* It is usually semisweet, though many firms market a dry version called *Gran Spumante* or *Riserva.* Sometimes the French term *brut* will also be seen on the labels of the very driest types. The quality of Asti Spumante can in no way approach that of French Champagne, even though many of the better varieties are often made with some admixture of wines pressed from Pinot Noir grapes, the variety used in Champagne. Because of the heavy duty on sparkling wines imported into this country, Asti Spumante can never be a really good buy. The price in the stores is often around $5 a bottle, which is not too far below the price of extra-dry or nonvintage *brut* Champagne. For those who like their sparkling wines sweet, however, some brands of Asti Spumante can be found for around $4. Because of their sweetness, these wines should be used only as dessert wines, and not served with the meal itself (unless you have a very sweet tooth). Among the best shippers of Asti Spumante are the firms of Martini & Rossi, Gancia, Cora, and Cinzano. There are many others, particularly among the very inexpensive brands, but those we have listed have the widest national distribution in this country.

We should mention briefly the other northern province of Italy, Lombardy, since some of its wines are seen in American shops from time to time. These are the wines from the Valtellina, a valley running eastward from the northern end of Lake Como. The red wines are sold as *Grumello*, *Inferno*, and *Sassella*, and all are made from the Nebbiolo grape. The white wine is simply called *Valtellina*, and is light in color and body and quite fresh tasting, though certainly not a great wine.

WINES FROM VENETIA

The province of Venezia, or Venetia, in English, produces a number of popular wines around the city of

Verona and Lake Garda. The best Italian white wine, *Soave,* is made a short distance east of Verona, and exported to this country by the two big shipping firms of Bertani and Bolla, both located in Verona. Soave is a very light wine and always quite dry. It should be drunk a year or two after the vintage, and old bottles that have been lying around in stores for three or four years should definitely be avoided. Though the wine is named for the village of Soave, around which the vineyards are located, the word also translates into English as "suave" or "mild," and correctly describes these wines. It would be difficult to say whether Bertani or Bolla makes the better Soave, but both cost the same ($2.45), and you can very easily try one against the other to decide which you like the best. When comparing wines like this, however, always be sure to have them of the same vintage, since otherwise one wine may be superior to the other simply because it was made in a better year and not because it came from a better estate.

The two famous red wines from Verona are *Bardolino* and *Valpolicella.* Bardolino is the lighter of the two, and is made from grapes grown along the shores of Lake Garda. Like the Soave, it should also be drunk young to enjoy it at its best. In the case of Bardolino, this would be around two years after the vintage, since red wines require a little more aging than whites. Valpolicella is somewhat heavier than the Bardolino, darker in color, rather mellow in character, and worth aging longer than either the Soave or Bardolino. Both of these red wines run about the same in price as the Soave and are widely distributed. There is also a very pleasant rosé from Lake Garda, known as *Chiaretto.* It is probably the finest of all the Italian rosés.

CENTRAL ITALY

South of Verona we come into the province of Emilia, where an interesting red wine called *Lambrusco* is produced. Slightly sparkling, the Lambrusco can be very pleasant as a table wine since it is dry and not sweet like most wines of this type. The vineyards are located near the city of Modena. (There is also a sweet version of Lambrusco, but this is once again in the sparkling Burgundy class and most people will not want to have it with their meals.) Another red wine, the *Sangiovese*, also spelled as two words, *San Giovese*, can be found in Bologna, but is not exported. It is a full-bodied wine, quite dry and hearty.

Passing through Tuscany, whose Chianti we have already discussed, we come next to the region known as the Marches. We shall take note of only one wine here, the *Verdicchio di Jesi*, which is produced near Ancona. Light in color and very dry, the Verdicchio also has a slight spicy quality about it that many people like. The wine often runs to 13 per cent alcohol, fairly high for a white wine. The best shipper of Verdicchio is the firm of Fazi Battaglia in Ancona.

West of the Marches and directly south of Tuscany is the province of Umbria. The only wine of interest here is the *Orvieto*, a white wine which is sold in both dry and sweet varieties. Bottled in a squat flasklike bottle of a different shape than those used for Chianti, called a *pulcianella* in Italian, Orvieto is popular among those who do not like their white wines too dry. The wines are pleasant enough in their way and have a nice bouquet and attractive color. They usually sell for around $1.50 a bottle and should not cost much more than this regardless of who ships them. The dry wines are usually marked *secco* on the label, and the sweet ones are marked *abboccato*. Sometimes the designation is in English, but not always.

In the area around Rome, two white wines are made, neither of which is of outstanding quality but must be mentioned nevertheless. The first of these is *Frascati*, coming from the vineyards to the south of Rome. It is the *vin ordinaire* of the Roman restaurants and one should not expect too much from it. Some Frascati is dry and some is slightly sweet, so that if you are ordering the wine in a Roman restaurant be sure to specify *secco* if you want the dry wine. Frascati has an attractive straw-gold color, a nice bouquet, and is only moderately high in alcohol—usually around 11 or 12 per cent. One of the main attractions of the wines as everyday table wines is their low price. Here in the United States they sell at about $1.50 a bottle and they are certainly not worth any more than that.

Somewhat north of Rome is the village of Montefiascone with its famous wine called *Est, Est, Est*. This wine owes its odd name to the amusing story of a German bishop who was once traveling to Rome and had a habit of sending his servant on ahead to select suitable inns along the way where the food and (especially) the wine were good. Wherever he found such an inn, the servant was to write on the front door in chalk the Latin word "*Est*," standing for the phrase: "*Vinum bonum est*," or in English: "The wine is good." He was supposedly so impressed by the wine of Montefiascone that he wrote three times on the door: "Est!—Est!—Est!" At any rate the wine still goes by this name today and no one would ever think of changing it. Like Orvieto, there is a dry and a slightly sweet version of Est, Est, Est, though we would not give either variety more than one *Est* ourselves.

In the province of Campania, which includes Naples and the islands of Capri and Ischia, there are some very pleasant wines produced, both red and white, and all fairly inexpensive. The most famous is the *Lacrima Christi*, which is grown in vineyards located on the slopes of Mount Vesuvius. Most of it is a fairly dry white wine, though some red is made and also a sparkling version of the white. With an attractive light golden color and a pleasant bouquet, the Lacrima Christi deserves its popularity as one of the best Italian white wines. The wines from the island of Capri are also excellent, but there is a very limited production, and most of what is sold as *Capri* really comes from some other region or from the near-by island of Ischia. To be sure of getting the real thing one would undoubtedly have to know one of the growers on the island and buy directly. The wine is dry and quite clean tasting—just right for a hot summer day. North of Naples is grown the *Falerno*, a wine famous in Roman days. Though the area where it is grown is still the same as it was then, the quality of the wine is no longer as good. The Romans apparently made a magnificent red wine in this region, though now it is the white Falerno which is the better of the two. It is a medium dry wine, golden in color, and, though pleasant, it is certainly not distinguished. The best red wine from the Campania province is the *Gragnano*, grown near Sorrento, and made in both dry and sweet versions. It is very light in body, but of a rich ruby color, and is certainly the best red wine from the Naples area.

DESSERT WINES

Italy produces a very famous dessert wine on the island of Sicily, which is known as *Marsala.* Much like Sherry and Madeira, Marsala is also a fortified wine, running to about 18 per cent alcohol, and ranges from dry to sweet. The finest Marsala is shipped by the Florio firm and sells for around $2 a bottle. The dry Marsala is used as an *apéritif* and the sweeter types are after-dinner wines. Many Italian recipes call for Marsala as one of the flavoring ingredients, and, since it is a fortified wine, Marsala will keep after having been opened so that one can always have it handy in the kitchen.

Both on the island of Sicily and on Sardinia, there is another sweet wine made, *Moscato*. As the name suggests, this is a Muscatel-type wine, quite sweet, and not to the average American's taste. There are Moscato wines made all over Italy, of course, and with some slight variations from region to region they are pretty much of a single type.

VINTAGES

Vintage dates on Italian wines are not so important as they are for the wines of France and Germany. More than anything else they should serve to indicate how old the wine is, and, especially in the case of white wines, whether they are too old to be still good. If your dealer has not sold one of his Italian wines very fast and he still has a large stock on hand, it may well be that the wines are too old. Most of the Italian white wines, and several of the reds, are best drunk young. They lose much of their charm with age, and you must therefore pay careful attention to what you are buying if you do not wish to be disappointed. With one of the great Chianti or Barolo wines, considerable age is usually desirable, but these are exceptions to the general rule. Since the Italian vineyards enjoy more favorable climatic conditions than those farther north in France and Germany, it very rarely happens that a vintage in Italy is a complete fiasco. Italians themselves do not pay much attention to vintages, and a wine is either good or it is bad. In actual practice, however, the bad vintages, if there ever really are any, are blended with wines of other years. You need not worry about consulting vintage charts, therefore, when buying Italian wines. Sometimes the Italian grower even has the problem of too much sunny weather during the growing season, and his wines do not develop enough acidity to make them completely harmonious and to give them "staying" power. In such cases he is allowed by law to add citric acid to the wines to make up for this lack of natural acidity. In Germany, where there is often not enough sun, exactly the opposite problem arises, and the wines often have too much acidity in poor years. Such are the problems of winegrowing, and every country must make laws which, while exercising a certain amount of control over the growers, always have to take into consideration the vagaries of nature.

IV

Portugal and Its Port and Madeira

PORT

IF INTERNATIONAL WINE LAWS were as well established and as strictly enforced as the international copyright laws, it would be quite unnecessary for us to begin a discussion of Port wine by saying that all true Port comes from a very limited area of Portugal, about forty miles from the city of Oporto—whence the name *Port* —and that the production and export of these wines is strictly controlled by the Portuguese government. Whatever is produced in California, New York, Ohio, Australia, or South Africa may try very hard to be *like*

Port, but it can never really *be* Port. Though it is produced in Portugal, we are often likely to think of Port as an English wine, and the phrase, "An Englishman and his Port," is just a way of saying that Port wine was at one time the English national drink, just as beer is often considered to be the German national drink. Times have changed since Port had its heyday in the last century, though England is still the biggest customer for these wonderful wines. The English climate is the best reason for having the decanter of Port always available, but the English style of what is now called "gracious living" played its part too.

Port wine warms as no other wine can, and on a cold winter evening it is the ideal drink to take the chill out of one's bones without producing any of the side effects of hard liquor. It is indeed unfortunate that Port is not more widely drunk and more widely appreciated in this country, and wine lovers are missing a great deal by not including several bottles in their wine cellars. Because our own American "Port" wines have become the symbol for all that is cheap and shoddy in wine making, there is no reason at all to throw out the baby with the bath water and condemn real Port wine to this same fate. The difference between real Port and American or other imitations is like the difference between day and night, and one should try two or three different bottles of the genuine product before making up one's mind about this wine. Port wine depends for its quality on the patience and skill of the shippers in Oporto, who maintain huge stocks of wines from many different vineyards and many different vintages in order to insure a continuity in their wines that the customer can depend on. Except in the case of "Vintage Port," which, like vintage Champagne, is the wine of one particular year, the Port wines of firms like Sandeman, Graham, or Cockburn will taste pretty much the same year in and year out. In other words, if one develops a fondness for Cockburn's No. 25 Port, for example, one can be fairly certain that this wine will taste the same five years from now, or ten years from now, as it does today. One is thus spared much of the inconvenience of worrying about good years and bad years when buying Port, as well as of bothering to know about various vineyards and their often difficult-to-pronounce names. Port wine always carries a good old English name, the name of the firm that ships it and stands behind it as a guarantee of quality.

There are over two dozen Port shippers of established reputation who currently bring wine into England and export it to America. Some of these firms are very small and their wines are not often met with in the average wineshop. Some of the larger ones, on the other hand, do considerable advertising in American magazines so that their wines are quite well known to the American wine-drinking public, even if they are not always at the top of the list as far as quality is concerned. There are three names that stand out among all the many producers as being the leaders in the quality production of Port wines. These three are the firms of Cockburn, Graham, and Taylor. The Taylor wines, unfortunately, cannot be imported into the United States, because there is an American firm by that name in New York State, which produces New York State Port wine as part of its operation. This means, therefore, that we have here in the United States the two firms of Cockburn and Graham as leaders in the field of quality Port wines. The Sandeman wines are also well known here, and are certainly the leaders as far as volume of sales is concerned. Sandeman has excellent wines, needless to say, and we do not wish to imply that they are in any way a second-rate concern. Just as with Champagne, the only names that you need to remember as far as Port wine is concerned are the names of two or three first-class shippers such as we have listed here. After that, the only decision to make is the type of Port that you wish to buy.

According to the method by which the wine is aged, Port is divided into three main categories: Tawny Port, Ruby Port, and Vintage Port. Vintage Port is not widely known or sold in the United States, though real Port connoisseurs consider it the only Port worth bothering about. Needless to say, it is much more widely appreciated in Great Britain than here in the United States, though the best wineshops in most large cities will usually carry at least one or two brands of Vintage Port, and you will usually be able to find it with a certain amount of searching and careful inquiry. As the name implies, Vintage Port is the wine of one particular vintage which is considered to be particularly outstanding. Not every year produces the same quality wine in Portugal, any more than it does in France or Germany, but since Port is a blend of the wines of several different years this does not matter much. When there is a really excellent crop in certain years, as a result of fine weather and ideal growing conditions, the producers in Oporto "declare a vintage," which simply means that they all agree to sell most of that particular year's wine by itself and not blend it with the wines of any other year. The wine is then bottled fairly young, that is, after two years in the cask, and is allowed to develop further in the bottle. This period of aging may go on for fifteen or twenty years, and it used to be the custom in England for a father to buy several dozen bottles of a Vintage Port when his son was born, and to then lay them away until the son's twenty-first birthday. A bottle of wine this old demands careful handling when it is opened, and Vintage Port in particular throws quite a sediment during the course of its life in the bottle. Obviously, this is *not* the wine for anyone in a hurry, nor should it be purchased in the afternoon, carried home, and opened that same evening! If you feel that you would like to partake of the pleasures of Vintage Port, be sure to let the bottle rest standing up for at least a week, completely undisturbed, and then open it slowly and carefully without shaking it up. The wine must then be decanted, or poured off into another bottle if you have no decanter, through a piece of cheesecloth to catch any small particles of sediment. Always keep a light behind the bottle so that you can see when the sediment begins to come out with the last little bit of wine. This last ounce of wine should be discarded, and one should definitely *not* go on the theory of "good to the last drop" when decanting Vintage Port, or any other well-aged bottle of wine for that matter. Remember that Vintage Port is not produced every year, and that the wines to look for and to drink now are such vintages as those of 1934, 1935, 1942, 1945, and 1947—certainly none any younger than these should be drunk in the 1960's, and of course the more recent vintages would be ideal (and much cheaper) for laying away. The 1955 vintage is an excellent choice for this purpose at present.

Ruby Port is next after Vintage Port as far as richness and sweetness are concerned. It is a delightful after-dinner wine in its own right, and is of course a perfect in-between wine to serve in the morning, in the middle of the afternoon, or in the evening when unexpected company drops in. It is served at room temperature, and since there is considerably less sediment in Ruby Port than there is in Vintage Port, the wine can be served directly from the bottle, though with such a lovely color it is really a shame not to decant it and let your guests enjoy the rich red color of the wine. Ruby Port is a blend of wines of different vintages and will therefore never carry a vintage date on the label. It is also aged longer in the casks before being bottled, so that it does not have to be kept for long periods of time in the bottle in order to achieve proper maturity. Ruby Port is a rich, full-bodied wine, and it is cheaper than Vintage Port, since there is a great deal more of it to go around. Because the wine is carefully blended from large reserve stocks which the shippers always keep on hand, you can buy any of the well-known Port wines of the leading shippers with complete confidence, and should not think that Ruby Port is merely a poor relation of Vintage Port. Many people find Vintage Port too rich, or simply do not want to devote the care and attention to handling and opening such a wine. In either case a Ruby Port is the logical substitute and will fill the bill just about as well.

Tawny Port is the lightest and the driest of the three major types of Port wine, and because of these characteristics it probably appeals to more people than either of the other two types—Ruby Port or Vintage Port. As the name implies, Tawny Port does not have the rich red color of either Vintage Port or Ruby Port, but is rather more of a reddish-brown color. This is due to the extremely long aging period of Tawny Port in the cask—twenty years being the standard length of time for a truly fine Tawny Port from a first-class shipper. This long period of aging in the wood gives the wine a delightful mild and mellow character which other types of Port never attain. Unfortunately, because of the costs involved in aging wine for such a long period of time, Tawny Port can never be cheap, and the prices of the best brands run around $4 to $6 a bottle. One often encounters very inexpensive Tawny Port wines, but these are not true Tawny Ports, since they have usually been made by blending White Port with Ruby Port to attain the desired tawny color. This practice is perfectly legal and honest, by the way, and all the reputable Port firms employ this method for making their less expensive lines of Tawny Port—

those, that is, that sell for around $2 or so a bottle. In all fairness to this delightful wine, however, you should try the real thing if you are to have any idea of what fine Tawny Port is like, for it is certainly worth the extra two or three dollars that it costs. Remember that Tawny Port is not a dry wine, nor a wine to drink with your meals. Though it is drier than either Vintage or Ruby Port, it is still basically a sweet wine. Because it is somewhat milder than the other types of Port, many people prefer a Tawny Port in the morning or afternoon when they would find a Ruby Port too heavy. For our warmer climate and generally warmer homes, Tawny Port would seem to be the ideal type of Port for American wine lovers. If you have never tasted anything but the American versions of this wine, a fine Tawny Port from one of the top shippers will really show you just what a great Port is.

Now and then you may come across a White Port, but not much of this wine is imported into the United States. It is mainly sold in the Scandinavian market and is also used for blending purposes as we mentioned before. White Port is of no particular merit and not worth any special discussion here, except to mention that its alcoholic strength is the same as that of any other Port—roughly 20 per cent—and those who think it is less "strong" than the red Ports are only deluding themselves. Alcoholic content, after all, does not have any relationship to the color of a wine.

For those who wonder why we cannot produce an American "Port" when we have been so successful with the production of other types of European wines, we should explain that the art of making Port wine is much more complicated than the making of ordinary table wines in northern Europe. Just the blending of the grapes alone is a major operation, for there are over thirty different types of grapes grown in the Douro region of Portugal, where the wine is produced. The

Tinta is the chief variety used, but the fact that Tinta grapes may be planted in California and used for the wine there is a long way from saying that the wine will be Port wine. Such blending operations with so many different varieties of grapes are unknown in Germany, for example, where all the great wines are made from the single Riesling grape, or in Burgundy, where they are made from the Pinot Noir grape. For those who are concerned with romantic traditions, it may be of interest to know that the grapes are still treaded by barefoot workers in large vatlike tanks called *lagars*. Portugal is one of the few countries where this ancient method is still employed.

To control the quality of the Port wines the Portuguese government has imposed very strict and well-enforced laws on the producers and shippers of these wines. To begin with, only those wines which come from the Upper Douro region, beginning at Barca D'Alva near the Spanish border and running forty miles west to Regua, may legally be called Port. The vineyards are on both sides of the Douro River and the area varies in width from ten to thirty miles. It is a beautiful river valley, and one feels transported back into the seventeenth or eighteenth century when traveling through this area, so little has it been modernized. The vineyard estates are called *quintas*, and several of the larger firms have lovely manor houses on their estates, where they often entertain their customers from abroad. The Cockburn estate, for example, is known as the Quinta do Tua, and the lovely Graham estate is called the Quinta dos Malvedos. In addition to the wines of their own estates, all the big shippers also buy wines from many of the smaller growers, and every little winegrower or vineyard owner has "his" Port firm to which he regularly sells his wines. Changes are not lightly made, and should a grower decide to sell his wine to someone else for one year, both his former buyer and his new buyer will want to have full particulars on just why a change is desired.

The Port wine trade is probably the most honorable and the most gentlemanly wine trade in the world. It is not at all unusual to hear one of the leading shippers praise his competitor's wines in the most enthusiastic terms, just as though his own wines did not even rate. Part of this gentlemanly and well-bred way of conducting the Port wine trade is due to the organization known as the Factory House. It actually is a large mansion which dates back to 1600, and is jointly maintained by the thirteen leading Port shipping firms who are members. On joining the Factory House, each firm must donate fourteen dozen bottles of its Port to the Factory House cellars, and also contribute three dozen of each of its Vintage Ports from then on. In this way, the Factory House has managed to build up a magnificent cellar of fine old Port wines of all the great vintage years. One of the interesting features of the building itself is the novelty of two identical dining rooms. Luncheon is served in the first dining room, after which the guests adjourn to the second dining room, taking exactly the same places which they had before, at exactly the same-sized table, and there they are served their Port. This has the advantage of providing a sort of "fresh start" for the Port wine, and however many cigarettes may have been smoked during lunch, the air is always clear and fresh for the enjoyment of the Port afterwards.

Since all the best shippers belong to the Factory House, we feel that a list of the complete membership will serve as a guide in buying good Port wine. Here they are in alphabetical order:

Cockburn Smithes
Croft
Delaforce

Gonzales Byass
Graham
Martinez Gassiot
Morgan Brothers
Robertson Brothers
Sandeman
Silva & Cosens (Dow)
Smith Woodhouse
Taylor, Fladgate, & Yeatman
Warre & Co.

Not all of these shippers have their wines on sale in the United States, and, since market conditions change from year to year, no purpose would be served by listing those currently available, especially since one shipper may have his wines in the New York State market, but not in California, or vice versa. Because of the difficulties encountered in many states with liquor control boards, there are many shippers who just cannot be bothered with promoting their wines in some of the more restrictive states.

Port Wine is at its best as an after-dinner wine, to be drunk leisurely in the company of a few good friends. It is certainly not a party wine, as it does require a certain amount of care and attention in handling. A decanter is almost a necessity for those who wish to indulge in Vintage Port, but it is certainly an added attraction to the service of Ruby or Tawny Port as well. For those who wish to show the actual bottle to their guests—a routine procedure for real wine lovers in many cases—the empty bottle can be passed around after the wine has been served, but the wine itself should be decanted an hour or two before dinner. If one is entertaining at a formal dinner with many different wines, or if the guests are not close friends, then certainly the empty wine bottle should neither be displayed nor passed around, since some of the guests would construe this as an attempt to show off or impress people with the cost of the wine. Remember, too, that Port should always be drunk from a good-sized glass. Most matched sets of glasses include so-called Port glasses that are far too small. There is no reason why a Port glass should be much smaller than any other wineglass, especially since one should never fill the glasses to the brim anyway. A large glass, half full, permits the drinker to swirl the wine a little in his glass and enjoy the bouquet. A tiny glass filled to the brim is not only totally useless but is also dangerous to rugs or carpets.

When we say that Port wine is drunk at room temperature, it would be well to bear in mind once again that this does not mean a room of 80 degrees Fahrenheit. In warm weather Port is much better slightly chilled, and certainly the less expensive types are not harmed by drinking them "on the rocks." The French regularly drink their Port in this way, with a twist of lemon peel, as an *apéritif*. It would be a shame to ruin a fine old Vintage or Tawny Port in this manner, and the cheaper wines should of course be used on such occasions.

There is certainly nothing more pleasant or relaxing after a nice dinner than a good glass of Port, and we can only hope that the custom of after-dinner Port will catch on in the United States as more people become aware of how delightful authentic Port can be.

MADEIRA

The island of Madeira, located about four hundred miles off the west coast of Africa, has been a Portuguese possession since the early part of the fifteenth century. Its wines have been famous for the past two hundred fifty years, though in the United States they are not now as popular or as well known as they were in colonial times. The Madeira wines have a distinct character of their own, but the easiest way to describe them to someone who has never tasted them is to say that they are somewhat like Sherry. The two wines are certainly enough alike in their general characteristics so that the one can be substituted for the other in any menu or recipe. This means that where a dry Sherry is called for, a dry Madeira will do just as well, and, where a sweet or Cream Sherry is wanted, a sweet Madeira can just as well be served in its place. Madeira is a fortified wine, that is, a wine of about 20 per cent alcohol, just like Sherry and Port. We do not mean to suggest that everyone should abandon Sherry in favor of Madeira, but the wines are definitely worth trying for their own sake, and have the added advantage of being generally less expensive than the best brands of Sherry. Fortunately, there is no longer any American "Madeira" being made in this country, so that if you buy any type of Madeira at all you can be sure that it is the authentic wine imported from the island of that name.

Just as Port became the "Englishman's wine," so Madeira was the American colonists' wine, having been far more popular here than it ever was in Great Britain. Washington, Jefferson, John Adams, and many other famous men of the period were all Madeira drinkers. The seaport cities of Boston, Philadelphia, New York, Charleston, and Savannah were the centers of the Madeira trade, and the great plantation owners in the South continued to import large quantities of the wine almost up until the time of the Civil War. Since Madeira is one of the longest-lived of all wines, there are still some bottles of these early nineteenth-century Madeiras in existence, and they can now and then be found for sale in some of the top wineshops in New York City. During this period the Madeira wines were always imported directly by the purchaser in barrels and then transferred into five-gallon demijohns which were stored in the attic of the house where they would be exposed to the extremes of heat and cold during the changing seasons. This method of storage had a mellowing effect on the wine.

In the days of the sailing ships it was found that Madeira wines which had been shipped around Cape Horn to the East Indies or China, and back again, were much better than the wines which had not been thus exposed to the rigors of the sea journey. Apparently the heat of the tropics and the motion of the ship improved the quality of the wine to a considerable extent, and the same results were soon being obtained artificially by heating and rocking the wines right in the shippers' lodges on the island of Madeira itself. This is the method employed today, where the wines are "baked" at a temperature up to 130 degrees for a period of six months or so. These "hot rooms" are called *estufas* in Portuguese, and are unique to the island of Madeira (unless we consider the "baking" process used for American sherry, which is not quite the same thing at all).

There are five main types of Madeira which are presently on the market. They are:

Rainwater—the lightest and driest of all
Sercial—very dry and light
Verdelho—not quite as dry as Sercial, and darker in color
Bual (also spelled Boal)—medium sweet and rich
Malmsey—very rich, full-bodied, and sweet

From this it can be seen that the *Rainwater* and *Sercial* wines would be best with the soup course at dinner or as an *apéritif*, while the *Bual* and *Malmsey* are best as after-dinner wines or served in the afternoon by themselves. The Malmsey Madeira reminds one very much of a Cream Sherry.

Though the island of Madeira escaped all man-made catastrophes of the past five hundred years, it did suffer two serious natural catastrophes during the middle of the nineteenth century. The first of these was a type of mildew called Oïdium, which struck the vines in the early 1850's. The second was the notorious Phylloxera, or root louse, which appeared in the 1870's, shortly before it struck the vineyards in France. This all but ended wine making in Madeira, but the vines were replanted on American roots, just as was done in France, and wine was soon being made once more. These two blights, however, combined with our own Civil War in between, served to put an end to the great popularity of Madeira in this country. As Americans once again become wine conscious, however, more and more of them will begin to try such off-beat wines as Madeira and find how delightful and useful they can be.

Madeira wines are no longer sold with vintage dates, but are now blended wines of several different years, just like Sherry and all nonvintage Ports. This means that one buys Madeira solely by type; there is, in other words, no need to worry about the year in buying Madeira, any more than there is in buying Sherry. Another attractive feature of the Madeira wines is that they do not differ too much from producer to producer. All the leading shippers are banded together in the Madeira Wine Association, and their wines are all handled at the one lodge in Funchal, the capital city of Madeira. Though we are listing the names of the most important shippers here, it is really of no particular importance whose wines you buy, since they will be basically the same. A Sercial from Blandy, for example, will taste just about like the Sercial from Cossart Gordon or Leacock, if, indeed, it is not the very same wine!

We should mention here that Rainwater Madeira was first brought to the United States in the year 1820, and, as the name implies, it is very light in color and thus supposedly looks like rain water. The other types of Madeira are all named from the grape varieties from which they are made.

Here are the most important Madeira shippers whose wines are usually found in American wineshops:

Blandy's Madeiras Ltd.
Cossart Gordon & Co.
Henriques & Henriques
Leacock & Co.
Rutherford & Mills
Shortridge, Lawton & Co.
Welsh Brothers, Ltd.

Any of these names on a bottle of Madeira is an authentic guarantee of quality and an assurance that you are getting the real thing. Prices run from around $2.50 to $3.50 for most Madeiras, so they are really not in the luxury class and can be enjoyed fairly often. The drier Madeiras are best served chilled and many people prefer the sweeter Bual and Malmsey chilled too. Since it is a very hardy wine, Madeira loses nothing of its character when served in this way, and one need have no hesitation in chilling the wine. All in all, Madeira is one of the easiest wines to serve as well as being one of the most versatile. Certainly every wine cellar worthy of the name should have a few bottles included in its inventory, and apartment dwellers with smaller stocks of wine on hand will find that it pays to keep one or two bottles of Madeira tucked away for unexpected guests, or those special meals where something different is called for.

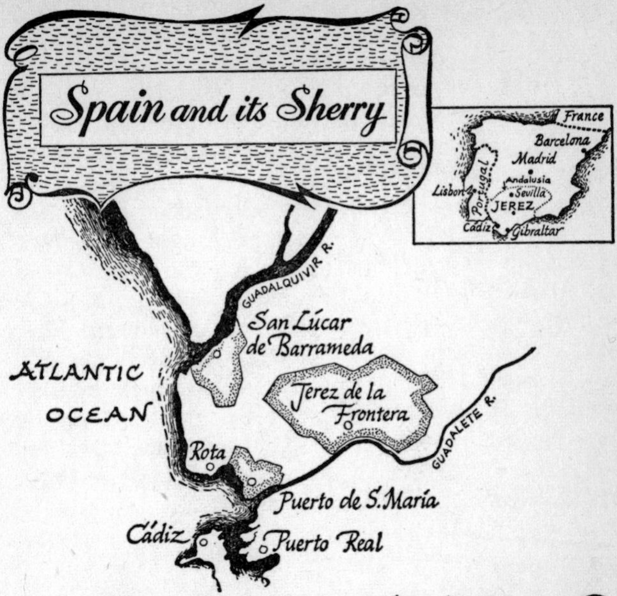

Spain and its Sherry

France
Barcelona
Madrid
Andalusia
Lisbon
Portugal
Sevilla
JEREZ
Cádiz
Gibraltar

GUADALQUIVIR R.
San Lúcar de Barrameda
ATLANTIC OCEAN
Jerez de la Frontera
GUADALETE R.
Rota
Puerto de S. María
Cádiz
Puerto Real

Portugal and its Port

France
OPORTO
Madrid
Lisbon
Portugal
Spain
Cádiz
Gibraltar

SPAIN
ATLANTIC OCEAN
PORTUGAL
Vila Real
CORGO R.
TUA R.
Oporto
Barca d'Alva
DOURO R.
Vila Nova de Gaia
CIMA CORGO

V

Spain and Its Sherry

SHERRY MUST CERTAINLY BE the most imitated wine in the world, for in addition to the authentic Sherry that comes only from Spain, we find New York State Sherry, California Sherry, South African Sherry, and Australian Sherry. This must certainly be some sort of a record as far as wine imitations go! Though there are many wines that "come close," real Sherry can never be duplicated exactly. The soils where the grapes are grown, as well as the methods by which the Sherry wines are made, are too distinctive to permit imitations ever to succeed more than halfway.

Located on the southwest coast of Spain, not far from the famous city of Cadiz, the Sherry region gets its name from the main town in the area, Jerez de la Frontera. That this derivation is not immediately seen is because the English word "sherry" is derived from the Moorish name for the city, *Scheris*, or *Sheris*. It must be remembered that Spain was under Moorish domination for about seven hundred years, and it was not until 1492 that the Moors were finally driven out once and for all. In the year 1264, however, the Christians gained a foothold in the area around Cadiz, and, since Jerez was the point of the furthest penetration, it was called Jerez de la Frontera, or Jerez on the frontier—the frontier, that is, between the Christian and Moslem parts of Spain. The region around Jerez had been known as a wine-growing area since pre-Roman times, and the Moors did not uproot the vines when they conquered Spain, but used the grapes to make raisins instead. Moslems are forbidden by the Koran to drink alcoholic beverages, but they were not so fanatical as to rip up all the vines that they found growing in Spain when they arrived. We may even suppose that a little wine was pressed in secret by some of the less devout followers of Mohammed, though there is no actual record of any such activity on the part of the Moorish conquerors.

The Sherry wines are produced in a roughly triangular area north of Cadiz, with the towns of Puerto de Santa Maria, Sanlucar de Barrameda, and Jerez de la Frontera serving as the three corners of the triangle. Some wines are brought in from outside this area, but the majority of the vineyards are close to one or the other of the three towns we have named. Altogether, the vineyards cover about twenty thousand acres of land or perhaps a little less. No other wine but Sherry is made in this part of Spain, and it is of course the wine of the region, in the sense that it is drunk by everyone right through a meal, or at any time of the day for that matter. The Jerezano, however, does not drink a sweet Sherry ever, but nearly always one of the drier, or even very driest types. The soil varies to a considerable extent from one part of the Sherry region to another. The best soil is the *albariza*, a white, chalkish type that makes considerable dust during the dry summer season, as anyone who decides to stroll through the vineyards at this time of year will find out to his sorrow. A sandy soil called *arena* is found in some areas, and there is a third type called *barro,* that is not so chalky as the *albariza,* being more of a reddish-brown clay. The same grapes when grown on *arena* soil will yield twice as much wine as those grown on the *albariza* soil, though not so high in quality.

The Palomino is the chief grape variety used for making Sherry, though about a dozen different kinds of grapes are grown throughout the Sherry region. Another rather special variety of grape is grown to be used in sweetening those wines that are intended to become Cream Sherry. This is the Pedro Ximenez, often called simply P.X. Some Muscat grapes are also grown for sweetening, but the P.X. is the most important grape used for this purpose.

Like Port, Sherry is not stored in underground cellars, but is kept in large buildings called *bodegas.* These buildings with their high columns and arched roofs almost make one feel that he is in a great cathedral—in spite of the countless rows of barrels on every side. The windows are covered with straw matting, but enough light gets in to keep the *bodegas* from being really gloomy, and there is enough circulation of air to keep them from ever getting musty or damp. They are always cooler in the summer, of course, than the outside air temperature, and many visitors do not notice what a difference there really is until they go outside after having sampled their way through a dozen different Sherries!

The basic principle of making Sherry which sets it apart from all other wines and methods of wine making is the so-called *Solera system.* It has been in use now for over a hundred years and has proved its success beyond any measure of doubt. In its simplest form it consists of just three rows of barrels, one above the other, with the new wine always being put into the top row while the bottles are filled from the bottom row of barrels. Since the bottom barrels are never emptied completely—never more than two-thirds in any one year—the wines are constantly being blended and reblended as they pass from the top row of barrels into the middle row, and from there into the bottom row. There is thus no "vintage" Sherry, since every bottle is a blend of the wines from many different years. If a Solera was begun in the year 1860, for example, there may well be a few quarts of the 1860 Sherry still in the barrels, and every bottle taken from this Solera will contain a few drops of the 1860 wine. This would not, however, give the shipper the right to call his wine an 1860 Vintage Sherry, and such a thing would of course never even be considered by any reputable shipper. In actual practice, the Solera system shows some variations from the simple description we have given here. To begin with, instead of there being only three stages through which the wines pass, there may at times be as many as six or eight. The barrels do not have to be stacked one on top of the other in exact sequence, but may well be in different parts of the *bodega* for the sake of convenience in filling them or in bottling the wines. In addition to the Solera itself, there is usually a junior version of the same thing, called the *criadera,* in which the young wines are first aged. A new wine often goes through two or three of these *criaderas* before it is introduced into the top row of barrels in the Solera proper.

The whole purpose of the Solera system is to assure continuity in the various types of Sherry that a shipper is known for. It is fortunate that younger wines take on the characteristics of older wines to which they are added and not vice versa, since otherwise the Solera system would never work properly and the wines would constantly be changing from one year to the next. As it is now, the consumer can be sure that his favorite

Sherry will taste the same five years from now as it does today. All the Sherry casks used for the Soleras are made of American oak, by the way, and we export more oak to Spain, in terms of dollar value, than we import in Sherry. These casks are very much sought after by whiskey distillers since they give the necessary color to whiskey, which is of course as clear as water when it is distilled. The Sherry that has soaked into the wood of the barrel is enough to impart this color, believe it or not, and no Sherry is actually mixed with the whiskey. The most popular brands of Sherry must be prepared in such large quantities that glass-lined tanks are usually used for the purpose of blending the wines, instead of the smaller oak barrels that hold only about six hundred fifty bottles of wine. The tanks are *not* used for aging the wines in the Solera, but only for blending the wines for shipment after they have been withdrawn from the Solera. Most Sherry is made up of wines drawn from several Soleras, though the proportion taken from each one must be the same at all times if the particular brand of Sherry being made up is to maintain a constant style.

All Sherry is described by type as well as by brand name. Each of the leading shippers produces a whole range of Sherries from very dry to very sweet, but the same type of Sherry is not too different from one producer to the next. To begin with, the two most obvious divisions of Sherry are dry and sweet. The dry wines are of a type called *Fino,* and the sweet wines belong to a type called *Oloroso.* Each of these two types has two subdivisions. Listing them all in a simple table from the driest to the sweetest, we have the following types of Sherry that are commonly sold in the United States:

Manzanilla—the very driest
Fino—dry, but not as austere as Manzanilla

Amontillado—medium dry

Oloroso—darker in color and higher in alcohol than the other Sherries, Oloroso is always sweetened before being put on the market. Cream Sherry is of this type.

All Manzanilla Sherry comes from Sanlucar de Barrameda, where it seems to take on the tang of the salt air. If it is stored in Jerez instead of Sanlucar, the wine develops into a regular Fino for some strange reason. The village of Manzanilla itself no longer produces the wines sold under its name, though that is where the wines first came from. Those who like an extremely dry Sherry should certainly try Manzanilla. It is a wonderful *apéritif*, served well chilled.

Fino Sherry is always very expensive since it requires aging through many Soleras to be really good. It is about the driest type Sherry that most people like and is always light in color and delicate.

Amontillado is considered to be the perfect cocktail Sherry and the best Sherry to serve with the soup course at dinner. The name comes from the village of Montilla that, like Manzanilla, gave its name to a type of wine that it no longer makes. It is darker in color than a Fino, but a true Amontillado is never as dark as an Oloroso.

Oloroso is the sweetest type of Sherry that we can buy. It has the P.X. wine added to it to attain this sweetness, since in the cask it is still dry, though not so dry as the Fino-type wines.

There are several hundred firms doing business in Jerez, and all the best ones belong to the Sherry Shippers' Association. We could not begin to list all the members of this association here, but instead will give the names of those whose wines are most often found in the United States. The wines of the following six firms are the easiest to find here, together with wines shipped by John Harvey & Sons of Bristol, England. Harvey

& Sons do not have bodegas in Spain, but only buy their wines from the producers there and ship them to Bristol for bottling. Here are the principal Spanish firms:

Duff Gordon & Co.
Gonzalez, Byass & Co.
Pedro Domecq
Sandeman Bros. & Co.
Williams & Humbert, Ltd.
Wisdom & Warter, Ltd.

Following our description of the various types of Sherry, the Duff Gordon wines range as follows: *Pinta*, the driest, a Fino. *Nina*, less dry, but also a Fino type. *Amontillado*, here called "Club Dry," and finally two Oloroso types: *No.* 28, medium sweet and *Duff Gordon Cream*, the richest and sweetest of all.

Williams and Humbert classify their wines as *Bone Dry*, a Fino, followed by *Pale Dry*, which is a little less dry than the Bone Dry. After these come *Amontillado*, probably the lightest and driest of all the various firms' wines of this type; *Dry Sack*, the driest type of Oloroso; *Medium Sweet*, as the name implies, a somewhat sweeter Oloroso; and finally *Canasta Cream* which corresponds to Duff Gordon Cream above.

Taking Pedro Domecq as a third example, we have the following series of wines: *La Ina*, a Fino; *Guitar*, also a Fino, but a little less dry; *Ideal Pale*, medium dry; *Amontillado*, here called "Primero," and then two Oloroso types, *Double Century*, which is medium sweet, and *Celebration Cream*, the sweetest of all, and like the Duff Gordon Cream and Williams and Humbert Canasta Cream in style.

It is interesting to note that, though the Harvey firm is famed chiefly for its *Bristol Cream*, which is certainly on a par with the other Cream Sherry types that we have just mentioned, they list in their English catalog twenty-five different brands of Sherry, ranging from the very cheapest up to the Bristol Cream, their finest. Only a half-dozen of these wines are shipped to the United States, but in Great Britain almost every London club has its own particular blend of Sherry and no other will do. Here we are not confronted with such a large selection of wines from each shipper and find it much easier to make a selection from among a half-dozen different types than from among two dozen.

It is not possible to say with any certainty which firm has the finest Sherry, but we can point out a few wines here that are well thought of among Sherry experts and not always too well known to the average consumer, who seldom knows any Sherry by name other than Harvey's Bristol Cream. Among the very dry types, we have already mentioned Manzanilla, and one of the best wines is shipped by Pedro Domecq. Their outstanding Fino wine, *La Ina*, is superb and is now becoming much better known than it formerly was. Gonzalez, Byass & Co. also have a justly popular Fino under the name of *Tio Pepe*. Among the Amontillado types just about all the firms produce an outstanding example, and which one you select will be largely a matter of availability and personal preference. Excellent Cream Sherries are the Celebration Cream of Pedro Domecq, and the Duff Gordon Cream.

Sherry is a fortified wine of about 20 per cent alcohol when shipped to this country and this means that the wine will keep reasonably long after the bottle has been opened. You should not let the wine stand around for six months or a year, however, since it will certainly become stale and unpleasant by then. A month is about as long as we usually like to keep Sherry once it has been opened. Most Sherry throws a sediment in the bottle and should therefore be decanted before using it if at all possible. Since many American wine drinkers don't know what sediment in a wine is and become alarmed when they find it, some of the Sherry shippers are now treating the wines intended for shipment to the United States and Canada so as to remove all sediment from them. Just about every wine merchant in this country has had the experience of people returning a bottle of wine with the comment that there was "something in it," when it was simply the natural sediment that the wine throws down during its further development in the bottle.

Sherry should always be served chilled, though never ice cold. The Fino-type wines are *apéritif* wines and the Oloroso types are dessert wines. Many people serve the Cream Sherries at cocktail parties, since they are the most expensive and therefore have a certain amount of status in terms of actual cash outlay, if not in terms of the host's or hostess's knowledge of Sherry. Who wants to stand around drinking the sweetest of all Sherries on an empty stomach and then have to eat dinner afterwards? How much nicer a fine Amontillado would be at such a time, or even a Fino such as La Ina! We are not a Sherry-drinking nation, of course, and we still have a long way to go in learning about the various types of these magnificent wines. The service of Sherry is fortunately very simple and uncomplicated, since there are no vintage dates, vineyard names, or even town names to worry about. Once you have become acquainted with the principal wines of the leading shippers you will have nothing else to learn and you need then only select the type of Sherry that is most suitable for your needs at any particular time.

VI

Various European Wines

INTRODUCTION

ALMOST EVERY COUNTRY in Europe produces wines of one sort or another even if they do not always attain the great qualities of the French or German wines. In many countries the wines are not well enough known to have a large export market, or they may be exported for blending purposes, either legal or illegal, as the case may be. One well-known example of the latter type of blending is the case of the Yugoslavian Riesling wines which often appear in this country as German Liebfraumilch. Many of the table wines from Switzerland, Hungary, or Spain are quite good, but, because they lack the snob appeal or the fame of their northern neighbors in France and Germany, they are not very much in demand in the United States.

As prices for the French and German wines continue to rise, however, these "lesser" wines from other European countries are often very good buys.

HUNGARY

Now that Hungary has become one of the Russian satellites, the wines are not so popular as they once were. They are still imported into the United States, however, and the firm of Vintage Wines, Inc., in New York City has sole distribution rights from the Hungarian government. The two most popular Hungarian red wines are the *Egri Bikavér* and the *Nemes Kadar*, both quite full-bodied. There is a Riesling wine produced too, and this is spelled *Rizling* on the Hungarian labels, though the wine is by no means in the same class as the fine German wines made from this grape. Another white wine is the *Szurke-Barat* from the Badacsony region. By far the greatest and most famous of the Hungarian wines, however, is *Tokay*. They should not be confused with wines using this name and coming from California, since there is no similarity whatsoever between real Hungarian Tokay (or *Tokaji*, as it is spelled on the bottle labels) and the California wine using this name! There is a dry Tokay called *Szamarodni*, and a more distinguished sweet type known as *Aszu*. In former times, when Hungary was still part of the Austro-Hungarian monarchy, the Tokay Aszu ranked among the greatest of the world's sweet dessert wines. The wines are still quite good, of course, but they lack the loving care that was given them in the days of the monarchy. Somewhat like a French Sauternes or a German *Beerenauslese,* the Hungarian Tokay Aszu is not made in quite the same way as these two famous wines, though the principle of the overripe grapes is employed here too. Instead of being made entirely from overripe grapes, as is the case in Sauternes, or in the making of a German *Beerenauslese,* there is a basic dry wine to which these overripe grapes are added. The ordinary dry wine is usually kept in casks of about thirty to thirty-five gallons, to which the juice from several baskets of the overripe grapes is added. These baskets are called *puttonyos* in Hungarian, and yield about seven gallons of wine. An Aszu wine may have anywhere from three to five *puttonyos* of the overripe grapes in it, and the more it has the sweeter it will be. Five *puttonyos* would mean that the dry wine was blended with almost an equal portion of the sweet *Auslese*-type wine. Sometimes a special wine may be made with seven, eight, or nine *puttonyos* added, but this is rare. The label will always state just how many *puttonyos* have been added to the wine, and a Tokay Aszu of five *puttonyos* will naturally be sweeter than one of only three. There was once a small quantity of a Tokay *Essence* made from the overripe grapes, much like a German *Trockenbeerenauslese,* but this wine was usually reserved for the imperial court and was never sold on the regular wine market.

⁂

SWITZERLAND

We do not often think of Switzerland as a wine country, and yet there are vineyards throughout the French-speaking part of this country that produce some very pleasant wines. There are many different types of grapes grown in Switzerland, and both red and white wines are made. Some of the best whites come from the area around Neuchâtel, and they are characterized by a slightly "prickly" quality, called *pétillant* in French, as a result of not being completely fermented. An attractive red wine from this region is the *Cortaillod,* which is something like a light Burgundy wine in character.

In the southern part of Switzerland, in the region known as the Valais, there are several wines of above-average quality that are worth keeping in mind. The best Swiss red wine is produced here as well as two very good whites. The red wine is known as *Dôle,* or sometimes as *Dôle de Sion,* from the town of Sion, near which the vineyards are located. The German Riesling grape yields a nice white wine known as *Johannisberg,* after the famous Rheingau estate in Germany, Schloss Johannisberg, from where the original Riesling vines are said to have been imported into Switzerland. Our own California Riesling wines use the name Johannisberg too, though usually with the word "Riesling" following. (The Swiss do not do this and their wines are known simply as Johannisberg.) As an ordinary table wine of no great distinction, the *Fendant* is probably the best known of all the Swiss white wines. It can be quite pleasant to drink on a warm summer day and should never cost over $2 a bottle if it is to be worth buying in this country.

Not far from Lausanne, in the Lavaux district, there is another very good white wine to be found, known as *Dézaley*. It is a light and fragrant wine, and many people consider it to be one of the very finest of the Swiss wines, even though it is not as well known as the Fendant or Johannisberg wines from the Valais region.

SPAIN

In addition to Sherry, Spain also produces a number of quite passable table wines, both red and white. The best of these come from the province of Catalonia in the northern part of Spain, and particularly from the Ebro Valley. It is here that the *Rioja* wines are made, with the red being the best of all Spanish table wines. The top producer is the Marqués de Riscal, and the Bodegas Bilbainas is also highly regarded. The red Riojas are much like the Bordeaux wines of France in character, and are made according to established French methods of wine making, since the Ebro region was originally settled by French winegrowers. The white wines are never completely dry and usually tend to be slightly sweet. Some are sold with the French designations such as Chablis or Sauternes, but none is ever as dry as a real French Chablis. The Spanish table wines are usually good values in the United States, since they rarely sell for much over $2 a bottle for the very best types. Vintages are unimportant in buying these wines, and one should not use a guide to French vintages when buying Spanish wines. The weather is often entirely different from the rest of Europe, and 1959 was a very good example of this. While France and Germany were enjoying almost three months of sunny summer days, Spain had one of the rainiest summers on record!

VII

The Wines of the United States

INTRODUCTION

THERE IS NO OTHER wine-producing country in the world where native wines are held in such low regard by the average consumer as American wines are by our own wine-drinking public. This is indeed an unfortunate situation, not only from the point of view of the wine drinker, but also for the producers of the best American wines, who are, to say the least, fighting an uphill battle to have their wines accepted by a larger and broader segment of the population than they are at the present time. As far as the really good American wines are concerned, we can say quite frankly that most wine drinkers in this country just don't know what they are missing. A wine lover in a typical American city may have access to, and knowledge of, any numer of fine French and German wines and yet be completely ignorant of the names of the outstanding producers of American wines or even what kinds of wines they make. Imagine a Frenchman knowing the names of a dozen outstanding German wines and having several dozen bottles of them in his *cave,* and yet knowing nothing of his own native wines! This example is admittedly a little farfetched, yet should serve to point up the absurdity of a situation in which the citizens of a major wine-producing country (for we *are* a major wine-producing country, believe it or not!) feel obliged to import great quantities of second-rate and inferior table wines simply because they have heard somewhere or other that their own domestic wines are no good.

Lest we be accused of chauvinistic attitudes in our statements about American wines, we should like to make it quite clear at the outset that not *all* American wines are worth drinking by any means. For every bottle of really good American wine made each year, there are several dozen bottles of poor and downright bad wines made that are certainly not worth our serious attention or interest. This is true, however, in every wine-producing country, but we do not recognize the really poor foreign wines here in the United States, so that the over-all picture becomes a little distorted at times. All too often we tend to think of France as a land of nothing but Château Margaux, Chambertin, or Dom Pérignon, whereas these wines, and other great wines like them, are only a tiny portion of an immense wine production that exceeds a billion and a half gallons annually. Or think how many millions of gallons of Liebfraumilch are produced in Germany each year in comparison to the few hundred gallons of such fine wines as Steinberger, Wehlener Sonnenuhr, or Scharzhofberger!

Before making any sort of comparison of American wines with their European counterparts, we must be quite sure of just what is being compared and of what exactly is being claimed for the native product. Even the most loyal drinker of American wines will admit, if he is completely fair-minded, that the great Bordeaux and Burgundy wines of France, and the great Rhine and Moselle wines of Germany, are unmatched anywhere else in the world. The qualifying word here, however, is "great" and in everyday terms of dollars and cents this means wines costing from four dollars to fifteen dollars a bottle. Few of us, though, are in a position to drink such wines every day, and the relative merits of a Château Lafite compared to a Château Mouton are likely to be of merely academic interest to the average person. For ordinary drinking we must usually come down a step from the great to the good, and it is in this category that American wines can play an important part in the daily enjoyment of wine with meals, for the best ones are very good indeed.

It is important to remember that winegrowing in America is a fairly young industry when compared to the two-thousand-year-old traditions of Europe. Serious winegrowing did not get started in this country until 1769, when the Franciscan monk Junipero Serra planted the first vineyard at the Mission San Diego in California. Early colonizers in the East, such as William Penn and Lord De La Warr, had no success with their plantings of the European vines and had to abandon all hopes of ever developing vineyard areas in their colonies. Though quality wine production has been thriving in California and New York for the last fifty to seventy-five years, it has been only in the last fifteen or twenty years that the American wine industry can really be said to have come of age. Tremendous progress has been made since the repeal of Prohibition, and improvements are still taking place all the time. The state universities in California and New York have large departments devoted to research and development in their agricultural schools, and they have been of immense help to the growers in determining just what varieties of grapes will grow best in each area. Certainly the general standards of knowledge and development in the field of grape growing and wine making are as advanced here as they are in Europe. In short, American wines of the best types are as good as, or better than, many European wines being brought into this country. They are well worth buying not only on the basis of economy, but also on the basis of quality.

Before discussing American wines in any detail we must first divide them into two distinct groups: those grown in the East, mainly in New York State and Ohio, and those grown in California. This is not only a geographical division, but, more important, a division into two basic types of American wines. New York State and other eastern wines are made from native American grapes, whereas the California wines are made from European grapes whose vines were brought over in the last century from the various wine-producing countries of Europe. The species of grape that is native to America is known as the Vitis labrusca, and all our well-known grape varieties such as Concord, Delaware, Elvira, or Catawba are of this type. The European species of grape is known as the Vitis vinifera, and the famous grape varieties of France and Germany—the Riesling from the Rhine and Moselle, the Pinot Noir from Burgundy, or the Cabernet Sauvignon from Bordeaux—are of this type.

It is obvious from this division that those who are looking for the closest approximation to the European wines must turn to California as their source of supply, while those who would like to try some of the many interesting and excellent wines made from our own native grape varieties should try the New York State wines. The eastern climate is too cold in the winter for the majority of European grape varieties and these have been found to do best in California, especially in the area around San Francisco. Our own hardier Concords, Delawares, and Niagaras thrive in the Finger Lake region of New York without suffering any ill effects from the cold winters there. Some of the American grapes have been crossed with European strains to produce new varieties combining the best qualities of both, and the Taylor Wine Company has recently marketed such a wine under the name *Lake Country Red.*

NEW YORK STATE

Since New York State wines bear no family resemblance to any of the famous European wines, we can only urge that they be judged on their own merits and accepted for just what they claim to be and nothing more. The taste sensations are entirely different from those that one has learned to associate with European wines, and a comparison with well-known types of wine from Bordeaux, Burgundy, or the Rhine is completely pointless.

The top-ranking producers of New York State and other eastern wines are rather few in number, and a couple of them have such a limited production that their wines are not always easy to find, even in large cities. The Boordy vineyard in Riderwood, Maryland, owned by Mr. Philip Wagner, is a real pioneer, and Mr. Wagner is to be commended for the great amount of research and development of hybrid grape varieties which he has undertaken. He produces an excellent red and an excellent white wine, but away from the Baltimore area one usually has difficulty in finding them.

Another one of the smaller producers is the High Tor Vineyard in Rockland County, New York. They market a red, a white, and a rosé wine, but since their production is also rather limited, the wines are usually difficult to come by in most stores. The wines are excellent examples of what good native American wines can be, however, and are well worth the attention of the interested wine drinker.

The bulk of the New York wine industry is controlled by four large producers: Great Western Producers, Inc., the Taylor Wine Company, Gold Seal Vineyards, Inc., and Widmer's Wine Cellars, Inc. Great Western is known chiefly for its champagnes, although other wines are produced as well. At the present times, three types of Great Western champagne are on the market: *Brut Special,* the driest of the three, *Special Reserve,* slightly less dry, and *Extra Dry,* still sweeter than the first two in spite of the name. This follows the practice of the French, where "Extra Dry" actually means slightly sweet.

The Taylor Wine Company is the largest of the big four, and though it produces a full range of table wines, sherries, and ports, it is the champagne here, too, which is the biggest seller. The Taylor Company markets only two types of champagne, a *brut,* which is of course the driest, and a slightly sweeter one called, *Dry, Royal*

Quality. This would correspond to a French Extra Dry, as mentioned before.

The Gold Seal Vineyards are uniquely distinguished in having as their president Charles Fournier, who was formerly associated with the French Champagne firm of Veuve Clicquot. As one might expect under these circumstances, the *Charles Fournier Brut* champagne is outstanding and certainly the best New York State champagne produced. The firm also markets a line of cheaper champagnes under the Gold Seal label, but it is worth paying a little more to get the Charles Fournier Brut. In addition to his champagne, M. Fournier has also marketed a dry white wine known as *Fournier Nature,* which is slightly *petillant,* or "prickly," on the tongue. This wine is less expensive than the Fournier champagne, but still has a little sparkle to it that reminds one of the wines from Neuchâtel in Switzerland. It is not a great wine by any means, but it is an interesting one. As far as the regular table wines are concerned, the two that are outstanding from the Gold Seal vineyards are their *Keuka Rosé* and the *Delaware*. The *Delaware* is a white wine, medium dry, and a fine example of what a native American wine can be.

A former associate of Mr. Fournier, Dr. Konstantin Frank, has now established his own vineyards of European Vinifera grapes at Hammondsport. This is a quite remarkable and historical achievement for New York State wines, and at the present time Dr. Frank has excellent *Johannisberg Riesling, Gewürztraminer,* and *Pinot Chardonnay* on the market. His first red wine, a *Cabernet Sauvignon,* will be available in 1967. Sold under the name of Vinifera Wine Cellars, Dr. Frank's wines are well worth searching out, though the production is still rather limited in quantity.

Last but not least of the big four in New York State

is Widmer's Wine Cellars, located at Naples, New York. The present owner of the firm, Mr. William Widmer, is a graduate of the German Wine Growing School in Geisenheim, in the Rheingau. Mr. Widmer's concern for quality over quantity has kept his vineyard operations somewhat more limited than they might have been had he wished to go in for cheap, mass-produced wines, but this is so much the better for the wine-drinking public who can thus depend on the Widmer name as a guarantee of quality. Foremost among the Widmer wines is their sherry, especially the one known as *Widmer's Special Selection Sherry*. This wine is probably the finest sherry produced in America today, and can certainly hold its own against many of the cheaper imported sherries. It sells for around $1.95 a bottle, whereas the regular Widmer sherries retail for around $1.55 a bottle. These are also tops in their field and well worth your attention if you are looking for inexpensive but good domestic sherries for everyday use. There is a dry cocktail sherry, a regular sherry, and a cream sherry with the price being the same for all three varieties. The reason for the excellent quality of the Widmer sherries lies not only in the care with which they are made, but, more important, in the length of time that they are aged—four full years in the cask. Most cheap sherries made in the United States today are produced and bottled within six months' time, and even the better-grade wines are rarely kept longer than two years in cask.

Not only is the length of time in which the Widmer sherries are aged an important factor in producing top-quality wines, but also the very unusual method by which this aging process is carried out. The wines are not stored in underground cellars, as one might expect, but rather in fifty-gallon oak barrels on the winery roof, completely exposed to the elements. This exposure to summer sun and winter cold for four years mellows the wines in a way that no other process could possibly duplicate. It reminds us of the custom of shipping Madeira wine in the holds of sailing ships during the nineteenth century, by which method the wine would be exposed to extremes of heat and cold and the motion of the sea for a year or so, thus mellowing it and aging it better than could be done on land in the same period of time. Whether you purchase the regular Widmer sherries or the Special Selection Sherry, you can at least be sure that you are getting full value for the money and are buying one of the finest sherries produced in America today.

As well as being the outstanding producer of sherry in New York State, Mr. Widmer also leads the field in the production of New York State *varietal* wines, that is, wines made from a specific variety of native American grapes. Each wine bears the name of the grape variety from which it is made instead of being called just New York State Rhine Wine or New York State Burgundy. There is a round dozen of them as follows:

WHITE WINES

Elvira
Dutchess
Delaware
Vergennes
Diana
Moore's Diamond
Catawba
Salem
Riesling (*not* the German Riesling)
Lake Niagara

RED WINES

Isabella

ROSÉ WINES

Seibel-Rosé
Lake Roselle (not a varietal, but rather a blend of several different grape varieties)

To those who have never drunk American wines these names will mean little or nothing; we can only suggest that you try them and judge them on their own merits. Most of the wines are dry white dinner wines. The two exceptions are the semisweet *Lake Niagara,* which reminds one vaguely of a Sauternes, and the *Lake Roselle,* for those who want a rosé wine which is not too dry. The Lake Niagara is excellent as a dessert wine with fresh fruit and is also intended as a dinner wine for those who do not care for a dry wine with their meals. It goes without saying that these varietal wines are aged in the regular way, and *not* on the winery roof as are the sherries. Sherry, after all, is a fortified wine, that is, a wine to which brandy has been added to bring its alcoholic content up to 20 per cent as against the average of 12 per cent for table wines. It is only because of this additional alcohol that sherry keeps so long when it is opened, and that it can be aged on the winery roof in all kinds of weather. (Table wines could never endure such an aging process, even though there would be no practical reason for trying to age them this way in the first place.)

Mr. Widmer has recently produced two wines made from the Missouri Riesling grape which have been sold as *Riesling Spätlese* and *Riesling Auslese.* It is claimed that the same type of fungus which attacks the grapes in Europe and produces the German *Auslesen* and the French Sauternes has been found on the grapes in New York State, and these wines are made from such grapes. If you have drunk a fine German *Spätlese* or *Auslese* wine, you will be very disappointed when you try the Widmer wines bearing these names. We feel that the experiment has been an unfortunate one since an experienced wine drinker expects an *Auslese* wine to be sweet—and these wines definitely are not. If the wines were at all similar to their European counterparts there would be some justification for calling them *Spätlese* and *Auslese*, but as the wines are produced now the names are completely misleading.

All of the big producers whom we have named thus far produce cheaper wines as well as the varietals, and these are sold simply as New York State Burgundy, New York State Rhine Wine, and so on. They could just as well be called New York State Red Wine or White Wine and let it go at that. The names Rhine, Burgundy, Chablis, and the like are totally meaningless when attached to wines that are nothing at all like the originals. Perhaps the day is not far off when such wines will bear strictly American names, or at least names which do not trade so openly on the famous wine names of Europe. How much better it is, for example, that Widmer's Lake Niagara is sold by that name rather than under some such name as "Château Widmer Sauternes." (There is no law that would prevent Mr. Widmer from calling his wine that if he chose to do so.) The California producers who cater to the Italian market in this country have had a great success with Italian-style brand names such as *Paisano* and *Fior di California*, to name just two of the most popular. The wine, which is sold in half-gallon and gallon jugs as well as in the regular-sized bottles, thus has a European-sounding name, yet does not presume to call itself California Chianti or California Bardolino. Let us hope that more and more of the big producers will follow this trend! For some reason the United States has never seen fit to sign any international agreements protecting wines and wine names. Such agreements are the rule in Europe, and no German winegrower, for example, would ever dare call his red wine German Burgundy, any more than he can call his sparkling wines Champagne. Even Great Britain, which produces no wine at all, has agreements with the wine-producing countries to protect their names. The foremost example of this is the treaty with Portugal, which states quite simply that no wine can be sold in Great Britain as Port unless it comes from the delimited area of Portugal where the genuine Port wines are produced. All other wines, whether they come from South Africa, Australia, or anywhere else, must be called "Port-type" wines, and the word "type" must be printed in the same size letters on the label as the word "Port" itself.

We do not expect every wine we drink to be a great wine, but we can and should expect every wine to be a good and authentic wine. The sooner we can do away with imitations the better off we shall be, and the sooner our American wines are marketed under their own region-of-origin names without misrepresentative European associations, the better for the wine trade in the United States, and the consumer who is looking for a good honest bottle.

CALIFORNIA

When we come to California, we are really in a wine paradise, for here all the greatest American wines are grown—wines that can hold their own with the fine wines of France, Germany, and Italy. The wine situation in California is completely different from that in New York State and other eastern vineyard regions. Not only is the production of wine much larger—making up almost 90 per cent of the wine produced in

America—but there are also several different types of climate in which grapes are grown, ranging from the hot inland valleys to the cool coastal region around San Francisco. California certainly has every right to call itself the "Wineland of America," both from the point of view of quantity and that of quality—though the two rarely go together. Concerned as we are here with finding wines of first-rate quality, we shall concentrate on the San Francisco area, for it is in this part of the state that all the finest California wines are grown. Climate and soil conditions have been found to be almost ideal in this region, and a really poor vintage is rare. Although "Every year is a fine wine year in California," is not 100 per cent correct, only the years which *are* fine years are bottled as vintage wines at the top-ranking estates. In actual practice this means that one need pay no particular attention to the vintage dates on California labels unless one intends to lay the wines away for several years. Under no circumstances, however, should a European vintage chart be used as a guide to California wines. Europe and California are approximately six thousand miles apart and one could hardly expect the weather conditions to be identical in both places in any given year.

In Europe, the weather can cause extreme variations in the quality of the wines, from downright poor to utterly magnificent. One sees vintage dates on California wines, of course, but they are there only for the information of the consumer, so that he will know how old the wine is. If the vintage does not come up to standard for any reason, it will not be sold under the producer's label at all, but will be disposed of in bulk to the producers of the cheap mass-produced wines. Remember, then, that if you see a vintage date on a bottle of California wine you can be sure the wine is good, since only the best wines carry such vintage dates in the first place.

Though many hundreds of grape varieties are found in California, all the best vineyards around San Francisco are planted with the classic varieties from France and Germany, such as the Cabernet Sauvignon from Bordeaux, the Pinot Noir from Burgundy, or the Riesling from the Rhine and Moselle. The wines made from these grapes are referred to as *varietal* wines to distinguish them from the cheaper wines which are labeled simply California Burgundy or California Rhine Wine, for example. A varietal wine must be made from at least 51 per cent of the grape variety claimed for it on the label, but it goes without saying that all the best producers use just about 100 per cent of the variety named on the label. The law is lax in requiring only 51 per cent of a particular grape variety to be used for a wine bearing a varietal name. A Cabernet Sauvignon would certainly not taste very true to type if 49 per cent of the wine in the bottle were some other kind of red wine mixed with it! The leading winegrowers are generally of the opinion that the time has not yet come when such names as Pinot Noir or Riesling on a bottle of California wine are sufficient to tell the prospective consumer just what he is getting. They have, therefore, kept the general or generic description of the wine on their labels as well. The generic description means the general type of wine, such as claret, Burgundy, Rhine Wine, Sauternes, or Chablis. Though usage varies from one producer to the other, you will often find that a name such as Pinot Noir appears on the label in large letters, and under it, in smaller type, the words "California Burgundy." Thus the person who doesn't know that *Pinot Noir* is the name of the grape from which the great red Burgundy wines are made is able to tell from the generic name just what kind of wine he is getting. This method is best employed on the attractive new labels being used now by the Inglenook Vineyard Co., in Rutherford. The varietal name appears in very large type, as, for instance, CABERNET SAUVIGNON. Under this, in parentheses, are the words "Classic Claret," which will of course identify the wine for those who know what claret is, but do not know that the Cabernet Sauvignon is the great grape variety of Bordeaux. Some of the producers have already stopped using this secondary, generic description on their labels, feeling that the varietal name alone is quite sufficient. Many producers look forward to the time when the varietal names alone will be sufficient to describe the wine contained in the bottle, but at present the American wine-drinking public still pretty much expects to find the old familiar European names on its domestic wine labels, even though the wines so described may not bear the slightest resemblance to the European prototypes.

The production of the finest California wines is largely in the hands of seven first-rate producers, with one or two others on the outer fringe trying to capture their share of the market by large-scale advertising. In alphabetical order these seven producers are:

Almadén Vineyards
Beaulieu Vineyard
Buena Vista Vineyards
Charles Krug Winery
Inglenook Vineyard Co.
Louis M. Martini
Wente Brothers

There are several other top-notch producers whose production is very limited, and the wines are not very easy to find outside of California. The best of these is Martin Ray, but the wines are quite expensive. We shall therefore concern ourselves with the seven producers named above, since their wines, though not available in all wineshops, have national distribution.

Because of the commercial requirements for any nationwide distribution, each of the vineyards produces a whole range of red and white wines, as well as sherry and port in many cases. It would be much better for all concerned if each producer made just one or two types of wine, as is the case in the European vineyards, where no one would ever consider trying to produce Burgundy on the Moselle, or Rhine Wine in Bordeaux. However, the economics of the wine business in this country make it necessary for each producer to have what is called a "line," that is a full range of various types of wine, so that the wholesalers can satisfy all demands with the wines of just one producer. Otherwise, they would have to carry the Pinot Noir produced by A, the Cabernet Sauvignon produced by B, and the Semillon produced by C, with all the extra paper- and book-work which this would entail. Those who have access to all the wines of the "big seven" can soon pick their favorites by comparative tastings of the same type wines from three or four of the different vineyards. It is not possible for us to state here that so-and-so has absolutely the best Cabernet Sauvignon of the group, since qualities vary from year to year. A vineyard which might have come off third best in a tasting held this year could very well be at the top of the list next year. We shall, however, point out the wines for which each vineyard is noted, as well as certain wines which we feel are of more than usual interest. From there on, it is simply a matter of personal taste and a question of availability of the wines in the particular part of the country where you live. Remember that in most stores it is possible to order wines which are not ordinarily carried in stock, so do not give up too easily if you don't find them readily available in your own local wineshop.

The Almadén Vineyards, located south of San Francisco, at Los Gatos, is the oldest of the fine wine producers in California, having been established in 1852. It is also the largest producer of varietal wines in the United States, and has certainly done more than all the other leading producers put together to have the best wines of California accepted as fine wines in their own right. The founder of the Almadén Vineyards, Charles LeFranc, came to California from France as a forty-niner, more interested in discovering gold than in growing wine. He soon realized that the chances of growing rich by panning gold were not so great as he had at first thought them to be, and that a better and more certain living was to be made by farming in the Santa Clara Valley. Encouraged by his success with produce and fruit production, LeFranc sent to France for cuttings of the best French grape varieties, as well as oak casks and other equipment necessary for wine making, and by the year 1880, he had over one hundred thirty acres of vineyards with an output of one hundred thousand gallons of wine a year. After LeFranc's death, and the untimely death of his son in an automobile accident in 1909, the Almadén Vineyards did not again regain their old reputation until 1941, when Louis Benoist of San Francisco purchased the entire operation as well as some additional vineyards near by, known locally as ranches rather than vineyards. Thus one refers to the original Almadén Vineyard as the Almadén *Ranch*, and the other vineyards are known as the Howell Ranch, the Valliant Ranch, and so on. Just recently, Almadén has acquired a new vineyard property in San Benito County, known as the Paicines (pronounced Pie-*see*-nays) Ranch. About two thousand acres in size, the new Paicines Ranch has been planted almost entirely in varietal grape varieties in order to increase Almadén's production of these wines, as well as to replace vineyards in the original Almadén area which had to be torn up to make way for housing developments. When the suburbs and residential areas began to encroach upon the original Almadén Vineyard area, it soon became apparent that vineyards could no longer be maintained there. Land that has a value of fifteen thousand dollars an acre for building purposes is *not* the sort of land where one grows Pinot Noir or Cabernet Sauvignon grapes for wine.

The new Paicines Vineyard is the largest fine wine vineyard in the world. Planted entirely in ungrafted French wines, it now produces more varietal wines than all the other Almadén ranches put together, and more Grenache Rosé, for example, than is produced in this grape's native district of Tavel in France. More Cabernet Sauvignon will be produced than in any of the great châteaux of Bordeaux, and twice as much Pinot Noir as grows in the great vineyard of Chambertin in Burgundy. These statistics in themselves mean nothing at all if the wine produced in the new vineyard is not of first-rate quality. Judging by the great amount of study and planning that went on before the new vineyard was planted—experts from the University of California advised on the planting of the various grape varieties in the different sections of the vineyard, selecting the site where each type of grape would do best—we have every reason to expect that it will yield fine wines. The results of the first harvests have been very promising, even though the wines made from such young vines will not match the quality of wines made from the mature vines two or three years from now.

The varietal wines produced by the Almadén Vineyards include all the major types of red and white wines. They are as follows:

WHITE	RED
Traminer	Cabernet Sauvignon
Johannisberg Riesling	Pinot Noir
Pinot Chardonnay	
Pinot Blanc	PINK
Chénin Blanc	Grenache Rosé
Sauvignon Blanc	
Grey Riesling	
Sylvaner	
Dry Semillon	

In addition to the varietal wines, Almadén also produces some excellent table wines for everyday use. These are made from blends of various grapes and are designated simply as *Almáden Mountain Red Claret* and *Almadén Mountain Red Burgundy*, and the white wines as *Almadén Mountain White Chablis* and *Almadén Mountain White Sauterne*. They can be obtained in half-gallon and gallon jugs like many other California wines, and are excellent for large informal parties where a good sound wine is wanted though not a really great one.

The Almadén champagne is bottle fermented in the true French manner and has long been considered one of the top-ranking American wines of this type. Just as with French Champagne, the *brut* is the driest and the extra-dry is a little sweeter.

Because of the ever-increasing popularity of rosé wines, the *Almadén Grenache Rosé* continues to be one of the leaders in the field. The Grenache is the same grape variety as is used for the famous Tavel rosé wines of France, and it certainly produces every bit as good a wine in California as it does on its native soil. With some French rosé wines now costing over $3 a bottle, the Almadén Grenache Rosé is certainly well worth trying—and at only half the price of the $3 French wines. Rosé wines, no matter where they may be produced, are never really "great" wines, and it is certainly silly to pay prices for them that one would pay for a good Bordeaux or Burgundy.

Since the Almadén Vineyards is the largest producer of varietal wines in the United States, its wines are often more easily found in wineshops than some of the other varietals from California.

To the north of San Francisco, in the famous Napa Valley, is the magnificent Beaulieu Vineyard. *Beaulieu* means "beautiful place" in English, and the Beaulieu Vineyard is exactly that. Founded in 1900 by a Frenchman, Georges de Latour, the estate is today owned by his daughter, the Marquise de Pins. She and her husband, the Marquis de Pins, divide their time between Beaulieu and her husband's ancestral home in France, the Château de Monbrun. They frequently tour the wine-growing regions of France in order to keep abreast of the latest developments there, and Beaulieu in a sense reflects the best of the two worlds. Certainly it is the nearest thing to one of the great Bordeaux wine estates that one can find in this country. The Beaulieu Vineyard wines, usually called "BV" for the sake of simplicity, are among the finest made in the United States. They are served at formal dinners in honor of visiting royalty and heads of state when it is desirable to show off our best native wines, and they are even listed on the wine list of the Hotel Georges V in Paris. A visit to the Beaulieu cellars and vineyards should convince even the most skeptical and blasé wine drinker that American wines *can* attain high standards of quality.

The full range of BV varietal wines is as follows:

RED	WHITE
Cabernet Sauvignon	Pinot Chardonnay
Georges de Latour Private Reserve Cabernet Sauvignon	Sauvignon Blanc
Pinot Noir	Sylvaner
	Johannisberg Riesling

PINK

Grenache Rosé
Beaurosé (a rosé wine made of a blend of various grape varieties)

In addition to the above varietal wines, there is also a BV Burgundy, a Chablis, and a dry and a sweet Sauternes. These are all blends of various grape varieties intended to produce good, sound table wines at a reasonable price.

The *Georges de Latour Private Reserve Cabernet Sauvignon* is the pride of the BV estate. It is given more aging in bottle than the regular Cabernet Sauvignon, and is also made from grapes grown on the choicest vineyard sites. It sells for around $3 a bottle and well repays laying away in one's wine cellar for further development. Wines of this quality should of course be treated just as one would treat a fine Bordeaux wine, since they *really are* fine wines in their own right and not just run-of-the-mill table wines. The same holds true for the *BV Pinot Noir,* an outstanding wine of the Burgundy type.

All BV wines carry the phrase, "estate-bottled," which in California means just what it does in France: the wine was made at the vineyard from grapes grown on the estate, that is, no grapes were bought from other growers nor was any other grower's wine blended in with the BV wine. The phrase, "produced and bottled by———," means that only 75 per cent of the wine need come from the estate named on the label, and if the phrase, "made by———," is used, only 10 per cent of the wine need be the grower's own. It goes without saying, of course, that any California wine carrying a vintage date is required by law to be 100 per cent of the year so named. If a grower feels that he has to blend the wines of another year with a certain vintage in order to make up for shortcomings in the wine, he can no longer use a vintage date on his labels.

In recent years Beaulieu has brought an excellent champagne onto the market, and many people feel that it is one of the closest to the real French product that can be found in this country. The production is still small, however, and the BV champagne cannot always be found in all parts of the country, though it is certainly worth looking for.

The Sonoma Valley to the west of the Napa Valley, and at about the same distance north of San Francisco, is the home of the Buena Vista Vineyards. This was where the Hungarian Count Agoston Haraszthy, usually called the "father of modern California viticulture," first laid out his vineyards in the middle of the last century. In 1861, Count Haraszthy was sent to Europe by the governor of California, and during the course of this trip he gathered over one hundred thousand cuttings from the various European vineyards which he planted in California after his return. Over three hundred varieties of grapes were represented, all carefully tagged, and Count Haraszthy had hoped to catalog them all and determine where each variety would grow best. Unfortunately the count was soon beset by all sorts of financial troubles and he left California for Nicaragua, where he planned to operate a distillery. His career there was cut short one summer day in 1869, when he was devoured by alligators while trying to cross a jungle stream! The cuttings which Haraszthy had so carefully tagged were soon scattered all over the wine-growing regions of California, and no one paid attention any longer to the names of the various grapes or where they came from. Thus much of Count Haraszthy's great work went for naught, and winegrowing and wine drinking in the United States suffered a setback from which we are only now really beginning to recover. The Buena Vista Vineyards were purchased in 1943 by Frank H. Bartholomew, the president of United Press International, and he has since restored the property and its vineyards to first-class condition. The following wines are produced:

RED

Cabernet Sauvignon—estate-bottled
Burgundy
Pinot Noir
Zinfandel

PINK

Rosé Brook—estate-bottled from
Cabernet Sauvignon grapes
Grenache Rosé

WHITE

Johannisberg Riesling
Pinot Chardonnay
Sylvaner
Traminer
Grey Riesling
Green Hungarian
(all the above are estate-bottled)
Chablis

Buena Vista also produces a *brut* champagne made from Pinot Chardonnay grapes and bottle fermented in the authentic French manner.

It is interesting to note that the Zinfandel wine, now one of the most popular of the everyday table wines of California, was first grown here at the Buena Vista estate by Count Haraszthy. The origin of the Zinfandel grape remains a mystery, however, and no one has yet been able to locate this grape variety in Europe, or find out what country it came from. It is now assumed that the Zinfandel is a cross of two or more varieties of European grapes, since no actual counterpart of the Zinfandel is known in Europe today. There are many brands of Zinfandel wine made in California, but those from here in the Sonoma Valley, or from the Napa Valley, are generally considered to be the best. They are charming, fruity wines, and many wine drinkers have found that they are really outstanding for everyday use, instead of some of the more highly touted (but less good) European wines for twice the price.

Returning once more to the Napa Valley, we come first to the Inglenook Vineyard Company in Rutherford. Located next door to the Beaulieu Vineyard which we have already discussed, Inglenook is also one of the very finest producers of California varietal wines. Among those who know fine California wines it is always a matter of great interest each year to see whether Beaulieu or Inglenook will have the best Cabernet Sauvignon wine. Both producers strive to produce the very finest wines, and in one year Inglenook may excel while in the next vintage Beaulieu may be at the top. It is obviously impossible to say which is the best, any more than a French wine authority could say whether Château Mouton or Château Lafite produced the finer Bordeaux wine. When dealing with wines of this quality it hardly matters which one is really the best, and most wine drinkers who know these wines lay away quantities of both of them so that they may have the pleasure of comparing them in the years that follow. One should not make the mistake of thinking that these wines—

whether from Inglenook, Beaulieu, or any of the other top producers—are merely California *vin ordinaire.* Nothing could be further from the truth and a fine Cabernet Sauvignon from one of the top estates will certainly repay laying down as much as a fine Bordeaux wine will.

Inglenook was founded in 1879 by a Finnish sea captain named Gustave Niebaum. During the 1860's Captain Niebaum had his own ship with which he engaged in the fur trade in the then Russian Territory of Alaska. Niebaum was not only very intelligent (he became a full-fledged ship's master when he was only nineteen) but also a shrewd business man. When the United States purchased Alaska from Russia, Niebaum took more than a half-million dollars' worth of furs into California and sold them there. He continued to prosper as a fur trader, but at the same time he was developing a considerable interest in wines and wine making. In the course of several voyages to Europe, Niebaum had a chance to visit most of the leading wine-growing areas on the continent. He was convinced that wines of equally fine quality could be made in California, and for this purpose he brought back large numbers of cuttings from the best vineyards. In 1879 he purchased the Inglenook estate and in the course of the next ten years he made it into one of the finest wine-growing estates in the country. Captain Niebaum lived until 1908, after which his widow took over the operation of the estate, and on her death it passed to a nephew.

There are two important factors to remember in connection with the Inglenook wines. First of all, they are estate bottled—still somewhat of an unusual thing in California—and this means that the wines were made only from grapes grown on the Inglenook estate. Second, the vintage date on the label not only shows when the wine was made, but it also guarantees the quality as well—unlike European wines, where the vintage date tells only when the wine was made. When Inglenook has a bad year and certain wines do not come up to their strict standards, the wine is sold off in bulk to other producers and no Inglenook wine of that particular type will be made at all in that year. It might happen, for example, that the Pinot Noir grapes did not do so well one year, even though the other grape varieties flourished. If such were the case, there would be no Inglenook Pinot Noir made at all in that particular vintage. As a result of this method of marketing their wines, the Inglenook people can always be sure that the bottles that carry their label are of outstanding quality. This is a great benefit to the consumer, since he need have no concern about the various vintage years, knowing that the wines are good if they are on sale under the Inglenook label in the first place. The following wines, all estate-bottled, are made at Inglenook:

RED

Cabernet Sauvignon
Pinot Noir
Red Pinot
Gamay
Charbono

PINK

Navalle Rosé (made from Gamay grapes)

WHITE

Pinot Chardonnay
Traminer
White Pinot
Riesling (actually a Sylvaner)
Semillon (semisweet)
Navalle White Wine

The oldest wine estate in the Napa Valley is the Charles Krug Winery at St. Helena. (There is no connection, by the way, between this firm and the Krug Champagne firm in France.) Charles Krug came to California from Germany in 1852, and after trying his hand at panning gold he turned his attention to winegrowing. He purchased his first vineyard in 1858, and in the autumn of that year made the first commercial wine ever made in the Napa Valley. By the 1860's his wines, all made from European cuttings, had become so good that he was soon made a state viticultural commissioner.

When Charles Krug died in 1894, his estate was sold to a friend, James K. Moffitt. The Moffitt family finally sold the estate in 1943 to the Mondavi family, on the strict condition that the former high reputation of the Krug wines would be maintained, or rather restored, since the years of Prohibition had seen no wine production at all. The sons of the original purchaser, Cesare Mondavi, who died in 1959, now manage the Krug Winery. Robert Mondavi is the business manager of the winery, and his brother Peter is the cellar master. Both, however, are Stanford graduates and have had additional study in viticulture at the University of California. The present high quality of the Krug wines is ample proof of the knowledge and experience of the Mondavi brothers, and anyone who might be inclined to think that the Krug Winery is a Johnny-come-lately type of operation could not be more mistaken. The Krug wines are aged in wooden casks, just as in Europe, and then bottled when they are considered to be properly developed. If the wines are not immediately bottled when they are ready they are stored in glass-lined tanks after their aging in wood has been completed. This method enables the cellar master to remove the wine from the wood at exactly the right point in its development. The additional storage in the glass-lined tanks is for all practical purposes the same as storage in bottles, but is more convenient for the wine maker than having many thousands of bottles to handle and store in his winery. In addition to the excellent varietal wines produced at the Charles Krug Winery, there are also several fine generic wines—that is, wines called simply "claret," "Burgundy," and so on. Here is the full list of the Charles Krug varietal wines, all made entirely from the variety of grape named on the label:

RED

Cabernet Sauvignon
Gamay
Pinot Noir
Mountain Zinfandel

PINK

Vin Rosé (made almost entirely from Gamay grapes, but sometimes has some Grenache added)

WHITE

White Pinot
Chénin Blanc (slightly sweet, rather like a German *Spätlese*)
Grey Riesling
Johannisberg Riesling
Sylvaner
Sauvignon Blanc (sweet)
Dry Semillon (has a small percentage of Sauvignon Blanc added)

Probably the Krug *Chénin Blanc* is the most popular of all their wines and many other California producers are now going into large-scale production of this wine too, though it will be many years before they can overtake the Krug Chénin Blanc in quality, if they ever do at all. Distinguished by a very slight sweetness, the Chénin Blanc is an outstanding wine in every respect. It is the ideal wine for people who "talk dry" but "drink sweet." Those who enjoy some of the good Loire wines from France, or the German *Spätlese*-type wines will certainly enjoy the Krug Chénin Blanc.

Our final Napa Valley producer is the winery of Louis M. Martini, also at St. Helena. Long considered to be one of the very finest producers of California varietal wines, the Martini winery was founded in 1906. The present Martini estate is made up of three separate vineyards, each one planted with choice varietal grapes of the types that will do best in the soil of that particular vineyard. The *Cabernet Sauvignon* is certainly the greatest of the Martini red wines, just as it is at Beaulieu and Inglenook. Those fortunate enough to live in California, and able to order directly from the winery, may obtain choice wines of older vintages which are not often available in other states. The regular Martini wines are of course excellent in every way, and the wine drinker with adequate storage space can lay away his own supply of these wines from current vintages, just as he would with any other fine wines.

For everyday drinking, where good, sound, yet inexpensive wines are wanted, the *Martini Mountain White Wine* and *Mountain Red Wine* are both excellent. These are superior table wines, properly aged, and of very pleasant character. Far superior to any of the 97 cents or $1.29 imported wines which are so readily available in the stores, the Martini Mountain wines are well worth keeping on hand for daily use. In addition to the regular bottle size, these wines are also available in half-gallon and gallon jugs, making them convenient for large parties, picnics, and the like.

The following are the leading Martini varietal wines:

RED

Cabernet Sauvignon
and
Cabernet Sauvignon Special Selection (made in outstanding years only)
Mountain Barbera
Mountain Zinfandel
Mountain Pinot Noir

WHITE

Johannisberg Riesling
Mountain Gewürztraminer
Mountain Sylvaner
Mountain Folle Blanche
Mountain Dry Semillon
Dry Chenin Blanc

PINK

Napa Gamay Rosé

The wines listed above as "mountain" wines are grown in Martini's Monte Rosso Vineyard, over one thousand feet up in the Mayacamas Mountains, where the volcanic soil and the cool climate combine to produce fine quality wines of several different types. If the Cabernet Sauvignon is the finest red wine of the Monte Rosso Vineyard, the *Folle Blanche* is certainly one of the finest whites. It is a crisp, dry, delicate wine which goes well with seafood and any such dishes where one might otherwise serve a Chablis-type wine. Another worthwhile wine coming from this vineyard is the *Zinfandel*. This can be a real value for anyone able to store the wine properly for a few years, since it improves a great deal with bottle aging. A light, fruity wine when young, and costing only $1.80 a bottle, it matures into a delightful medium-bodied wine with five or six years of additional aging.

South of San Francisco, at Livermore, in Alameda County, we have one of the finest producers of white wines in the entire United States. This is the Wente Brothers winery, founded in 1883. It is interesting to note that the founder of the Wente estate, Carl H. Wente, who came to the United States from Germany in 1880, learned most of the wine-making art from Charles Krug, up in the Napa Valley. His son, Ernest Wente, and his grandson, Karl L. Wente, now manage the winery, which has been considerably enlarged since Carl Wente bought his first fifty acres of vineyards in 1883. Because the soil at Livermore is quite gravelly, very much like the Graves district of Bordeaux, the Wentes concentrated mainly on the famous grape varieties of that region, the Semillon and the Sauvignon Blanc. Other varieties were added later, but the *Wente Sauvignon Blanc* still remains their finest wine. A few acres have been planted with red wine grapes, the Gamay and Pinot Noir, and there is now an excellent *Wente Vin Rosé* available, too, together with a small amount of the two Wente red wines. Here is the full list of the Wente wines currently available:

Dry Semillon	Pinot Blanc
Haut Semillon (sweeter)	Chablis
Sauvignon Blanc	Pinot Noir
Grey Riesling	Gamay Beaujolais
Pinot Chardonnay	Vin Rosé

The *Grey Riesling* is the best known of the Wente wines and is not as expensive as the Sauvignon Blanc, which costs around $2.50 a bottle. The Grey Riesling is not the German Riesling grape, which is always sold as Johannisberg or White Riesling, but rather a French grape called the Chauché Gris. The name Grey Riesling is certainly much easier to pronounce and to remember, but it is unfortunate that it causes confusion with the true Riesling grape from Germany. The Wente Grey Riesling is a very pleasant table wine, light and dry, but not really a great wine like the Semillons or Sauvignon Blanc.

Most of the Wente red grape varieties are planted in new vineyards in the Arroyo Seco Canyon, only about fifteen miles from the Pacific Ocean. Additional white wine acreage is laid out there, too, but thanks to an almost ideal climate with warm days and cool nights, the Pinot Noir and the Gamay Beaujolais are yielding such fine wines that they will soon make Wente as admired for red wines as they now are for white.

In addition to the vineyards that we have discussed here in some detail, there are also many fine wineries in California which operate on a smaller scale so that their wines are not always so easy to obtain. Those who live in the West often have the opportunity to take a trip through the vineyard country and visit their favorite estates, where they can purchase some of the wines which they particularly like. We are listing five other vineyards here, therefore, which are well worth remembering and whose wines are among the very finest in California. Most of them were started as a labor of love by wealthy businessmen who wanted to try their hand at making wines of their own in small quantities. No expense has been spared by these owners in their attempts to make the very finest quality wines. Here, then, are five small gems of vineyards and the wines in which they specialize:

Hallcrest Vineyard, near Felton in Santa Cruz County, south of San Francisco via U. S. route 101. This vineyard is owned by Chaffee E. Hall, a San Francisco attorney. Only two wines are produced: *Cabernet Sauvignon* and *Johannisberg Riesling.* Though the vineyard has only been producing since 1946, the wines are already of outstanding quality and will no doubt improve even more in the coming years.

Hanzell Vineyards, near Sonoma, north of San Francisco. The late James D. Zellerbach, former U. S. Ambassador to Italy, was the owner of this vineyard that also produced only two wines, in this case *Pinot Noir* and *Pinot Chardonnay.* Since Mr. Zellerbach was a "Burgundy man," he devoted all his attention to these two classic Burgundian grape varieties. The first wines were made in 1956, but with his death in 1963, Mr. Zellerbach's attempt to produce a really great *Pinot Noir* will be left unfinished.

Martin Ray, near Saratoga in Santa Clara County, south of San Francisco. A successful stockbroker who turned to wine making in 1936, Martin Ray produces what are undoubtedly some of the very finest wines being made in the United States today. These are wines that rank with many of the finest European growths, and though the prices for the table wines are around $4 and $5 a bottle, and $10 a bottle for the champagne, the wines are certainly worth it. Mr. Ray spares no expense in his efforts to make absolutely the finest wines possible, and the vintages that are not up to his exacting standards are disposed of to other growers. Since quality is the only thing that interests Mr. Ray in his wine making, no attempt is made to advertise these wines or to make them popular. Fortunately, however, they are available in New York City at the shop of M. Lehmann & Company, so that distribution is not restricted entirely to California. Mr. Ray grows three varietal grapes: *Cabernet Sauvignon* and *Pinot Noir* for his reds, and *Pinot Chardonnay* for his white. Various vintages of these wines sell at different prices and often carry special names. Since these designations change from time to time, there would be no point in listing them here. Suffice it to say that they are all outstanding.

Mayacamas Vineyards, about halfway between Napa and St. Helena, north of San Francisco. Owned by Jack F. M. Taylor, probably the only Englishman growing wine in California, the Mayacamas Vineyards produce two varietal white wines and three rosés. The Taylors specialize in making an outstanding *Pinot Chardonnay,* and also produce a *Chénin Blanc* as their other white wine. The rosé wines are *Cabernet, Gamay,* and *Zinfandel.* Some ordinary table wines are also produced, but these are sold under a different label and not as Mayacamas wines. The Taylors have been making wines since 1941, so of course their vineyards are well developed by this time and fully mature. The vineyard "went public" in 1958, when it became a corporation with the intent of increasing wine production to about double what it had been up until then.

Souverain Cellars, at St. Helena, north of San Francisco. Owned by J. Leland Stewart, the Souverain estate produces mainly *Cabernet Sauvignon, Zinfandel,* and *Grenache Rosé.* Mr. Stewart has a close working agreement with a couple of other near-by growers and obtains grapes from them for wines which are then made at the Souverain Cellars winery. There are four white wines available under the Souverain label, as well as the reds that we have already mentioned. The specialty among the whites is the *Green Hungarian,* and the other three are the *Johannisberg Riesling,* the *Sylvaner,* and the *Chénin Blanc.*

Since the names of the various varietal grapes used in California are not familiar to the majority of readers, we are listing here the most often encountered types, together with their European origin. In this way you will be able to see from a quick glance at this table that the Pinot Noir, for example, is a Burgundy-type wine.

GRAPE NAMES AS USED ON CALIFORNIA LABELS	EUROPEAN VINEYARD REGIONS WHERE THESE GRAPES ORIGINATE
Cabernet Sauvignon	Bordeaux (for red wines—claret)
Pinot Noir	Burgundy (for red wines)
Grenache (always a rosé)	the Tavel region of Southern France
Zinfandel	no exact counterpart in Europe
Gamay (often a rosé wine)	Beaujolais region of France
Johannisberg Riesling	the Rhine and Moselle in Germany
Gewürztraminer	the Palatinate in Germany and Alsace in France
Sylvaner	all parts of Germany and in Alsace
Pinot Chardonnay	Burgundy (for white wines) and Champagne

GRAPE NAMES AS USED ON CALIFORNIA LABELS	EUROPEAN VINEYARD REGIONS WHERE THESE GRAPES ORIGINATE
Pinot Blanc	Burgundy (for white wines)
Semillon	Bordeaux (for white wines)
Sauvignon Blanc	Bordeaux (for white wines)
Chénin Blanc	the Loire Valley in France
Folle Blanche	the Cognac district in France
Traminer	the Palatinate in Germany and Alsace in France

Try to remember the names of the varietal wines in which you are particularly interested and you will soon find your wine buying much easier when shopping for the fine California wines. After a little experience in using these names they will be perfectly easy to understand and a tremendous aid in finding exactly the type of wine you want for any particular occasion. In addition to the varietal wines, keep in mind as well the less expensive, everyday wines such as Louis Martini mountain wines, the Krug "Napa Vista" wines, and also the Buena Vista or Martini Zinfandel as substitutes for some of the fraudulent Beaujolais which seem to be flooding the United States right now. Any wine drinker who is limited in the amount he can afford to spend on his wine cellar should certainly lose no time in getting thoroughly acquainted with the top-quality wines of California. Even those, however, who can afford a $5 bottle of wine every day will find that there are still some California wines of interest to them. The amateur wine snobs who buy only imported wines will no doubt continue to buy the $1.49 French and German wines of dubious origin, but, to those who are sincerely interested in finding quality wines at reasonable prices, the wines of California certainly have far more to offer.

VIII

Buying and Storing Wine

EVEN THOUGH the United States imports large quantities of fine European wines every year, it is not always easy to find such wines in all parts of the country. New York and San Francisco are our two biggest wine-drinking centers, but they cannot be regarded as typical, since there is a considerable foreign-born population in New York City to raise the per capita consumption there, and in San Francisco far more of the local wines are consumed than European, which is of course to be expected. The greatest drawback to finding good wines in the United States today is the lack of first-class retail shops around the country. Many states must be written off altogether, since their laws forbid the sale of wines except in state-owned and state-operated stores. These so-called "monopoly" states carry very limited selections of fine wines, if indeed they have any at all, and the sales personnel are not usually allowed to make recommendations or to suggest specific wines to the customers. Every state has restrictions of one sort or another and it is forbidden just about everywhere to transport wine or other alcoholic beverages across state lines—just as though each state were a separate country. In those states where there are privately owned retail shops, the lack of qualified salesmen to staff them is almost as much of a problem for their owners as the various state and federal regulations with which they have to comply. It is unfortunate that there is such a gap between producer and consumer because of all this, but the selling of wine has never been considered a profession in this country as it is in England. In the United States a "job in a liquor store" is just that, and any knowledge of wines the salesmen may have is usually culled from the various pamphlets and booklets that the importers distribute, or from talking to the importers' representatives when they make their rounds from store to store. Whereas in Great Britain, because of its proximity to the continent, most wine merchants and salesmen have visited the leading vineyards of Europe and have acquired a first-hand knowledge of wines, most of their American counterparts could hardly care less about wines and would much prefer a good highball anyway. In some of the top-notch stores the owners have gone to considerable trouble to train their men in the proper appreciation of wines, but, when there is no real interest in the subject on the part of those being trained, this knowledge can at best be merely superficial. Do not, therefore, expect the salesman in your local liquor store to know all about wines and to be able to discuss their merits with you to any considerable extent. He is much more interested in getting you to take one or two of the wines with which his shop happens to be overstocked, or on which he may be making a little commission himself, than he is in finding out about your likes and dislikes. He will assure you that the $1.29 "special" is really worth much more and that you would indeed be wise to buy a case while there is still some of it left. There are, of course, many stores around the country where there is a serious attempt made to sell good wines and to give the customer value for his money. We are listing a few of them here, though unfortunately the list does not cover the entire United States for one reason or another. Either no quality stores were known to us in a particular area or else there was state-monopoly operation only. Here, then, is a list of about a dozen cities where there are quality wineshops or liquor stores with outstanding wine departments:

Atlantic City, New Jersey: Caldwell's Liquor Store, 3301 Atlantic Avenue

Boston, Massachusetts: Berenson Liquor Mart, 70 Summer Street

Chicago, Illinois: Armanetti's, 7324 North Western Avenue

Clayton, Missouri: European Import Co., 23 North Bemiston Avenue

Dallas, Texas: Centennial Liquor Stores—several branches

Denver, Colorado: Hoffman's Liquors, 1801 Glenarm Street

Kansas City, Missouri: Berbiglia's, 208 Westport Road

Milwaukee, Wisconsin: Keller's Beverage Center, 509 West Center Street

Minneapolis, Minnesota: Haskell's Liquors, 23 South 7th Street

New Orleans, Louisiana: Martin Wine Cellar, 3827 Baronne Street

New York, N.Y.: Luria's Wine & Spirits, 1217 Madison Avenue; Sherry-Lehmann, 679 Madison Avenue

Shreveport, Louisiana: Cuban Liquor Co., 1149 Texas Avenue

Southern California area: The Jurgensen stores are found in several cities and can be highly recommended.

Many people who live in the "monopoly" states do not realize that their state liquor control boards will often issue them a permit to "import" a few cases of wine from another state. Or, barring this, they are often willing to order wine from the importers at the customer's special request and on the payment of a deposit. Though we cannot begin to list all importers of fine wines, there are several whom we should call to your attention here as being particularly worthy of note. If you know that a particular wine is imported by one of these firms, they will be glad to advise you as to how you go about getting it in your own state.

On the West Coast, the leading importer is Henry J. Vandervoort & Co., 10 Lombard Street, San Francisco 11, California.

In New York City there are:

Dreyfus-Ashby & Co., 350 Fifth Avenue, New York 1, New York (Importers of Comte de Vogüë Burgundies, among others)

Kobrand Corporation, 134 East 40th Street, New York 16, New York (Louis Jadot Burgundies, fine German wines, and Taittinger Champagne)

Seggerman Slocum, Inc., 35-02 Northern Boulevard, Long Island City 1, New York (This firm handles the wines selected by Alexis Lichine, the Krug Champagnes, and excellent German wines)

Frank Schoonmaker, Inc., 14 East 69th Street, New York 21, New York (For any wine sold as a "Frank Schoonmaker Selection")

Frederick Wildman & Sons, 21 East 69th Street, New York 21, New York (Exclusive representation of the Romanée-Conti Domaine in Burgundy)

All of the above-listed concerns import wines of the very highest quality, as well as some medium-priced ones. They of course have no dealings with fly-by-night operators, nor will you find any of the bargain-priced wines on their lists. The best stores around the country all carry wines from these importers, since they are among the main sources of supply for top-quality wines in the United States.

Do not expect to get fine wines at bargain prices. It is impossible, for example, to get a real Beaujolais wine of any quality for much under $2 or $2.50, as we have mentioned in our discussion of those wines. If a store is featuring a selection of wines for 97 cents or $1.29, you should not expect them to be much more than just drinkable, if they are that. Always remember that the duty and import costs are the same for a dollar bottle of wine as they are for a ten-dollar bottle, so that you are getting proportionately less value for your money when you buy the cheaper bottle than when you buy the expensive bottle.

Do not buy pretty labels, but rather examine the label closely to see exactly what the wine is, who bottled it, and whether it is really worth the price being asked for it. Avoid buying white wines or Burgundies that are too old. Sometimes a store will mark down such wines for a quick clearance, but this does not mean that you have to take advantage of the bargain. Most white wines begin to lose their freshness after about five years or so and there is no reason to buy them any older than this. Rosé wines should only be a year or two old at the most. Burgundy much older than ten years will often start to lose in quality, but Bordeaux wines may be much older and still be magnificent. Such bottles rarely are offered for sale, however, and, when they are, the buyer must be quite sure about what he is getting. If the wine was not of a great year to begin with, no amount of aging is going to improve it.

Any serious wine lover should give some attention to laying down a supply of good wines in a suitable storage place, and not just buy a bottle or two as he needs them. There is usually a 10 per cent saving in buying wines by the case—either twelve regular bottles, or twenty-four half bottles—and one then has the assurance that there is always a supply of wine on hand when it is wanted. A basement that is reasonably cool or a cellar storage space of any kind where the temperature does not go much below 40 degrees or much above 70 degrees is just about ideal. It should be dark, neither too damp nor too dry, away from vibrations of any kind, and fairly well ventilated so that it does not become dank or musty. Those who live in city apartments will rarely have access to such cellars and must usually be content with storing a case or two of assorted wines in a closet. It is now possible to buy wine racks in many stores which will hold anywhere from twelve to sixty bottles. The rack can be placed in the back of a closet, or stored in any convenient place away from the heat and light. The twelve-bottle racks can often be built up, one on top of the other, as your wine collection grows. One should not store much more than a six-month supply of wine in an apartment, however, since temperatures are never as low as in a regular cellar.

Keeping a "cellar book" or a record of the wines you buy and drink can be a very practical as well as interesting hobby. One of the easiest ways to do it is to buy a good-sized scrapbook and paste in the labels from the bottles after you have soaked them off. Write your comments and the price you paid underneath, and you will have a very accurate record of how much you spend and what you drink over the course of the years. Saving the label is also handy if you want to reorder a wine, since often we tend to forget names of shippers or growers, or even the name of a château or estate if it is new to us and in an unfamiliar language. Do not expect to be able to obtain the same vintage of a particular wine three or four years after you first bought it! If you like a wine when you first taste it, and feel that you can afford to stock up on a supply of it, buy a case or two then and there, but don't expect your wine merchant to still have it in his shop two or three years later! Prices are always at their lowest when the wines are just put on the market and before they have developed enough to be ready for drinking. Those who can afford to lay down a stock of wines and have the proper facilities for long-term storage are thus able to save considerable money, while at the same time building up a fine collection of wines for future enjoyment. This is particularly true of the red Bordeaux wines, and to some extent of the red Burgundies, too. Those who bought the great 1959 vintage when orders were first being taken in advance of delivery were not surprised to see the prices almost double for many of the wines within about a year's time. This was an exception, to be sure, and wine prices do not ordinarily increase so much in so short a time, but the trend is always upwards in the case of really fine wines since the demand is greater than the supply.

When a particularly fine vintage is announced in the press and by wine merchants, there are always a few wine drinkers who rush to their local shops and want to begin drinking it at once. Some people actually think that wines are ready to drink a week or two after the grapes have been pressed! All the major wineshops had this experience in the fall and winter of 1959 and 1960, when many of their customers asked for the 1959 wines, which they had been reading so much about, even while these wines were still fermenting in the casks in France and Germany. Such a complete lack of knowledge about wines and wine making is not unusual in this country, needless to say, but even wine drinkers of some experience tend to drink up the great vintages much too soon. The fine Bordeaux wines of 1952 and 1953 were just about coming into their own in 1961 and 1962, yet they had all but disappeared from the market. Many shops are now selling the 1961 vintage Bordeaux, which will probably be drunk up before it is ready too. It seems that most Americans simply do not have any interest in laying away wines for proper development, even when they lack the excuse that they haven't a proper wine cellar.

An entire lifetime is not really enough to learn about wine, but the words "connoisseur" and "expert" are bandied about so easily that just about anyone who can pronounce the words on the wine label is considered to be an authority. A similar situation exists with eating, where just about anyone who likes good food is now considered to be a gourmet. As far as wines are concerned, we think it would be more to the point to refer to a person who likes wine, and knows a little about it, as a "wine lover" or even "wine amateur." Let us leave the terms connoisseur and expert to people like Frank Schoonmaker or Henry Vandervoort, with whom wine is a full-time occupation and not just a hobby or a sideline.

The fact that we are not all connoisseurs or experts, however, does not mean that we cannot enjoy talking about wine, sampling wine, and generally enjoying wine as often as possible. Wine lovers often get together for informal wine tastings of their own, either for the purpose of deciding what particular wines they want to buy for their own cellars, or simply for the pleasure in trying several different wines against each other. Such comparative tastings of wines can be very helpful in increasing one's ability to distinguish between two different wines from the same vineyard area, or even from different wine-growing areas altogether if one is in the beginning stages of wine drinking. By the time you are fairly well along in your wine-drinking career you should certainly be able to tell Burgundy from Bordeaux, or Rhine wine from Moselle wine, for example. The most important thing of all, however, is to be able to tell good wine from bad wine. To know where a wine comes from one need only look at the label on the bottle, but to know whether the wine is good or not requires actual tasting and is not something that can be determined just by looking at the label or holding the bottle up to the light.

If you organize a wine tasting for a group of friends, try not to have too many wines, but concentrate on just three or four of a similar type. There is nothing to be gained by trying a Moselle wine against a Burgundy, or a Bordeaux against a sherry, but you *will* learn a lot if you try three or four Bordeaux wines against each other, each one from a different township, for example, though all from the same vintage. Another interesting variation is to try the same wine in different vintages if you can find them at your local wine shop. Don't let the tasting develop into a general mix-up, but rather see that each glass has some means of identification on it—a number or a letter—that corresponds to the same number or letter which you have marked on the bottle. Serve bread or rolls, perhaps with cheese, so that everyone can neutralize his palate between samplings. Strong-tasting or highly seasoned foods should be avoided when one is trying to sample wines.

As far as the proper glasses for serving wine are concerned, the most important thing to remember is that they should always be large enough to give everyone a reasonable portion of wine without filling the glass to the brim. In the usual matched set of crystal which most brides get as wedding presents, the water goblets are about the right size for red wines, and the claret glass may be about right for white wines. The other sizes are usually not much good for wines at all. The finest wineglasses are generally acknowledged to be those made by the firm of Baccarat in France. They are very expensive, however, especially when sold in this country. The average price for a regular wineglass is around $5, with some of the large Burgundy glasses running as high as $10. There are other wineglasses, however, that are considerably less expensive, and in addition to those imported from Europe, there is an excellent series designed by Frank Schoonmaker that is available in many shops around the country. These glasses retail at about $1.50 each and there is one for each type of wine as well as an

Illustrated above are the glasses generally used for various kinds of wine. (A smaller size of the red wine glass is used for white wines.) Although the finest glasses are undoubtedly those made by the French firm of Baccarat, it is possible to buy American versions of many of these glasses for considerably less. The main thing to bear in mind is that wineglasses should be large enough to hold a reasonable quantity of wine even when only half full. They never should be filled to the brim. Colored glasses, no matter how fine in quality, never should be used for wines.

all-purpose glass for those who would rather not bother with different glasses for different wines.

A well-designed wineglass curves in toward the top and not outward in a V-shape as so many domestic wineglasses do. There is a typical glass for red Bordeaux wines (claret), a smaller version for the white Bordeaux wines, and a different-shaped glass, lower and wider, for Burgundy. Glasses for German wines have a longer stem and a smaller bowl, while those for Champagne are best when tulip-shaped. The wide, saucer-style, or *coupé* Champagne glass, customarily sold as a part of matched sets in this country, should be avoided whenever possible. It offers too much surface of the wine to the air and the Champagne gets flat that much quicker. If only our American glassmakers could be persuaded to stop making these glasses and to switch to the tulip shape instead! Sherry wine is best served in the chimney-style glass with a short stem, much like a brandy glass. Port wine should be served in a regular wineglass about the size used for the white Bordeaux wines, and not in a tiny cordial glass that only holds an ounce or two. Many people like to have the large brandy snifters for their after-dinner Cognac, but a regular brandy glass will serve the purpose just as well. Colored glasses, no matter what shape or how expensive, should never be used for serving wine. Likewise, plain, unadorned glasses are much to be preferred to ornate cut glasses. The design, or rather lack of design, on a glass has nothing to do with its quality. Many of the finest Baccarat glasses are completely plain, yet they are by no means cheap.

IX

Serving Wine

THE PROPER SERVING of a bottle of wine is no more complicated than the proper serving of lunch or dinner. Degrees of formality vary, of course, just as they do with meals, and the service of wine can range from the cheapest domestic wine poured from gallon jugs into water tumblers at the kitchen table, up to the rarest vintages served by a *sommelier* and drunk from Baccarat crystal at an elegant and formal dinner. There are times and places when we would just as soon have the gallon jug and the waterglasses as the more elaborate service by a wine steward. On the other hand, it should not be considered snobbish or affected to serve three kinds of wine at dinner if one is able to afford the necessary expenditure and is interested enough in wines to go to the trouble of arranging a meal to compliment them. For most of us, however, the everyday enjoyment of wine lies somewhere between the two extremes of utter simplicity and elaborate service, and the average wine-drinking American is usually content to serve just one wine at dinner, or perhaps two if there are guests and something special is planned.

Let us say at the outset that the service of any wine

should be as unobtrusive as possible and that one should not try to make a production out of it. If wine is ever to be accepted as an everyday part of our lives it has to be treated in an everyday manner—not in a careless manner to be sure, but certainly without any pretensions or affectation. The more common the wine, the more important this is, since nothing could be more ludicrous than to go through an involved and complicated wine-opening ritual for a dollar bottle of ordinary wine. If a group of serious wine lovers are tasting a rare or unusual vintage it is quite another matter, but in the everyday use of wine in the home the less pretense the better. A certain amount of care and attention to what one is doing is necessary, no matter how cheap or how expensive the wine, since no one wants bits of cork in his glass, or the sediment from the bottom of the bottle, but this is no more difficult to see to than preventing tea leaves from getting in the teacup or coffee grounds in the morning cup of coffee.

The most important piece of equipment for any wine lover to have is a decent corkscrew, yet how often we see the host struggling with a small, ineffective corkscrew attached to a can opener! Whether you are drinking 98-cent-a-bottle wine or $8-a-bottle wine there is absolutely no excuse for not opening the bottle properly. A first-rate corkscrew costs about $2.50 and can be obtained in any specialty shop and even in wineshops in some states. The straight corkscrew that is often a part of expensive and elaborate bar-equipment sets is the worst kind of all to use and should be avoided. Not only does it depend on brute force to get the cork out, but it can also be dangerous if the neck of the bottle should ever break or splinter—something which rarely happens, but is a possibility nevertheless. The better corkscrews all remove the cork by leverage and are perfectly easy and uncomplicated to operate. Most of them are imported from Europe (where the importance of a good corkscrew is well understood) and they give long and satisfactory service If the cork in the bottle is dried out or rotten it is very apt to crumble no matter what type corkscrew is used, and in such cases the only solution is to strain the wine through cheesecloth after the cork has been removed in the best way possible.

To open a bottle of Champagne, where no corkscrew is required, may be a difficult task for those who have not had much experience with Champagne-type corks. The main point to bear in mind is that the bottle should be opened gently, and not with the loud bang which so many people love to hear. The more you pop the Champagne cork, the more gas from the bottle will escape into the air and your Champagne will get flat. After removing the foil and the wire covering over the cork, the bottle should be held firmly in one hand while the cork is gently twisted out with the other. It is better to hold the bottle at a slight angle rather than straight up in order to prevent the wine from bubbling over. If the bottle is handled gently and the Champagne is properly chilled, it should *not* foam up when the cork is removed. If there has been a considerable struggle to open the bottle and the wine has been badly shaken up, then the worst may be expected and one should have the towel handy!

Most Port and Sherry wine bottles now have a replaceable cork for which no corkscrew is required. These corks, though not ideal for long storage of the wine, do have the advantage of making it easy to reclose the bottle after it has first been opened. We feel, however, that such wines should be decanted anyway, making this type of cork unnecessary, but until that distant time when every wine drinker has a decanter at hand, such corks will no doubt continue to be used. Fine wines intended for long storage, such as Vintage Port, will always have regular corks of particularly fine quality and they are often covered with sealing wax as well.

The top of the bottle should always be wiped clean after the foil or other covering over the cork has been removed. Use a damp cloth and wipe carefully around the top of the cork before inserting the corkscrew. After the cork has been removed, the top of the bottle should be wiped clean once again, but very carefully so as not to wipe any particles of cork or dirt into the wine. Be careful too not to use a soaking wet cloth that drips water into the wine. Usually a damp paper towel is the easiest thing to use and saves unnecessary soiling of good kitchen towels.

If the whole operation of opening the wine can be performed in the kitchen before dinner guests arrive, there will be much less danger of a last-minute fiasco and the wine can then be served easily and calmly when everyone is seated at table. Even when a servant is present, it is always better for the host to serve the wine himself unless the meal is a formal one where this would be out of place. Bear in mind, when pouring, that wine is always served from the right, and not from the left as is the custom with food. This is obviously a much more convenient side than from the left, since the wine glasses are always placed at the right of the person using them, and to serve the wine from the left would involve reaching across in front of those seated at the table—awkward to say the least.

It is customary for the host to always pour a little of the wine in his own glass first, not only to taste it to see if it is good, but also—and more important—to catch any stray little pieces of cork in his glass before serving the wine to his guests. Though this very necessary operation can be made into quite a ritual by a real wine snob, it is much better, and also more enjoyable for the host's later enjoyment of the wine, if the sampling is first done in the kitchen when the wine is opened. After all, no one enjoys drinking wine with little pieces of cork floating around in it, and there is no reason why the host should be made to suffer this fate any more than his guests. If one is willing to sacrifice a little of the ritual and be practical about the whole thing, an extra glass in the kitchen for sampling will make the later service of the wine at the table more enjoyable for the host who certainly has as much right to enjoy his own wine as his guests have. For those who still feel that they would like to go through the sampling performance at the table in front of their guests, the entire operation can be repeated later, but there will then be no danger of the host getting any little particles of cork in his glass.

It is not necessary to be a first-class wine expert to tell whether a wine is bad or not when you open the bottle. The smell and taste—usually sour or musty—are obvious at once to even the most inexperienced wine drinker. For someone who has been drinking only sweet domestic ports and muscatels, his first bottle of good table wine may seem to be "sour," whereas it is actually just a pleasantly dry wine. This is simply a matter of acquiring a taste for dry wines, and a little experience in sampling various kinds is the only sure way to avoid a mistake in the beginning stages of wine drinking. In actual practice one very seldom encounters a bad bottle of wine, and there is no need to be too concerned about the problem. A quick look at the cork before opening the bottle is often enough to tell whether a bottle will be bad or not. If the cork has shrunk away from the sides of the bottle, or if it pushes into the bottle when you insert the corkscrew, then chances are that the cork has dried out and that the wine may be bad. One precaution is simply to avoid buying wines at close-out or bargain sales of any kind, particularly white wines of older vintage such as 1953, or even 1959 in many cases. When buying imported wines there is more danger of getting a poor or defective bottle among the lower-priced wines than among the great, classic wines of France and Germany. The cheap wines are usually closed with small, second-rate corks which aren't meant to last too long, and they may soon shrink or dry out and let the wine spoil. This is especially true of many of the so-called Chianti wines from Italy, which sell for 97 cents or $1.29 in most wineshops. Because of the shape of the straw-covered bottles, these wines are usually stored in an upright position rather than on their sides like regular wine bottles, and the corks dry out that much faster. We hesitate to think how much spoiled or really sour wine has been sold in this country as Italian Chianti to people who are unaware of what Chianti really tastes like!

Rosé wines, too, are often kept far too long in wineshops so that they lose all their freshness and fruitiness—their two greatest attributes. One should definitely avoid any rosé wine more than a year or two old, and for those who have access to a good wineshop doing a considerable amount of business in California wines—where there is rapid turnover of stock, that is —it would certainly be more sensible to buy a good California rosé from a producer such as Wente, Charles Krug, or Beaulieu, than to buy imported rosé wines left over from the 1958 or 1959 vintages. Remember that rosé wines are never really great wines, so there is little to be gained by buying an imported rosé when our own California rosés are just as good and often much better.

The use of a wine basket to hold the bottle at the dinner table is a custom which many people enjoy, even though the basic purpose of the basket is completely misunderstood. The wicker wine baskets which all gourmet shops sell, and which many wine lovers feel they simply must have if they are to be considered true wine connoisseurs by their friends, were originally intended to transport a bottle of wine in a horizontal position from the wine cellar to the kitchen, where the wine would then be opened and *decanted*. The older and more venerable the bottle, the more important this kind of handling was thought to be. Indeed, one of the best wine merchants in London opens the Vintage Port for his customers right in his cellars where the bottles have been stored, and thus avoids any shaking or unnecessary movement of the bottles. After the wine has been decanted into new bottles it is shipped to the customer, together with the empty bottles from which it was poured if the customer so requests. Such a practice would be impossible in the United States, since most states forbid open bottles in any stores selling wines and liquors. In serving young red wines or any white wine, a basket can do no harm, but red wines which have aged for some years and consequently have a certain amount of sediment in them should be decanted all at one time and not put in baskets to be tilted up and laid down again each time a glass of wine is poured. If you are serving your wine directly from the bottle you will find it much better to stand the bottle up for a few hours before opening it, and to keep it in this position on the table when the wine is not being poured. Any sediment thus has a chance to collect in the bottom of the bottle, and you are much less likely to get any of it in your glass than if you lay the bottle on its side in a basket. In addition to the straw baskets for bottles, there are also metal holders on the market which are meant to serve the same purpose. Many hostesses find these holders, which are usually made of brass or silverplate, to be attractive table ornaments, but most people will find that it is easier to pour wine when one has a firm grip on the bottle than when it is in such a holder. Such gadgets as baskets and holders can do no harm, of course, except in the case of well-aged red wines, as we have mentioned, and if some people feel that it gives more "atmosphere" to their wine drinking we should probably not find fault with their use.

Next to the corkscrew itself, the most useful extra that the wine drinker can have is a good decanter. Many of the Victorian cut-glass monstrosities that are still around would be enough to turn anyone against all decanters, particularly in a home with modern furnishings. There are many beautiful ones available, however, which are quite modern in every respect. Foremost are the Baccarat designs, which sell for around $15. There are also many lovely designs in the famous makes of Swedish glassware such as Orrefors and Kosta. Nothing could be more attractive on a modern dinner table than one of these beautiful decanters filled with a fine red wine. From a more practical point of view, however, the decanting of the wine eliminates the possibility of anyone's getting any of the sediment or cork particles in his glass. White wines and sparkling wines are never decanted since they do not ordinarily throw a deposit while they develop in the bottle. All fine red wines, as well as Sherry and Port, will develop sediment as they age, however, and should be decanted. Most of the cheap wines, both domestic and foreign, have usually been so filtered and refiltered that they won't require decanting. (These wines will not develop much in the bottle either and should be used fairly soon and not laid away.) Any of the fine Bordeaux or Burgundy wines will be better if decanted before serving, and with Vintage Port it is an absolute must.

To decant a bottle of wine is a perfectly simple

operation and does not require an English butler to perform it properly. Try to have a light behind the bottle of wine as you pour it, so that you can see when the sediment is beginning to come out with the wine and you can then immediately stop pouring. A safer way to decant is to pour the wine through a clean piece of cheesecloth that has been loosely stretched over a funnel. The cheesecloth will then catch any of the sediment or cork particles in the wine that you may not see. Many wine lovers have two or three decanters and keep one or two of them filled with Sherry, Port, or Madeira, while the other one is reserved for table wines.

Wine coolers were much more popular in the days before the modern refrigerator, and there are many beautiful examples in English silver from the early nineteenth century. Some of them are not too ornate to be easily adaptable to modern settings. More readily available, though, are the modern designs in teak, brass, and stainless steel, many of which double as ice buckets for cocktail party use. A wine cooler is usually not necessary for the enjoyment of a prechilled bottle of wine, though in the summertime it is often useful to have one for keeping white or rosé wines properly chilled. White wines and Champagnes will get cold in about a half hour when placed in the ice, and one should be careful not to overchill them when using a cooler. Very sweet wines, such as Sauternes or the German *Auslesen*, can be chilled somewhat longer, but dry table wines should never be left in the cooler until they are ice cold. Since most coolers are not tall enough to accommodate a full-sized bottle of wine, you can perfectly well turn unopened bottles upside down in the cooler without harming the wine, so that the top third of the bottle will be chilled too. If the wine has been prechilled, this will of course not be necessary, and after the first two glasses of wine have been served there is no longer any problem anyway. In chilling the wines in a refrigerator allow two or three hours for a bottle to attain the proper temperature—and never put wine in the freezer compartment!

The question of the proper temperatures at which various wines should be served is often much misunderstood in this country. The expression "room temperature" is usually the cause of all the trouble. This is simply because European homes are not heated to the same degree that is customary in the United States, nor do any of the authorities on the subject ever take into account that many wine drinkers in this country live in warm, sometimes almost subtropical, climates where the room temperature might well be 90 degrees at times. Fine red wines from Bordeaux should never be served at over 70 degrees, and this would apply equally, of course, to the Cabernet Sauvignon wines from California, since they are the same type. The heavier Burgundies should be a little cooler than this, say around 65 degrees, and in Burgundy itself many wine experts drink their wines at cellar temperature, which would be around 60 degrees. The famous Beaujolais wines are often drunk slightly chilled, also around 60 degrees. With our tendency toward overheated homes and apartments in the United States, there is usually more danger of a red wine being too warm than too cold. After all, a wine will soon warm up in the glass if it happens to be a little cool, but there is no way of cooling it once it has been served. (It is probably necessary to mention here that you should never put ice in a glass of wine unless it is the very commonest and cheapest sort!) If you have no real wine cellar and you feel that your red wines are a little too warm, the only solution is to put them in the refrigerator for a half hour before serving them.

This will not chill them but will merely bring them down from a temperature of perhaps 80 degrees to the more enjoyable 65 or 70 degrees. Do not store wines, by the way, where they are exposed to high temperatures for long periods of time.

Cooling white wines is rarely a problem, but it should be remembered that the sweeter the wine, the cooler it should be served. Dry table wines are at their best when well chilled but not ice cold, whereas a great Sauternes would be simply cloying in its sweetness if it were not served quite cold. Rosé wines and *brut* Champagne should be well chilled too, and the sweeter types of Champagne, such as extra-dry, can be served colder than the *brut*. A well-chilled wine should be understood to mean a temperature of around 50 to 55 degrees, and a cold wine would be in the low forties. If a wine is served too cold it will have no flavor left at all, and one might just as well drink ice water.

While Port is always served at room temperature—English baronial hall room temperature, that is, not New York apartment room temperature—Sherry is usually served chilled. Many people drink Sherry at room temperature too, but the dry types are more refreshing if served slightly chilled, and certainly the sweet Cream Sherries are much more enjoyable chilled than at room temperature.

Those who drink brandy after dinner will find that the warmth of their hands cupped around the bottom of the glass is quite sufficient to release the bouquet of a fine old Cognac. It is utter nonsense to buy a brandy warmer in order to "warm" the brandy over a flame. Such a gadget cannot be considered as anything more than an affectation and a rather silly one at that.

In estimating the quantities of wine needed for any given meal one must first know whether the people who are to drink the wine are merely going to sip at one glass during the entire meal, or if they are real wine drinkers. At a women's luncheon, for example, one bottle of wine probably would be sufficient to serve from six to eight persons. A regular-sized bottle can be considered as containing six to eight glasses of wine, depending on the size of the glasses used. A half-bottle, therefore, would yield three to four glasses and is often quite enough for the average couple having wine with their dinner. At more elaborate meals, where several different courses are being served, the wine consumption may be anywhere from a half-bottle to an entire bottle per person. If the meal is planned as a gourmet dinner with five or six courses and four or five kinds of wine, the average amount used might even reach two bottles per person without anyone becoming in the least bit intoxicated. Such a meal would stretch over a period of four or five hours, needless to say, and would be planned around the various wines being served. In more everyday situations, we should say that one bottle of wine will usually be sufficient for four persons at dinner. If all are serious wine drinkers two bottles will probably be necessary, since many people regularly drink a half-bottle of wine with their dinner and do not feel that this is in any way excessive.

Nothing could be more embarrassing than to run out of wine halfway through a meal when guests are present, and if you are unsure about how much you will need it is always best to have an extra (unopened) bottle in reserve so that it can be brought out if necessary. On the other hand, do not constantly fill the glass of someone who does not seem to be enjoying his wine. Many people will accept a glass of wine at dinner just to be polite, when actually they don't really want it at all. It is necessary to use a little discretion in serving guests who may be visiting you for the first time, so that you neither force unwanted wine on anyone nor encourage anyone to drink to excess. Serious wine drinkers are concerned about the quality of the wine they drink rather than the quantity, and anyone who is obviously drinking too much should not long be tolerated in the company of the real wine lover.

X

Vintages

AMERICAN WINE DRINKERS have the habit of giving far too much attention to vintage charts and not enough attention to the actual bottle of wine that they may be about to buy. There is obviously no point in worrying about the year the wine was made if it is only a third-rate wine of questionable origin. Likewise, the very greatest wines are never sold under their own château or estate labels if the vintage turned out poorly. Such wines are always sold off in bulk to the shipping companies who use them in their blends of regional wines.

Though it may be interesting to read, a vintage chart which lists wines no longer available in the shops or restaurants is of no value to anyone except the wine historian. Who would want to drink a bottle of 1928 vintage Champagne now in the 1960's, even if he could find it in a store? Most white wines are past their prime after ten years, as are many of the red Burgundies. We have decided, therefore, to limit our discussion here to wines made after 1950, pointing out which ones are worth looking for and which ones will repay further keeping. No attempt has been made to rate the wines by any system of numbers.

Champagne: There is no great advantage to be had in buying old vintages of Champagne. More often than not they turn out to be flat when purchased at liquor stores here in the United States. The 1961 and 1962 vintages are the ones to look for now. Champagne always comes on the market about five years after the vintage. The 1964 will be in the stores in late 1969.

Bordeaux: Nineteen fifty-five is the finest year to look for here and should be drunk now. 1962 is very fine and can be drunk in 1967. The 1952 St. Émilions and Pomerols and the 1953 Médocs are ready for drinking during the early 1960's, though they are becoming hard to find. Nineteen sixty was a good-average year, but not great. Drink it now and do not lay away for future use. The great 1959 and 1961 wines will not be ready for drinking until well into the sixties. It would be a shame to start using your 1961's much before 1969 or 1970 at the earliest. The red Bordeaux wines of great years are usually not available until three years after the vintage. The 1961 white Bordeaux wines are ready now and need not be kept. The 1952 and 1953 whites are now generally too old to be worth buying.

Burgundy: Presently, 1959 is the best year for current use. Do not bother looking for older Burgundies than 1955. If you are able to put away a few bottles for future use, buy the 1961's and keep them for another few years so that they can develop properly. Nineteen fifty-nine and 1961 were both superb, and, though the 1961's are now on the market in the United States, they should be given a few more years to develop. They should be at their peak around 1967 and 1968, though they will certainly last longer than that if properly kept. The 1961 white Burgundies are excellent, but are rather expensive. The 1959's were very good but did not keep too long. They are now all pretty well past their prime.

Germany: The only two vintages worth looking for at present are the 1964 and the 1966. Older wines may still be good if they are of the great *Beeren-* or *Trockenbeerenauslese* class, but otherwise they should be shunned. The German wines, as well as most French white wines, are now brought on the market when they are a year old and sometimes only ten months after the vintage. The quality of freshness thus attained does not make the wines long-lived, and nothing is to be gained by long-term storage. The regular German wines, as well as the *Spätlese* category, are probably at their best when they are two years old, and only wines in the *Auslese* class or better should be drunk when they are much older than four or five years.

XI

Brandies and Liqueurs

AFTER A GOOD DINNER, a fine brandy or liqueur with the coffee has always been considered the perfect finishing touch. Brandy is nothing more than distilled wine, and the finest of all brandies comes from the region around the town of Cognac in the western part of France. It is interesting to note that the wines used for the distillation of Cognac are very poor and thin, and it is said that this is the main reason why Cognac came into being. The growers simply had to find some other use for their wines, since they weren't good enough to drink as is. In any case, the Cognac brandies are now supreme in quality in the entire world, and though we have California brandy, German brandy, and Spanish brandy, to name just a few, none can compare to Cognac. You should remember that all Cognac is brandy, but not all brandy is Cognac! The Cognac-producing region of France is carefully delimited by the French government, and it is divided into six subareas graded according to the quality of the brandies they yield. The Cognac brandies are all sold under brand names, just like Champagne, so that it is not necessary to remember the names of all the different vineyard sections. The top two, however, often cause some confusion, since they are called *Grande Champagne* and *Petite Champagne*, even though there is no connection with the sparkling wines produced in eastern France, in the famous Champagne region. If a bottle of Cognac is sold as *Fine Champagne Cognac*, it must be made from brandies distilled from the wines of these two vineyard sections and at least 50 per cent of it must come from the Grande Champagne area.

In addition to the character of the wines used to make Cognac, the methods of distillation, and, above all, the proper aging in oaken casks all contribute to the fine quality of the brandy. Much depends, however, on the skill of the blender, since the bottle of Cognac that you buy is made up of brandies drawn from many different casks. Each firm tries to keep its various types of Cognac the same over the course of the years, and the blending is therefore a skilled art. No one can say with any certainty that one particular firm has the best Cognac of all, but there are several leading producers whose brandies can always be relied upon. Many of the firms have English names, since they were founded by English or Irish families in the eighteenth century. One of the very finest of these, for example, is Hine, still pronounced just the way it is spelled, and *not* with a French pronunciation of "Een." The Hine brandies are not too well known among American drinkers, though they have long been appreciated by Cognac enthusiasts in Europe. Hennessy, Martell, Courvoisier, Rémy Martin, and Bisquit Dubouché are the best-known brands of Cognac in the United States.

Most firms have several different qualities of Cognac which they market. The "three star" is the cheapest and sells for around $8 a bottle. It is the everyday type of Cognac and the kind to use in cooking or for flaming various desserts and other dishes at the table. The three-star Cognacs are usually about ten years old. Next after three star is the V.S.O.P. or V.S.E.P. grade. These initials stand for "Very superior old pale" or "Very superior extra pale," even though the Cognacs are no longer sold pale, but now have caramel coloring added to them to make them darker looking. A V.S.O. P. Cognac is about twenty years old and sells for around $9.75 a bottle. It is an after-dinner Cognac to sip by itself, and is usually considered too good to use in mixed drinks such as brandy and soda, or to cook with. After the three-star category and the V.S.O.P. brandies, each firm gives its own names to other Cognacs which it sells, and which are superior to these two in quality. Hine calls its next higher quality *Triomphe,* Hennessy calls theirs *Bras d'Or,* Martell's is *Cordon Bleu,* and Courvoisier has a *Napoleon Fine Champagne.* Though Napoleon's name is used by many Cognac firms, and the Courvoisier firm has the registered phrase, "The brandy of Napoleon," on all their labels, the name means nothing at all today. No brandy continues to improve after it has once been bottled, and a bottle of Cognac which you may have been saving for the past twenty years will taste no different today than it would have had you opened it twenty years ago. Because of the high alcoholic content of Cognac, it is best not to leave it around too long in a decanter or after the bottle has been opened. It loses a little of its delicate quality if it is exposed to the air too long.

South of Bordeaux is the Armagnac region where another excellent brandy is produced. Armagnac is not as light and delicate as Cognac, and is usually considered to be fuller-bodied and with a stronger flavor than Cognac. Some of the leading producers in this region are the Marquis de Montesquiou and the Marquis de Caussade, both excellent and producing

Armagnacs of the highest quality. An average price for Armagnac is about $6.50 a bottle.

Liqueurs are usually brandies with various flavorings added to them. If the flavoring agent is a fruit, the drink is often called a "cordial" rather than a liqueur. Most of the well-known liqueurs are proprietary brand names such as Cointreau, Cherry Heering, Grand Marnier, and so on. Since tastes differ from one person to another and everyone will have one or two favorites of his own, we are listing here the best-known liqueurs without any attempt to rate one above the other or classify them in any way:

Bénédictine
Bénédictine and Brandy (B&B)
Chartreuse—green (110 proof)
Chartreuse—yellow (86 proof)
Cherry Heering
Crême de Menthe—white or green
Cointreau
Grand Marnier

In addition there is Drambuie, made with a Scotch whiskey base, and Irish Mist, made with an Irish whiskey base.

Since most of these famous liqueurs sell for around $9.50 a bottle, the best way to find out which one you like is to order them by the glass when eating in a good restaurant. When buying them for home use, it is usually best to buy half-bottles so that they don't stand around too long after they have been opened. This also allows you to have more variety for the same outlay of money.

BIBLIOGRAPHY

IT IS VERY DIFFICULT, not to say expensive, to keep up with all the new books on wine that are constantly being published. Some of them are aimed at the experienced wine drinker and others are strictly for beginners. Often there is duplication in the material covered and it is certainly not necessary to have every book that has been written about wine in order to be completely informed on the subject. Rather than a mere alphabetical listing, therefore, we have grouped a few books together as a sort of basic wine library, while the more advanced books are listed in a second group. A third group lists books that are mainly to be read for enjoyment rather than for instruction in the selection and drinking of wines.

THE BASIC WINE LIBRARY

Adams, Leon D.: *The Commonsense Book of Wine.* New York: David McKay Company, Inc., 1958. A very interesting book for the beginner, though strongly slanted in favor of California wines.

Lichine, Alexis (in collaboration with William E. Massee): *Wines of France.* New York: Alfred A. Knopf, 1955. Certainly the most useful book on French wines presently available.

Melville, John: *Guide to California Wines.* San Carlos, California: Nourse Publishing Company, 1960.

A most complete and authoritative guide to the fine wines of California, and a definite "must" for anyone living in that state who would like to know more about the native wines.

Schoonmaker, Frank: *The Wines of Germany.* New York: Hastings House, 1956. This book contains all the information you will ever need to have about German wines.

Street, Julian: *Wines.* New York: Alfred A. Knopf, 1961. An excellent, all-round guide to the wines of all countries, though not too detailed for the beginner.

FOR ADVANCED WINE DRINKERS

Allen, H. Warner: *Natural Red Wines.* London: Constable, 1951. The wines of Bordeaux and Burgundy are discussed in much detail, though most of the references are to vintages of the last century.

———: *Sherry and Port.* London: Constable, 1952. A very thorough discussion of the history and production of these two great wines. Well worth-while if you are a serious Port or Sherry drinker.

———: *White Wines and Cognac.* London: Constable, 1952. All French white wines are covered here, including Champagne, and also the white wines of Germany. A final chapter covers the making of Cognac and Armagnac.

———: *The Wines of Portugal.* New York: McGraw-Hill Book Company, Inc., 1963. The most recent of the "Great Wines" series has been done just as lavishly as the other three. It is a must for Port fanciers, but describes all other Portuguese wines as well.

Churchill, Creighton: *A Notebook for the Wines of France.* New York: Alfred A. Knopf, 1961. A very large book that not only lists and classifies all French wines in considerable detail, but also has space for your own notations on the wines you drink yourself. Contains excellent maps.

Croft-Cooke, Rupert: *Sherry*. New York: Alfred A. Knopf, 1956. The finest book available in English telling the history of Sherry, how it is made, and the stories of the leading shippers.

Massee, William E.: *Wines and Spirits*. New York: McGraw-Hill Book Company, Inc., 1961. A very informative book covering all major wine-producing countries and their best wines and also other alcoholic beverages as well. A good general guide book to all types of wines, liqueurs, brandies, and so on.

Roger, J.-R.: *The Wines of Bordeaux*. New York: E. P. Dutton & Co., 1960. A complete and detailed analysis of all the wines of Bordeaux, both red and white. A mine of useful information for the real claret lover.

Shand, P. Morton: *A Book of French Wines*. New York: Alfred A. Knopf, 1960. All the wines of France are covered here in considerable detail. Instructive and well written, this book is mainly for the serious wine drinker of some experience.

Simon, André: *The Noble Grapes and the Great Wines of France*. New York: McGraw-Hill Book Company, Inc., 1958. A beautifully printed book with magnificent color plates and excellent maps. All French wines are described with mention of the best vineyards in each area.

Simon, André: *Champagne*. New York: McGraw-Hill Book Company, Inc., 1961. All you will ever need to know about Champagne is here in a book equally as beautiful as the one above describing all French wines.

Simon, André and Hallgarten S. F.: *The Great Wines of Germany*. New York: McGraw-Hill Book Company,

Inc., 1962. Together with Mr. Hallgarten, an outstanding expert on German wines, André Simon has produced a third book in the same magnificent format as the two preceding ones. The color plates again are superb.

TO READ MAINLY FOR ENJOYMENT

Allen, H. Warner: *A Contemplation of Wine.* London: Michael Joseph, 1951. Various essays, some more interesting than others, covering many different aspects of wine-drinking, past and present.

James, Walter: *Wine—A Brief Encyclopedia.* New York: Alfred A. Knopf, 1960. Though certainly valuable as a reference work, this book has so many interesting and entertaining definitions that many wine lovers will want to read it straight through rather than just referring to it casually for the name of a wine or vineyard.

Oliver, Stuart: *Wine Journeys.* New York: Duell, Sloan and Pearce, 1949. A fascinating account of the author's search for old and rare vintages in the private cellars of French and German growers and connoisseurs.

Saintsbury, George: *Notes on a Cellar-Book.* London: Macmillan and Co., Ltd., 1951. One of the all-time classics on wines and wine drinking by a great English connoisseur. Professor Saintsbury died in 1933, so that the wines referred to are all of nineteenth- and early twentieth-century vintages.

Street, Julian: *Table Topics.* New York: Alfred A. Knopf, 1959. This book is as much about food as it is about wine, but the very interesting wine lore that it does contain makes us include it in this listing.

Waugh, Alec: *In Praise of Wine and Certain Noble Spirits.* New York: William Sloane Associates, 1959. An excellent group of essays covering the author's experiences with various types of wines and his travels through the vineyard country of Europe. Instructive as well as entertaining.

FOR WOULD-BE WINEGROWERS

There are many wine lovers who would like to make a little wine of their own, but who feel that they lack the necessary technical knowledge and "know-how" to go about it properly. Fortunately, there are two excellent books available on this subject which will guide the novice winegrower through every step of wine making, from the selection of the proper grape varieties, and the pressing, to bottling of the finished wine. The first of these books is *A Wine-Grower's Guide* and the second is *American Wines and Wine-Making,* both by Philip M. Wagner and published by Alfred A. Knopf, New York.

Mr. Wagner is the foremost authority in the United States on the French Hybrid grape varieties. These are crossings of French and American vines with the best characteristics of both—the hardiness and resistance to phylloxera of the American vines combined with the flavor of the European grapes. The resulting wines thus have none of the "foxy" taste so often found objectionable in our native Concord, Niagara, and other wines. The French Hybrids should certainly be planted by anyone living east of the Rocky Mountains who would like to make his own wine.

Prospective winegrowers should write to Boordy Vineyard, Box 38, Riderwood, Maryland, to obtain price lists and a catalog of the vines available. The cost of a grape vine is between 55¢ and $1, depending on the quantity ordered. In general, vines are planted in the spring and do not yield their first harvest for wine until the third year, so that considerable patience is required of the beginner. The cost of such an undertaking is not as expensive as many people believe, as there is no need to buy elaborate equipment when making two or three hundred bottles of wine for personal use and enjoyment.

WILLIAM S. LEEDOM, who was born in 1928, recalls having been interested in wines even before he was legally permitted to buy them in Philadelphia, where he grew up. After attending the Carnegie Institute of Technology, he served in the Navy. While stationed near Baltimore, he took particular pains to test the merits of various Chablis with the renowned Chesapeake Bay oysters. In 1954 he left for Europe, where he completed his education at the University of Heidelberg, in Germany, and at Neuchâtel, in Switzerland. He remained in Europe for almost six years, studying and selling wines. Since his return to the United States, Mr. Leedom has worked in the wine business in New York City. Thus, he is able to bring to the general public an exceptional inside knowledge of wines and the wine trade.

THE TEXT of this book was set in *Electra*, a Linotype face designed by W. A. Dwiggins. This face cannot be classified as modern or oldstyle. It is not based on any historical model, nor does it echo any particular period or style. It avoids the extreme contrast between thick and thin elements that marks most modern faces, and attempts to give a feeling of fluidity, power, and speed. Composed, printed, and bound by THE COLONIAL PRESS INC., Clinton, Massachusetts. Cover design by Warren Chappell.